INVESTING IN SEPARATE ACCOUNTS

INVESTING IN SEPARATE ACCOUNTS

Erik H. Davidson
Kevin D. Freeman
with Brian O'Connell

McGraw-Hill

New York   Chicago   San Francisco   Lisbon   London   Madrid
Mexico City   Milan   New Delhi   San Juan   Seoul
Singapore   Sydney   Toronto

Library of Congress Cataloging-in-Publication Data

Davidson, Erik, 1962–
    Investing in separate accounts / by Erik Davidson and Kevin Freeman.
      p. cm.
    ISBN 0-07-138508-8
    Portfolio management—Handbooks, manuals, etc. 2. Investments—Handbooks,
    manuals, etc. I. Freeman, Kevin. II. Title.

HG4529.5 .D38 2002
332.6—dc21

                                                        2001055846

McGraw-Hill

A Division of The McGraw·Hill Companies

1 2 3 4 5 6 7 8 9 0   DOC/DOC   0 9 8 7 6 5 4 3 2

ISBN 0-07-138508-8

This book was set in Times New Roman by Wayne Palmer of McGraw-Hill Professional's Hightstown, N.J., composition unit.

Printed and bound by R. R. Donnelley & Sons Company.

McGraw-Hill books are available at special quantity discounts to use as premiums and sales promotions, or for use in corporate training programs. For more information, please write to the Director of Special Sales, Professional Publishing, McGraw-Hill, Two Penn Plaza, New York, NY 10121-2298. Or contact your local bookstore.

To the families of the victims of the World Trade Center tragedy—the innovative spirit of America's financial servies industry that your loved ones championed will not be extinguished.

To our wives (Lori and Marnie) and children (Sonja, Derek, David, Sarah, and Madysen). Your presence in our lives has given us true "wealth."

To our parents (Elizabeth, Ken and Mary Ann, Kerry and Sue). Thank you for the significant "investment" that you made in our lives over these many years.

To our God. May we live our lives in a manner worthy of the "price" that you paid so that we might have eternal and abundant life (John 10:10).

Contents

Acknowledgments

The creation of this book leveraged our combined experience and knowledge of the booming separate account market. However, without the instrumental participation of many other individuals, the book would have remained in our heads and never have made it to the readers' hands. Brian O'Connell, our coauthor, was a phenomenal partner in the writing process. His skill with the written word, as well as his understanding of the capital markets made him indispensible to the achievement of this dream. Jim Griffith embraced this dream as his own and made it a reality. Rob Flowers contributed to the dream's realization in ways too many to list. Keleigh Milliorn's articistic eye was invaluable. Stephen Isaacs and our friends at McGraw-Hill brought expertise and encouragement to us as we navigated unfamiliar territory.

We also want to take this opportunity to thank some of the many people and organizations that have supported us in our quest called "Separate Account Solutions, Inc." These include, first and foremost, our employees. Beyond them, our other "partners" include "Angel" investors, the Royal Bank of Canada (especially Grant Rasmussen), Accenture (especially Steve Schwarzbach), and a wide circle of friends who are constantly supporting and encouraging in a myriad of ways.

Foreword

Separate accounts are the next generation of money management services to the upwardly mobile investor. As financial market turbulence tests self-directed investors' patience and finances, investors are looking toward professionals for assistance. However, as investors' needs become more complex the standard packaged investment product, the mutual fund, becomes a less attractive alternative as the standard mutual fund's tax, diversification, and trading patterns are problematic for the mid to high net-worth investor.

Separate account products provide the proper balance between mass-market investment products and personalized money management. These structures allow the individual investor to have professional money managers monitor their personally tailored portfolios at a scale to make these products available to the mid-tier investor.

These advantages are making separate account products one of investment advisors' hottest offerings. While the large brokerage firms have been offering these products since the early 1980s, new technology achievements are allowing these products to be offered by a wider array of investment professionals, from independent investment contractors to financial planning firms, tax advisors, mutual fund firms, regional brokers, and traditional banks.

As separate accounts become more widely available, we believe that we will see unprecedented adoption of these products as they allow for a much more personalized investment experience at a time when more investors are seeking professional management and investment management firms are looking to better leverage their professional advice.

Larry Tabb
TowerGroup

Introduction

Bob Dylan once famously wrote,"The Times They Are a Changing."
Brother, he didn't know the half of it.

In the last fifty years we've landed men on the moon, launched the information and technology age, and crowned three (count'em, three) new home run kings. Wall Street hasn't been any different.

In fact, the last half of the twentieth century recorded a tremendous advancement in the way money was managed at the retail level. Individuals could access brokers and professional money management through a remarkable innovation known as mutual funds. This allowed people across the country to pool their investments, hire a professional, and be treated as an institution. The explosion of wealth creation was astounding; it now amounts to trillions of dollars.

The reason that mutual funds have been so successful is threefold. First, individuals of nearly every economic class desire professional money management. They recognize that successful investing requires time, expertise, and experience. Second, our economy has grown substantially, making more money than ever before available for investing. Third, the mutual fund vehicle was, without question, the most efficient means possible to deliver professional management to investors with smaller account balances. Before the advent of funds, only the very wealthy could afford the high costs of record-keeping and transactions involved with private money management.

The computer revolution changed everything. Imagine the difficulty of record-keeping by hand for investors just twenty-five years ago. It was difficult enough to keep track of small trades for brokerage firms. As a result, individual transaction charges were prohibitive for all but the wealthy. The same was true for professional managers who charge fees as a percentage of the assets managed. With the advancement of computers, however, both transaction charges and record-keeping costs have fallen to a mere fraction of their levels just a few years earlier. The door is now open for individuals with as little as $100,000 to have all the benefits of private money management through separate accounts. These benefits can include tax control, customization, lower costs, and better performance. As a result, separate accounts are rapidly revolutionizing the way money is managed. Already the growth in separate accounts has far surpassed mutual funds. By the end of this decade, separate accounts will represent trillions of dollars invested in this nation alone.

REASONS FOR THIS BOOK

We have written this book to introduce investors to the concept of separate accounts and explain how they can benefit from this revolutionary trend in the way money is managed. Even though we've been a part of this trend for over a decade, we were unable to locate a single book that covered the basics for investors. As a result, millions of people have missed out on the benefits of separate accounts while close to a million others may own separate accounts and not really understand their potential.

Anyone who owns a mutual fund or has the intention of investing seriously over his or her lifetime should read this book. It will explain in detail what separate accounts are and how they work. It will also explain the many benefits of a separate account approach and how to best take advantage of them.

Overall, we believe that separate accounts are the best kept secret in the money management world. Maybe it's because mutual funds have proven so profitable that brokers and money managers alike seem to push them. But, while funds may be easier for brokers and managers, what's best for the client is really what counts. By educating investors, we hope to cause them to explore the investment approaches that work best for them.

HOW TO USE THIS BOOK

The book is organized into thirteen chapters and is designed to provide a true "how to" manual with regard to starting and maintaining a successful separate account investment program. By way of illustration, we've included a dozen case studies that correspond to the issues we cover in the book (they appear at the end of the chapters). Each case study shows a real-life situation where investors need to understand and be educated regarding how to benefit from separate accounts. The thirteenth and final chapter looks to the future and some possible innovations that will further transform the investment industry.

Each chapter is filled with illustrations and examples to help clarify the contents. For example, Chapter 4 contains some very specific questions to ask a prospective money manager. This book is not about theory. It's written so that investors know step by step whether or not they should invest in separate accounts and how to do so.

In addition to the chapters, we have included a glossary and four detailed appendices. These tools can clarify the concepts of the book and provide concrete examples of how the process works. Separate accounts involve their own reports and information, and we want readers to see exactly what's involved with real-world examples.

After you finish this book we hope you don't just put it down. We hope you give it to your neighbor, your brother or sister, or even the annoying guy down the hall in Accounting (and of course, we don't mind if you tell them to buy a copy of their own).

We want everyone to know that we're at the cusp of a revolution in financial asset management. Separate accounts are rewriting history, even during these perilous political and economic times we're living in (we think especially so). Separate accounts are showing Americans that there is a better way of handling money and investments. We don't want you or anyone you know to miss out.

God Speed,
Erik Davidson
Kevin Freeman
Carmel, California
December 2001

1

THEY SHOOT MUTUAL FUNDS, DON'T THEY?

You behold a range of exhausted volcanoes. Not a flame flickers on a single pallid crest.

BENJAMIN DISRAELI

Like other monumental cultural trends, it was inevitable. In the past, generations lived and died in the same society with the same rules applied through life. Consider the railroad, which replaced the lumbering Conestoga wagons that transported freight across U.S. prairies. Or how about telegraphs, which originally sprouted along railroad lines? They soon gave way to the telephone, which in turn is giving way to wireless communication.

At the end of the nineteenth century, Americans bore witness to the motorized automobile. An aberration at first, automobiles soon dotted newly constructed urban roads and highways. After a fashion, Americans no longer had a need for the horse and buggy. So it goes with gasoline lamps giving way to electricity, rail travel giving way to the airplane, and the typewriter giving way to the personal computer. Good ideas in their day, all giving way to better ones.

So it's no surprise that the death of the mutual fund, too, was imminent. After all, mutual funds couldn't have gone on forever, could they? Like other cultural supernovas such as the steam engine, the horse and buggy, and the typewriter, mutual funds had to give way to a better idea. With the separately managed investment account, so they have.

ASCENT, AND DECLINE, OF FUNDS

Before explaining Wall Street's transition from the mutual fund to the separate account, which is what we'll spend the bulk of this book discussing, let's give credit where credit is due. Mutual funds made history. Their impact on everyday people's lives was huge. Most Americans under 50 years of age grew up investing in mutual funds. Most Americans over 50 years of age used them to retire comfortably.

How did mutual funds become such a force, both on Wall Street and Main Street? And why is that force waning? Let's have a look.

Founded in 1940, mutual funds gave average Americans the opportunity to invest like professionals. For a fee, investors could hire huge fund firms, with scores of savvy money managers, to invest their savings in pools of stocks called mutual funds. For the average working American, mutual funds were manna from heaven. They gave Americans an opportunity to have their portfolios managed by the nation's best and brightest financial minds at a price they could afford.

With the introduction of the 401(k) plan in the early 1980s, mutual funds really took off. Fund companies, both of the boutique and behemoth variety, plastered advertisements in newspapers and magazines and on television and radio. Each promised the best results, if only you invested your money with them.

As the bull market of the 1980s and 1990s barreled along, investors enjoyed the ride. But soon, as their portfolios mushroomed into six, and sometimes even seven, figures, investors began to grow weary of the tax inefficiency, out-of-control management, rising costs, and underperformance of their mutual funds. With the evolution of the Internet, which gave investors greater access to financial information than ever before, fund shareholders began exploring alternative investment options such as online discount brokerage trading and online banking programs. Soon, the idea of taking greater control over their financial destinies grew more appealing. Emboldened by their Web experience, newly empowered investors began taking their business elsewhere, both online and offline. Financial advisors became prevalent, and online trading became more commonplace.

From there, it was a short leap to separate accounts, which are individually managed investment accounts that gave investors more control over their investment portfolios at a lower cost and with greater tax benefits. Separate accounts require investors to pay one flat fee for asset management, a fee much lower than the commissions charged by mutual fund companies. At annual growth rates of over 31 percent each year from 1995 to 1999, separate accounts became the hottest investment tool anywhere. So hot, in fact, that Boston-based Cerulli Associates notes that separate account consultant program assets have risen to over $297.7 billion at the end of 2000, up from $92.8 billion in 1995. Meanwhile, interest in mutual funds began to wane. Sure, mutual funds still controlled in excess of $7 trillion through late 2000, with 83 million Americans participating. But distributions to funds slowed and withdrawals increased.

Soon the mass media began to catch on. According to an article entitled "The Death of Mutual Funds" that appeared in the September 2000 issue of *Red Herring*, "the open-end mutual fund—still the bastion of popular investing in America—came under heavy fire from a slew of competing investment vehicles like separate accounts that feature cost savings, tax efficiency, transparency, and customization. Ironically, those elements, now the seeds of the industry's decline, are the same ones that helped it blossom in the first place."

The fault, the article said, could be traced directly to the increasingly flaccid mutual fund sector. "The industry, however, has no one to blame but itself for its imminent fall from favor," according to *Red Herring*. "Most fund companies do business today very much the same way they did ten years ago, practically ignoring—and therefore not sharing with their investors—the many benefits that technology now offers."

As evidence that the fund industry's slide may not be temporary, but "lethal" as *Red Herring* notes, the article cites steadily declining contributions to mutual funds in recent years. Despite a fifth knockout year in a row for the

Sidebar I: Expensive Expenses

According to Lipper Analytical Services, which tracks these sorts of things, the average U.S. stock fund charges 1.43 percent of its assets per year for expenses. Although that's only $29 per year for a $2000 account, it's a whopping $1430 per year for a $100,000 account.

stock market and an apparent snapback in fund performance, people are putting far fewer dollars into mutual funds than they did a few years ago.

Back in the 1990s, mutual funds were still riding high. In fact, next to the personal computer, a good argument can be made that the mutual fund was the single most powerful commodity in the world during the second half of the twentieth century. That's why it's so sad to bid mutual funds good-bye.

Like most aging monoliths, cracks in the façade are showing. Erosion around the edges is becoming only too apparent. And thanks to the Internet, which has leveled the playing field to the point where retail investors have as much access to good investment information as do professional investors, Americans are beginning to take a darker view of the venerable mutual fund.

WHERE'S THE BEEF?

Given recent net contribution and redemption figures like the ones cited in the *Red Herring* article (Figure 1-1), mutual funds appear to be in big trouble. But those aren't the only reasons. Let's examine a few more.

FIGURE 1-1

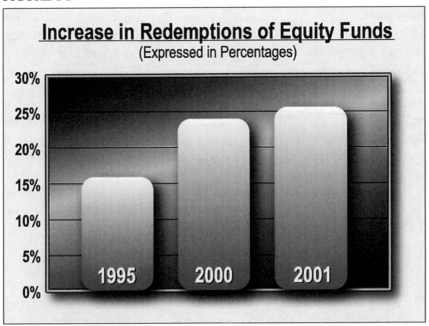

Choice

While Americans have poured trillions of dollars into mutual funds in recent decades, they've done so primarily because they didn't have any other choice. Until recently, the only way small investors could afford a diversified portfolio of stocks or a professional money manager was to pool their money with others in a fund.

But with a rise in investor income levels, thanks primarily to the long-running bull market, the stakes have become higher for Americans. Aside from the individually managed flavor of separate accounts, they also fall easily into the budgets of a burgeoning number of American investors.

Taxes

Imagine a nascent mutual fund investor say a 28-year-old systems analyst opening her year-end mutual fund statement for the first time. Now imagine the sticker shock when she finds out her year-end fund-tax bill reaches $900, even though she has never sold a single share of her fund.

Chances are that's because a new manager came in and sold many of the fund's holdings, triggering the tax bill. Yep, those capital-gains distributions can be a killer. Ignites.com, a Web-based fund-tracking newsletter, states that, on average, taxes cost fund investors 2.3 percent annually, which can be well over 10 percent of their average total returns.

When our investor wakes up, she'll recognize something that investment professionals have know for a long time: Open-end mutual funds are often tax inefficient. Long-term shareholders expecting to profit from the benefits of a lower capital-gains tax bracket (20 percent) for holdings kept more than a year might be surprised to see a large tax bill when April arrives. Worse, investors might actually have to pay capital-gains taxes even if the fund posts overall losses. This happens because investors have no control over what and how often their fund managers are buying or selling, regardless of how long they hold the fund.

A January 24, 2000, *Business Week* article entitled "Mutual Funds: What's Wrong?" argues that mutual funds have no choice about distributing their gains, but critics argue they don't do enough to lower them. One way is through better bookkeeping. Just as a tax-savvy investor would reduce the size of a profitable block of stock by selling the highest cost shares, fund companies need to do the same. "Yet not all funds follow the 'highest in, first out' accounting. They should. Joel S. Dickson, a tax specialist at

Vanguard, says studies show that HIFO accounting can save shareholders as much as 1% a year in costs," reports *Business Week*.

Another way to cut the tax bill is to trade less often. "The average equity fund has a turnover rate of 90%, which means that a $1 billion fund does about $900 million worth of trades each year. Besides triggering gains, trading incurs commission costs of about 5 cents a share—that's much higher than most individuals pay for online brokerage," notes *Business Week*. Why so high? In part, by paying higher commissions, investment management companies can also use some of the commission—called "soft dollars"—to pay for research, data services, or even newspapers and magazines. "Think of it this way: It's sort of like frequent-flier miles for the fund managers, except they use the shareholders' money," the article concludes.

Tax woes are particularly hard on more affluent fund investors. One reason is that mutual fund managers typically focus on overall fund performance (a strategy that may not be in alignment with an individual investor's tax circumstances). Effective tax planning will include timing security sales to utilize capital losses or to defer the realization of capital gains. Before acquiring a particular mutual fund, investors should recognize that mutual funds generally do not provide the same tax-planning flexibility as do separately managed accounts.

Another reason is that if an affluent investor holds shares in a mutual fund that has significant unrealized gains within its portfolio, he or she may incur an accelerated income tax liability. A mutual fund with significant unrealized gains has embedded income tax liabilities that are generally borne by each of the fund's shareholders once the gains are realized by the fund, despite the fact that not all shareholders will benefit from the capital gain. In an extreme instance, an investor who purchases shares of a fund with an imbedded income tax liability could incur a significant income tax liability as a result, even though the fund has not appreciated in value subsequent to the purchase. Determining whether a fund has significant unrealized capital gains before making an investment is especially critical for investors with more of their hard-earned cash invested in the fund.

Fund Costs

Fund costs hardly mattered when returns were in the double digits all those years. But when the Dow has tumbled more than 10 percent in 1999 and 2000, and with the tech-heavy NASDAQ tanking during the same period, investors

Sidebar II: Waterlogged Inflows
According to the May 2000 edition of *Institutional Investor*, by way of Financial Research Co., mutual fund inflows declined from $18 billion per month in 1998 to $12 billion in 1999. Fifty-three percent of all fund companies experienced net outflows for 1999. New mutual funds also fell from 1998 to 1999, the magazine reports, from 718 to 420.

may be taking a longer look at fund fees. Investors pay roughly 1.5 percent annually, on average, for the "convenience" of investing in a mutual fund.

Traditionally, when it comes to lowering fund costs, mutual fund firms have long sported a tin ear. Apart from the introduction of index mutual funds in 1976 by John Bogle, legendary founder of the Vanguard Group and the father of low-cost investing, money managers have done little, if anything, to trim costs for fund investors. In fact, while the rest of the investment industry is moving toward lower costs, mutual fund companies are raising them. According to Morningstar, average annual equity fund expenses have risen to 1.55 percent of invested assets through June 2000. The fact that most of these increases are usually used to fatten the paycheck of the mutual fund managers is a real slap in the face of fund investors.

There used to be a time when mutual funds were the cheapest way for the average American to enter the equity market. That's no longer true. The costs of setting up a stock portfolio, so prohibitive in the not-so-distant past, have dropped dramatically as the Internet has triggered economies of scale that allow online brokerages to charge transaction fees as low as $8 a trade. Some Web sites are even offering commission-free trades based on an advertising-sponsored model. In addition, most financial Web sites are giving away news, portfolio tracking, equity research, and real-time stock quotes, bringing the price of retrieving information down to, well, zero.

Another reason for rising expense ratios is 12(b)-1 fees. These fees, which show up in the expense ratio, pay for the fund's advertising or distribution costs or to compensate those who sell the fund. Fees for a 12(b)-1 can be as little as 0.25 percent or as high as 1 percent per year, and they come right out of the fund's assets.

Market Impact

Commissions are not the only costs involved in trading; there's also what is commonly called "market impact cost," which is an additional cost incurred when the fund's buy or sell order itself changes the price of the stock. For example, if a mutual fund wants to sell a large block of stock, it may have to accept a lower price to do the trade. Likewise, if the fund is shopping for a large block of shares, it will have to pay more for it.

According to the *Business Week* article, market impact cost is not something you find in a fund's financial statement. But it can be detected through analysis of the trading records. The cost to shareholders can be as high as 1 to 5 percent a year, depending on the size and liquidity of the stocks that a fund trades and the style of trading. Funds that invest in small-cap stocks have higher impact costs than those that buy large-caps, according to Nicolo Torre, a managing director at BARRA Inc., an investment consulting firm. And funds that practice a momentum strategy—buying what's hot—usually end up paying more than value investors that buy and hold. The only way to cut market impact costs, he says, is through fewer trades. "Ten percent of the trades reflect 90% of the market impact cost," Torre tells *Business Week*. "Halve the number of trades, and you can significantly lower the fund's market impact cost."

Disclosure Limits

You wouldn't buy a new car without getting in and driving it—at least you shouldn't—but mutual fund companies don't want you to even look under hood, let alone take a test drive.

According to Securities and Exchange Commission rules, mutual fund companies have to disclose their holdings at least twice a year. Quite a few don't go beyond the bare minimum requirement. This means the information you see when you check your favorite fund's top holdings on the Web is outdated, to say the least. In fact, given the high speed at which managers are changing their portfolios these days, it could be flat-out wrong. According to Morningstar, the typical turnover on a stock portfolio today is in excess of 90 percent a year, which implies that the average fund manager is buying stocks with a 12- to 15-month time horizon.

Fund companies are also beginning to rely more on "window dressing." In the *Red Herring* article "Death of Mutual Funds," the author points out that window dressing is a "common industry trick" that allows fund managers to spruce up their portfolios by purchasing some of the best performing stocks in a given period shortly before releasing their holdings to the SEC. "By doing so," states the article, "the portfolio will look pretty good to investors' eyes, even though the fund may have missed out on most, if not all, of the run-up in those top-performing stocks it now holds. The practice is legal, albeit sleazy. The saddest part is that there's no practical way to know for sure which funds are doing it and which are not."

Fund Performance

Funds could win back investors if they improved their returns. Sure, from 1995 through 1999—before the market began to decline—the average fund earned 19 percent a year. But poor performance in 2000 and 2001 has negated a lot of those gains fund investors earned in the 1990s. (Chart 1.1).

Too Many Funds

Another way to improve returns is to shut a fund's doors to new investors before it gets too large to manage effectively. This is especially critical for funds investing in small companies, where too much money crimps returns. At what point does size start to slow a fund? It could be as little as $100 million or $200 million for small-cap funds and several billion dollars for large-caps.

Many funds need to close down—period. John Rekenthaler, research director for Morningstar, estimates that at least half of all equity funds are below $50 million in assets, probably not profitable for their sponsors, and with little likelihood of ever getting much bigger. Liquidating or merging them would go a long way toward cleaning up the clutter of funds that daze and confuse prospective investors and would lower overhead for the firms.

That would give fund companies latitude to lower expenses for share-holders, who by and large haven't benefited much from the economies of scale that go with the sixfold increase in assets over the past decade. As we said earlier, the average expense ratio for equity funds is 1.55 percent, up from 1.45 percent a decade ago. Bond fund expenses have shot up, too, from 0.84 percent to 1.08 percent.

Gone in 60 Seconds

Mutual funds have also become more sensitive in recent years to traders who dart in and out of the funds. In some cases, the traders have been booted out, and in others, redemption fees have been instituted to discourage short-term switching. Industrywide, redemption rates are on the rise.

CHART 1.1

Fund category returns in 2001

Domestic Stock Funds (03-31-01)								
Approx # of Funds	Total Assets ($Bil)	Category	3 Mo (%)	1 Yr (%)	YTD (%)	3 Yr (%)	5 Yr (%)	10 Yr (%)
6495	--	**Domestic Stock**	**-12.76**	**-16.03**	**-12.76**	**3.18**	**10.86**	**12.56**
234	39.5	Small Value	0.76	13.27	0.76	0.84	11.23	12.75
145	11.3	Specialty-Real Estate	-1.56	21.42	-1.56	-0.54	9.37	9.30
266	72.6	Mid-Cap Value	-2.98	10.72	-2.98	4.64	12.09	13.76
253	36.7	Small Blend	-4.94	-0.73	-4.94	2.13	10.81	13.01
64	6.3	Specialty-Natural Res	-4.96	13.49	-4.96	4.58	7.98	9.56
781	274.3	Domestic Hybrid	-5.31	-5.38	-5.31	3.20	8.93	10.25
766	533.2	Large Value	-5.63	0.20	-5.63	2.35	11.57	13.01
96	26.8	Specialty-Utilities	-6.52	-5.64	-6.52	7.19	13.66	12.28
79	16.7	Specialty-Financial	-6.89	19.49	-6.89	3.54	16.66	20.36
62	7.9	Convertibles	-7.50	-15.59	-7.50	5.60	10.30	11.97
225	36.8	Mid-Cap Blend	-9.48	-10.82	-9.48	1.73	11.02	13.05
1125	771.3	Large Blend	-13.01	-21.11	-13.01	1.79	11.75	12.50
476	99.3	Small Growth	-17.98	-32.50	-17.98	2.28	8.21	12.06
935	670.7	Large Growth	-19.96	-35.66	-19.96	3.33	11.58	12.52
97	46.5	Specialty-Health	-21.33	1.99	-21.33	13.76	12.93	15.40
531	167.0	Mid-Cap Growth	-22.38	-37.09	-22.38	6.01	10.31	12.60
40	9.0	Specialty-Communications	-25.34	-52.23	-25.34	4.06	13.55	16.33
320	88.1	Specialty-Technology	-34.82	-61.64	-34.82	10.07	14.20	19.42
--	--	**Standard & Poor's Midcap 400**	**-10.80**	**-6.95**	**-10.80**	**8.88**	**16.30**	**16.06**
--	--	**Standard & Poor's 500**	**-11.80**	**-21.70**	**-11.80**	**3.05**	**14.18**	**14.41**
--	--	**Russell 2000**	**-6.50**	**-15.30**	**-6.50**	**-0.89**	**7.76**	**11.81**

International Stock Funds (03-31-01)								
Approx # of Funds	Total Assets ($Bil)	Category	3 Mo (%)	1 Yr (%)	YTD (%)	3 Yr (%)	5 Yr (%)	10 Yr (%)
1761	--	**International Stoc**	**-12.15**	**-28.68**	**-12.15**	**-0.73**	**2.83**	**5.65**
70	23.8	International Hybrid	-4.45	-7.05	-4.45	3.30	5.64	8.22
33	1.6	Specialty-Precious Metals	-4.97	-7.02	-4.97	-12.52	-18.38	-5.48
37	1.4	Latin America Stock	-5.08	-24.36	-5.08	-7.59	3.35	--
99	3.5	Pacific/Asia ex-Japan Stk	-6.39	-36.55	-6.39	-0.90	-7.35	4.70
176	14.8	Diversified Emerging Mkts	-6.72	-37.84	-6.72	-8.58	-4.96	0.19
51	4.3	Japan Stock	-8.58	-42.18	-8.58	6.18	-2.33	-2.58
52	2.9	Diversified Pacific/Asia	-9.39	-40.27	-9.39	0.65	-5.99	3.94
294	154.4	World Stock	-13.81	-25.70	-13.81	1.25	7.66	8.10
781	228.5	Foreign Stock	-14.31	-28.68	-14.31	0.51	5.47	7.23
168	21.1	Europe Stock	-16.38	-27.12	-16.38	-0.86	9.22	9.88
--	--	**MSCI World ex US ND**	**-14.00**	**-25.90**	**-14.00**	**-0.45**	**3.72**	**6.00**
--	--	**MSCI Europe, Australasia, Far East ND**	**-13.70**	**-25.90**	**-13.70**	**-0.56**	**3.43**	**5.90**
--	--	**MSCI Emerging Markets ID**	**-5.62**	**-36.80**	**-5.62**	**-8.42**	**-7.01**	**1.71**

Taxable Bonds (03-31-01)								
Approx # of Funds	Total Assets ($Bil)	Category	3 Mo (%)	1 Yr (%)	YTD (%)	3 Yr (%)	5 Yr (%)	10 Yr (%)
2190	--	**Taxable Bond**	**2.57**	**6.89**	**2.57**	**3.97**	**5.85**	**7.29**
330	84.9	High Yield Bond	3.83	-3.70	3.83	-2.15	3.65	8.92
570	179.7	Interm-Term Bond	3.04	10.68	3.04	5.65	6.49	7.62
123	21.5	Long-Term Bond	3.01	9.78	3.01	4.65	6.48	7.85
238	42.8	Short-Term Bond	2.86	9.80	2.86	5.97	6.05	6.54
139	22.0	Short Government	2.53	9.46	2.53	5.62	5.78	6.26
285	75.7	Intermediate Government	2.41	11.26	2.41	5.87	6.40	6.96
40	3.3	Emerging Markets Bond	2.35	5.95	2.35	1.46	9.53	--
158	26.7	Multisector Bond	2.00	2.77	2.00	1.39	5.32	7.93
65	7.3	Long Government	1.95	11.98	1.95	6.02	7.14	8.38
76	32.9	Ultrashort Bond	1.44	6.20	1.44	5.43	5.82	5.57
166	15.1	International Bond	-0.64	1.89	-0.64	1.95	3.79	5.30
--	--	**Lehman Brothers Mortgage- Backed Bond**	**2.73**	**12.66**	**2.73**	**6.98**	**7.59**	**7.78**
--	--	**Lehman Brothers Government Bond**	**2.52**	**12.33**	**2.52**	**7.09**	**7.51**	**7.95**

Municipal Bonds (03-31-01)								
Approx # of Funds	Total Assets ($Bil)	Category	3 Mo (%)	1 Yr (%)	YTD (%)	3 Yr (%)	5 Yr (%)	10 Yr (%)
1812	--	**Municipal Bond**	**1.85**	**9.45**	**1.85**	**4.06**	**5.33**	**6.52**
178	50.0	Muni National Interm	2.06	8.97	2.06	4.29	5.21	6.30
34	7.0	Muni New York Interm	1.96	9.70	1.96	4.65	5.47	6.47
303	79.7	Muni National Long	1.93	9.52	1.93	3.75	5.38	6.66
267	15.4	Muni Single State Interm	1.92	9.07	1.92	4.16	5.05	6.28
103	16.5	Muni Short	1.89	6.67	1.89	3.97	4.31	5.14
91	17.2	Muni New York Long	1.82	10.49	1.82	4.23	5.58	6.71
682	50.3	Muni Single State Long	1.82	9.79	1.82	3.98	5.45	6.63
34	4.4	Muni California Interm	1.79	9.26	1.79	4.83	5.59	6.59
120	36.3	Muni California Long	1.36	10.49	1.36	4.36	5.80	6.79
--	--	**Lehman Brothers Aggregate Bond**	**3.03**	**12.53**	**3.03**	**6.87**	**7.48**	**7.98**

Posted 03-31-01
Russel 2000 and Lehman Brothers Aggregate Bond data are updated monthly.

Slowing down the trading also enables funds to be more fully invested and keep less cash in the till for redemptions. That cash is a drag on performance because it earns less than it would if it were invested in stocks. Over the long haul, lower cash levels should improve returns.

The World Wide Web

Another serious problem facing mutual funds is that they don't translate well in the Internet era. The technology of funds is so archaic that investors can do little more with funds on the Web other than check daily prices, buy,

> ### Sidebar III: Too Many Stocks Spoil the Broth
> According to the fall 1997 edition of the *CFA Digest*, mutual fund companies are overdoing it when it comes to diversification. The magazine says that the majority of a portfolio's nonsystematic, or diversifiable, risk can be eliminated at portfolio sizes, with holdings of 20 stocks a common occurrence (although holdings of 100 stocks are out there, too). The average growth mutual fund (at the time) held 78 securities, the magazine reports, thereby limiting any diversification potential.

and sell. Basically, that's the same thing as eBay does with Beanie Babies and other collectibles. Fund investors can't, however, do meaningful things such as take tax control, screen individual holdings, or even find out what stocks are in the fund on a real-time basis. In fact, end users can't even determine the price of the fund shares until after the market has closed for the day.

A study by Cerulli Associates estimated that 107 million U.S. households will have Internet access by 2003 versus 34 million in 1999. The survey showed a large correlation between the adoption of the Internet and the recent spectacular growth in the number of brokerage accounts. "Based on historical growth prior to the advent of the Internet," the report indicates, "we believe discount brokerages would have accumulated 12 million accounts by 1999, versus the 20.8 million that existed at last year's end." These brokerages are bringing investors one step closer to cheaper investment alternatives and one step further away from the clutches of the mutual fund industry.

If You Can't Beat 'em, Join 'em

Fund companies are beginning to take to separate accounts in a big way. AIM Management Group's nascent managed accounts division recently closed a first deal with First Union Securities under its new subsidiary, AIM Private Asset Management, to provide separately managed accounts from a mutual fund company. AIM portfolios became available through First

Union's separate accounts Master's Program in October 2000. AIM initially offered three of its own fund styles—core large-cap, blue-chip, and mid-cap equity—through First Union. In addition, the new AIM subsidiary signed on futurist Harry Dent, president of HS Dent Advisors, to manage a version of the Dent Demographics portfolio for private accounts.

At New York City-based The Dreyfus Corporation and its subsidiary, Dreyfus Service Corporation, company executives followed suit. A new separate account service that provides individually managed portfolios and related investment services through institutional channels such as broker-dealers or financial planners was rolled out in late 2000. The Dreyfus separate account team includes a product management team, a client service team, and a sales force that work directly with investment consultants to distribute Dreyfus investment management services.

They're not alone. Fidelity, Massachusetts Financial Services, and Oppenheimer Funds, among others, are all opening managed account divisions. The question is: Are they simply hedging their bets? Or are they opening their main profit centers of the year 2010?

A WORD ON MUTUAL FUND "WRAP"

As you delve more deeply into the separate accounts world, you're bound to run into mutual fund wrap accounts. Although not as old as separate accounts, wrap accounts grew from unsteady beginnings in the 1980s when financial giants like Fidelity and Smith Barney developed new fund profit centers in the burgeoning "fee-only" marketplace.

Cerulli Associates describes mutual fund wrap accounts as programs that are designed to systematically allocate investors' assets across a wide range of mutual funds. Services include client profiling, account monitoring, and portfolio rebalancing. An asset-based fee of around 1.25 percent is charged instead of a commission plus the cost of the funds used. Account minimums typically range between $10,000 and $50,000.

Aside from the absence of having a fund manager on board to choose stocks, the primary difference between mutual fund wraps and separate accounts is that, with separate accounts, taxes aren't as big an issue and investors have greater control over their accounts than mutual fund wrap investors do.

Overall, separate accounts are proving more popular than mutual fund wraps. According to the Money Management Institute, separate account assets reached roughly $400 million through 2000. Mutual fund wraps have grown at a slower, and lower, rate. Cerulli Associates reports that mutual fund wraps grew from $109 billion in 1999 to $289 billion through the fourth quarter of 2000.

A NEW ERA

The steadily increasing success of separate accounts notwithstanding, the mutual fund industry, which controls more than $7 trillion in equity, bond, and money-market funds, is in no immediate danger of withering away. Funds still meet the needs of millions with no interest in online trading or only modest sums to invest.

Still, the stocks of mutual fund companies are underperforming the stock market, and that's a signal that there are problems in the industry. "Mutual funds used to be the investment of choice," says A. Michael Lipper, founder of Lipper Inc., a fund data and research company. "Now, it's more the investment people use when they have no other choices."

CASE STUDY 1

Mutual Fund Problems

Settling down with her quarterly mutual fund statement one evening, Eileen Reilly grew concerned over how many different stocks had moved in and out of her fund in the preceding year. "I'm used to seeing some trading activity," said the 39-year-old who runs a graphics design business out of her home. "But that statement showed my fund was like a revolving door last year."

It turns out that Reilly had stumbled upon a grim trend in the mutual fund industry that could seriously impact the success of her fund. Too much trading—often triggered by Internet advice—has recently begun to harm long-term mutual fund investors. According to John Brennan, chairman of the Vanguard Funds, annual redemption rates for stock funds used to average about 10 percent—equivalent to an average holding period of 10 years. But by year's end 1999, they were approaching 40 percent a year—equivalent to a holding period of only 2.5 years. Rapid turnover punishes buy-and-hold investors who bear heavy transaction costs and are faced with unwanted tax burdens.

"I understand my fund manager was new and wanted to place his own personal stamp on my fund," adds Reilly. "But the extra capital-gains taxes and trading fees may have wiped out any benefits the new stocks added to the fund. I'm a person who likes stability, and when my mutual fund becomes unstable, well, that's a big red flag to me."

2

ASCENT OF SEPARATE ACCOUNTS

I called the New World into existence, to redress the balance of the Old.

GEORGE CANNING, BRITISH PRIME MINISTER, 1826

We told you in Chapter 1 that a growing number of mutual fund firms are hopping aboard the separate account bandwagon. Why? Partly because mutual funds are falling out of fashion with investors and partly because separate accounts are a superior alternative. With the average separate account size rising annually, that's where fund companies want to be—mutual funds or no mutual funds.

According to a 2000 report by Cerulli Associates Inc., the popularity of separate accounts goes hand in hand with the growth of fee-based investment advice, which has expanded sharply in the past few years. According to Cerulli, nearly 25 percent of the net new cash going into mutual funds during

Q1 of 2000 came through fee-based RIAs and mutual fund wrap programs (10.3 and 13.5 percent, respectively), instead of from sales commissions. In 1996, fee-based money accounted for just under 14 percent of new mutual fund cash (8.6 percent from RIAs, 5 percent from MP wrap).

According to a 2001 study (Figure 2-1) by the Money Management Institute (MMI) and TowerGroup, separate account assets could surpass $2 trillion by 2010 and will grow at a rate of $200 billion annually. In contrast, assets in stock and bond mutual funds (excluding money markets) were about $5.2 trillion at year's end and growing much more slowly. The February 23, 2000, issue of *The Wall Street Journal* ("Dreyfus Joins Push to Pamper Its Clients") made the following characterization: "Essentially, separate accounts are custom made suits in a world of off-the-rack department store brands."

What is driving all the hoopla over separate accounts? Easy. More control, better investment performance, a sensible tax structure, better use of Web tools than funds, and lower fees. But those are just the simple answers. For the real good stuff, let's take a detailed look at how separate accounts came to be—and why they're so in vogue today.

THE EVOLUTION OF INVESTMENT MANAGEMENT

For nearly as long as there has been a stock market, there has been a demand for advice on how to pick the best stocks. Pools of wealth were accu-

FIGURE 2-1

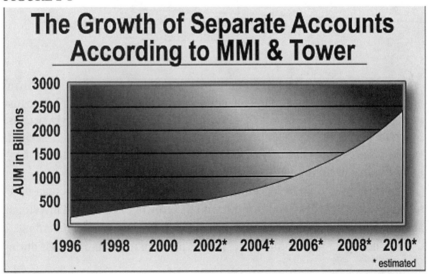

The Growth of Separate Accounts According to MMI & Tower

mulated and then used by bankers and businessmen such as Vanderbilt, Fisk, Rothschild, Morgan, Drew, Astor, Gould, Keene, Sage, Gates, Rockefeller, and others. These individuals made and lost (and sometimes made again) fortunes for themselves and their backers. It was largely an unregulated (and sometimes unscrupulous) enterprise.

In the early 1900s, the process of providing advice began to slowly shift to brokerage firms. Improved communications made it possible for the Wall Street brokers to maintain clientele across the country. In 1885, Burrill and Housman was formed in New York. It was later to become E.A. Pierce and Company. In 1915, Merrill Lynch and Company was formed. By 1940, the two had merged into what we know as Merrill Lynch today. Under the leadership of Charlie Merrill, stockbrokers became more than sellers of securities. Brokerage firms built research departments and provided market education and advice.

With the bull market of the 1920s, the desire for professional management was so strong that blind pools were formed offering individuals the chance to participate in market speculation. Never mind that the investors had no idea how the money was to be invested. That didn't matter nearly as much as who the blind pool operators were. In the best of cases, such investments were risky. Some represented outright frauds. With the tremendous bubble building in the Roaring Twenties, however, demand for pooled vehicles continued to increase.

It's no secret that the truly wealthy have always been able to afford professional assistance when investing. But pooled vehicles made it possible for average Americans to join the club. Sadly, however, investment accounts for the masses were largely unregulated. Stockbrokers also provided advice to the middle class, although their advice was often tainted by the sales commission they received (shocking, we know). It wasn't until the Investment Company Act of 1940 that professional management truly became widely accessible in the form of the modern mutual fund. Funds didn't become popular, however, until even later. As an example, noted mutual fund pioneer John Templeton began investing for clients in the 1930s, first with a brokerage firm and later with his own investment counsel firm for wealthy clients. He didn't get into the mutual fund business until 1954 when he started the Templeton Growth Fund. Even then, available mutual funds were numbered in the dozens.

Initially, funds were sold only by brokers. These brokers were paid a "sales load" amounting to as much as 8.5 percent of the initial investment. Over the past 60 years, the fund industry has grown and evolved substantially. Now, no-load funds are bought directly by investors without the services of brokers. The success of funds has been so spectacular that there are now

Sidebar I: The High Five

It seems that even when it comes to separate accounts, the old firms keep getting richer. The top five firms offering managed accounts are Merrill Lynch, Morgan Stanley Dean Witter, UBS PaineWebber, Prudential, and Salomon Smith Barney, which collectively hold approximately 70 percent of the overall market.

At the end of 2000, these top five managed account program sponsors reported $292.1 billion in assets under management (AUM), up from $245 billion at the end of 1999, but down slightly from $300.5 reported at the end of 2000's third quarter. According to Money Management Institute (MMI) spokesperson Christopher Davis, the figures are based on a survey of money managers and managed account sponsor firms conducted annually by the MMI, whose membership comprises the industry's leading program sponsors as well as their selected professional portfolio management firms.

The MMI reports that the industry's performance this year is all the more striking in that, in 2000, asset flows into equity mutual funds generally declined. Major equity indices also have generally declined in 2000 and 2001: the S&P 500 roughly by 20 percent and the NASDAQ Composite falling almost 50 percent from its high through May 2001.

more funds available than stocks listed on the New York Stock Exchange (actually, that's part of the problem with funds today—there are too many to choose from). Funds are available in every style and type. Index funds, foreign funds, convertible funds, sector funds, hedge funds, funds of funds, and others offer an extremely wide variety of alternatives. In addition, an entire industry has been built around providing advice and information regarding the professional managers of funds.

THE BIRTH OF AFFORDABLE SEPARATE ACCOUNTS

The terrain shifted about 30 years ago, placing separately managed investment accounts on firmer ground. In 1971, the Securities and Exchange Commission ruled that commissions were negotiable for any trade involving $500,000 or more. Four years later, fixed rates were abolished for trades of any size. This now famous ruling was put in effect on May 1, 1975, and is known as "May Day" in the financial markets. Discount brokerage was allowed for the first time, giving rise to powerhouse Schwab and eventually the deep discounters such as E*TRADE, Ameritrade, and other online brokers.

The ruling had another important effect. It allowed brokers to price their services in a variety of ways. Innovative E.F. Hutton seized the opportunity by pricing commissions as a percentage of assets for select clients rather than as a per trade charge. Because all commissions are "wrapped up" in an annual percentage of assets charge (typically 2 percent), they became known as "wrap fees." Hutton offered this new approach to clients who utilized professional managers to pick their stocks in separate accounts rather than funds. This made it more affordable for individuals to access separate account management. There was no longer a fear that brokerage commissions would consume a portfolio. The account minimums dropped sharply, as low as $250,000 in some cases.

Although clients became able to afford separate accounts in 1975, it wasn't until much later that most managers could afford to provide them. The cost of tracking investment portfolios remained high well into the 1980s due to its labor-intensive nature. In addition, the best-performing managers were growing their business very nicely with mutual funds. With the bull market's start in August 1982 (when the Dow Jones Industrial Average was still well below 1000), professional money management through mutual funds became a booming business.

GETTING CYBER-SAVVY

Technology-wise, the money management industry was slow in adopting the benefits of computerization. Certainly, computers were used to provide stock quotes. Computers were also used to keep track of mutual fund client rosters. For the most part, however, computers were not used in the areas of portfolio accounting, trading, and reporting. Yet, these were the precise areas which made it uneconomical to manage smaller separate accounts. Fortunately, that was about to change and change dramatically.

According to Jamie Waller of Citigroup Asset Management, in the 1980s, it was assumed institutional quality money management reporting would cost about $1000 per year per portfolio, and that was just for the systems overhead allocation (never mind paying the portfolio manager or the broker consultant and their back-office staff). Today, systems allow for sophisticated money management and reporting and trading solutions for under $100 per portfolio per year (and yes, the portfolio managers, brokers, and back-office people still need to be paid). Technology has paved the way for these cost reductions. A decade ago, an institutional manager would typically have one reconciler for each account. Today, separate account managers have leveraged their operations so that one person can reconcile between 5000 and 8000 accounts."

Thus, the advent of the computer age combined with the deregulation of commissions has allowed both clients and managers the ability to afford lower separate account minimums.

ADVANTAGES OF SEPARATE ACCOUNTS

To paraphrase Thomas Edison, success is 1 percent inspiration, 1 percent determination, and 98 percent perspiration. That was the recipe for the separate account industry, and its patience and commitment to the idea of separately managed accounts are really beginning to pay off for investors. But how are they better than mutual funds?

Separate accounts offer a number of distinctive advantages over mutual funds. Let's look at some of the more prominent benefits.

Customized Portfolios

First and foremost, separate accounts allow clients to have customized portfolios unavailable through funds. Clients may choose to not hold a particular company or industry in their portfolio for any number of personal or economic reasons. For example, executives at Microsoft might prefer not to have any Microsoft or other technology shares in their managed separate account due to high levels of ownership in their option or profit-sharing plan. In a mutual fund, it would be virtually impossible to have the fund avoid ownership in these companies. In fact, fund shareholders have to wait as long as 6 months just to learn what the fund owns.

Investing with Your Heart

With separate accounts, investors apply social or personal screens on their portfolios. When we were at Franklin Templeton, managers handled a number of Catholic charities that had a strict "no abortion" screen. As a result, the money managers avoided ownership of certain health-care providers for those clients. Templeton also had clients who were concerned about the impact of deforestation on the environment. Consequently, managers avoided ownership

> **Sidebar II: Not Wrapped Up**
> Contrary to some media reports, separate accounts are not necessarily wrap accounts. Wrap accounts can include mutual funds or stocks, whereas separate accounts contain only stocks and bonds.
>
> In general, wrap programs are fee-based managed investment arrangements. Clients never pay a commission. Instead, they pay an annual fee based on a percentage of assets, regardless of the number of trades or services provided. The programs typically come with advice services, such as investor profiling and asset allocation, and management services, such as automatic rebalancing, quarterly and annual reporting, and frequent advisor consultation. Separate accounts may or may not be based on a wrap fee. Some separate accounts charge a management fee for advice plus trading commissions.

in certain forest-products companies in their portfolios. Suffice to say, it would be impossible to enforce or even track these mandates in a mutual fund.

Taxes

Tax efficiency may be the most compelling argument in favor of separate accounts according to experts in the field. "Mutual fund turnover ratios have grown to an average of about 100% per year, from 10% to 12% per year, because many mutual fund managers trade aggressively to get every last basis point," says Len Reinhardt, chief executive officer of Lockwood Associates and a leading industry advocate for the use of separately managed accounts.

As a result, even buy-and-hold mutual fund investors can face yearly tax liabilities. They must also forgo the use of loss-harvesting strategies that investors in individual securities can use to reduce capital-gains taxes. Separate account managers, by contrast, can time a client's trades for optimal tax treatment based on the individual's specific needs. As we pointed out in Chapter 1, each year, mutual funds are also required to distribute the vast majority of any gains or income enjoyed by the fund. These distributions then become taxable at the shareholder level. This system was implemented due to its relative simplicity.

Unfortunately, it can also create some serious inequities. For example, the average mutual fund held 30 percent of its net asset value in unrealized gains as of year end 2000. These gains are distributed to shareholders in the year they are realized. Yet, it's possible that the shareholder wasn't in the fund when the gains were made, but only when they were distributed. As a result, shareholders have absolutely no control over their tax liability and in some cases are taxed on gains they didn't even enjoy.

Investment "Flows"

Perhaps one of the most important benefits of separate accounts is that unlike mutual funds, they are not subject to the inflows and outflows of other investors. One of the hardest things in managing a mutual fund has to do with managing the shareholders. Human nature is such that most investors panic when markets fall and become greedy when markets are rising. As a result, fund managers are inundated with net redemptions as markets bottom and excess inflows when markets are peaking. Unfortunately, this is the exact opposite of the adage to "buy low and sell high." Even more unfortunately, it impacts on every fund owner, even those who stayed the course and didn't buy or sell.

Cache

Separate accounts provide select clients with the cache of direct discussions with institutional money managers. "Some high-net-worth clients want to feel that they have something that distinguishes them from ordinary investors in mutual funds," said one advisor who uses separate accounts.

Imagine driving a car and taking the bus. Separate accounts are similar to a private car in which the manager drives the client directly to his or her destination. A public bus can also take passengers to destinations, but it must stop at various points along the way to let people on and off. All other things being equal, a private car typically offers a superior experience to the public bus (you get to control the radio, too).

SEPARATE ACCOUNTS GROW UP

These benefits are just now registering with the masses, and they're showing on the bottom line. In 1990, approximately $10 billion was managed in broker-directed separate accounts. By 1993, the industry had grown to nearly $70 billion according to Cerulli Associates. As we've indicated, that figure had risen to over $719 billion at the end of 2000.

A June 23, 2000, article in *The Wall Street Journal*, entitled "Managed Accounts Win More Fans; Product Moves Beyond the Rich," demonstrates the growth in the separate account market. One reason for this rapid growth is that the public is becoming more educated on the subject. For example, *The Wall Street Journal* notes: "Clearly, separate accounts have strong selling points. Unlike investing in a mutual fund and immediately being exposed to the fund's embedded capital gains, an investor has some say over stock purchases and sales in a separate account, giving him better control over his tax bills. Another advantage is that investors can say no to a stock they don't want to own—a tobacco company or defense contractor, perhaps—or one they already own in such quantity that they don't want any more."

In addition, fund managers are rapidly entering the separate account market for fear of losing customers. In the early 1990s, Franklin-Templeton was alone among the very large mutual fund companies offering separate accounts. As we mentioned in Chapter 1, many other larger players have announced or are exploring plans to enter the separate account business: MFS and Oppenheimer Funds have just begun to target separate accounts for sales. They join Janus, T. Rowe Price, Eaton Vance, Alliance, and John Nuveen.

In setting up separate account businesses, fund firms are catering to wealthy investors who want personalized attention and an upscale alternative to mutual funds with their tax-inefficient, one-size-fits-all structure.

BARRIERS TO SUCCESS

Before separate accounts are able to displace funds, however, they will have to overcome a few limiting factors. First, distribution of separate accounts is virtually dominated by the five largest brokerage firms. Combined, these five firms—Merrill Lynch, Salomon Smith Barney, USB PaineWebber, Prudential, and Morgan Stanley Dean Witter—control nearly 80 percent of the market according to Cerulli Associates.

These firms control the distribution or separate accounts and view them as their high-margin business to be protected at all costs. In fact, half of all trades are now completed online. The major firms recognize the advice component inherent in separate accounts, however, and recognize that the e-brokers will struggle to compete. Unfortunately, for clients and prospective clients, this factor has kept minimums high as the major firms have sought to serve wealthier investors where the margins are higher. Stockbrokers continue to promote funds for smaller accounts because the cost of service is lower.

This creates a stranglehold of distribution for separate accounts somewhat similar to limited shelf space in a grocery store. Only the existing brand names have space, and new entrants find it difficult to offer their products. In addition, the cost of distribution can be almost prohibitive due to the high demands placed by the broker channel.

Sidebar III: Brothers in Arms?

Can two competing investment tools live together without driving each other crazy? Ken Hyne, head of investment management at Advest Inc. in Hartford, CT, thinks so. Hyne tells *Bank Investment Marketing* in the August 1, 2000, issue that there's room for mutual funds and separate accounts in the same portfolio under the right circumstances.

"If someone has $500,000 to invest, they may want to buy large cap growth and value stocks and then use mutual funds for more niche exposure," says Hyne. One scenario the magazine presents is a separate account for managing securities and a mutual fund wrap account for the international portion of the portfolio.

Getting into the separate account industry isn't easy, however. Industry officials estimate that it takes more than half a year to build the obligatory wholesaling staffs and back-office systems to support separate accounts. And that doesn't guarantee shelf space on the separate account platforms at brokerages and banks.

Cost, as always, is an issue, too. At Templeton, the cost of a full-scale wholesaling effort for separate accounts was estimated to be more than $2 million per year. This can be prohibitive for many managers.

The second limiting factor is tied directly to the first. Although the cost of nearly every other financial services product has declined sharply in recent years, the cost of managed products such as funds and separate accounts has remained stubbornly high. Fund expense ratios remain around 1 or 2 percent (not including the trading costs of the fund itself), and the average separate account fee was still 2.11 percent in 1999.

Interestingly, however, the cost of the professional management in separate accounts has actually declined sharply. For example, separate account clients at Templeton paid 3 percent per year in the early 1990s, with the company retaining 2 percent of that and 1 percent paid to the broker. Less than a decade later, the average fee for clients industrywide was 2.1 percent, with 1.1 percent attributed to brokerage commission costs and distribution.

That's fairly amazing in the Internet era because the actual cost of trading has fallen sharply and distribution has also been sharply devalued.

The reason, of course, is the tight control of shelf space by the major firms. Having lost retail stock trades to e-brokers, these firms have kept separate accounts as their high-margin business. Individual brokers who sell these accounts average nearly $400,000 per year in income. What do they provide to warrant such an income? Many offer good asset allocation advice as well as monitoring the managers for clients. Too many, however, do little more than sit behind a mahogany desk, drink coffee with clients, wear stylish clothes, and help clients fill out forms.

Another serious problem with such limited distribution is that investors are forced to use the brokerage services of the program provider. Without competition, it's difficult to be certain that trade executions are as efficient as they should be. This scenario can be devastating to long-term performance. Unfortunately, because the only access to managers is through brokerage firms, directed brokerage is automatically assumed without any potential for trade competition. While it's relatively simple to fire your manager in the current separate account system, it's very difficult to fire your broker or even to hold your broker accountable for the trading activity. Actually, it's even difficult to monitor the quality of the trades due to reporting delays. Sadly, even managers find it difficult to do anything about trade quality. The major firms have too strong a lock on distribution.

These possible conflicts of interest can raise serious questions regarding the advice provided by brokers regarding managers. Until the distribution stranglehold is broken and fees come down, separate accounts will be unable to take their rightful place in fully displacing mutual funds. As a result, other products have cropped up as "competitors" to traditional funds. These include exchange-traded funds and, more recently, the ability for investors to buy customized baskets of stock from companies like FOLIOfn. While the customized baskets offer some value such as individual tax control and screening of unwanted securities (though ETFs don't), they ignore one of the true benefits of mutual funds and separate accounts: active professional management.

In addition to having greater appeal to investors, separate accounts also have greater appeal for brokers and managers. Brokers would find their commissions and margins squeezed even further if baskets or ETFs replaced mutual funds. Managers would lose their asset-based fees altogether. By supporting separate accounts, brokers can still enjoy trading commissions or wrap fees, and managers are still paid for assets.

Clearly, then, separate accounts are the logical successor to the mutual fund throne from every perspective. Institutional money managers have recognized this and are entering the separate account market as a result. The media have also taken notice and produced dozens of articles on this very subject this year alone. Finally, with a 30-percent annual growth rate, individual investors are beginning to catch on, too.

CASE STUDY 2

Consumers Turn to Separate Accounts

Bob Keane knew a raw deal when he saw one. And the more the 42-year-old computer programmer saw of his mutual funds, the less he liked them.

Keane had started investing in mutual funds in the late 1980s, accumulating a nest egg of nearly $450,000. But the funds' unavoidable taxable distributions have been a prickly issue for Keane, especially around tax time. "When you get those 1099s every January, it seems like you're getting hit with taxes on money you never see," he says.

Spotting a story in his local newspaper on separate accounts, Keane decided they deserved a closer look. An admitted do-it-yourselfer, Keane dug deeper into his mutual fund portfolio and was shocked to discover that not only was he getting taxed more for his fund portfolio than he would for a similar separate account portfolio, but he was paying more for it, too. "I discovered that I was paying about 2.5 percent in mutual fund fees as opposed to about 2 percent for a separate account holding basically the same stocks."

Keane opened his new separate account days later and was glad to hear that his tax picture would look better, too. "With separate accounts, I'll only pay capital-gains taxes when I sell stocks at a profit, not when a mutual fund manager unloads a holding bought long before she came to the fund." Keane estimates that if he had a separately managed account the year before, he would have netted $10,000 more after taxes.

3

WHERE DO YOU FIND SEPARATE ACCOUNTS?

An invasion of armies can be resisted, but not the invasion of ideas.

VICTOR HUGO

Innovation has long been a staple of American commerce. Take the National Bank of Detroit, which once offered its customers $10 each time they discovered an error in their checking accounts. The policy garnered 15,000 new accounts and $65 million in new assets within the first 2 months of the program.

Then there's cosmetics giant Estee Lauder, which was the first company to offer a gift with a purchase. From that idea, the company grew to a value of nearly $2 billion.

Sometimes innovation is built on someone else's idea. Henry Ford didn't invent the automobile; he just improved on it. Bell Laboratories may have invented the first transistor in 1947, but they didn't sell the first transistor radio. That honor went to Sony, which sold the first model in 1956.

That's the case with the separate account, an innovative idea built on the foundations poured by the mutual fund and brokerage industries decades ago. Taking the notion of professionally managed investment portfolios at an affordable price is a natural progression for both investors and the financial services industry.

Still, not many people know much about separate accounts, and certainly, not many individual investors understand what they are and where to find them. So far, we've covered some significant ground on the differences between separate accounts and mutual funds. But now it's time to separate the wheat from the chaff and bore in on how you can benefit more directly from one of the most innovative ideas in the history of financial services.

The first task is to figure out how separate accounts work. Then you'll need to know where to find separate accounts and evaluate what programs might fit your needs best. That's what Chapter 3 is about: charting a course to the best separate accounts available in the world.

HOW SEPARATE ACCOUNTS WORK

Before you embark on your separate accounts journey, take a minute to understand the terrain. And that means knowing how they work.

A significant benefit of many separate account programs is that they provide investors with access to money managers that might not otherwise be available. Another key feature of separate accounts is professional portfolio management. Portfolios are usually managed by institutional investment advisors (commonly referred to as money managers) on a discretionary basis. This means that investors delegate the day-to-day investment decisions to their managers. It is important to note that although investors assign the daily decision-making responsibility to their money managers, they do not in any way relinquish control over their portfolios.

With a separate account, your financial advisor assumes the role of a true consultant, assisting you in developing long-term investment plans and determining asset allocation strategies for your portfolio. To appreciate the real value of this unique approach to investing, it is important to understand the role of your financial advisor. Once the portfolio managers have been selected, consultants are then responsible for monitoring their clients' portfolios and meeting with them on a regular basis to ensure that their long-term goals and objectives are being met. Another important responsibility of your financial advisor/consultant is to coordinate the activities of each of the parties involved in the investment program. These include the program sponsor (brokerage firm or other financial institution), money managers, the investor, and the financial advisor. (We'll cover choosing an advisor in greater detail in Chapter 4.)

With separate accounts, advisors place your money with portfolio managers specializing in each of their preferred categories, going to them either directly or through a brokerage company. These companies, which handle assets that come to them through advisors, "wrap" together several services, including consulting, custodial, money management, and monitoring, all for one fee. Wrap-fee companies can be a good way for smaller investors to get the tax benefits of separate accounts while gaining a higher level of money management expertise, although they typically come with a high annual fee.

Some managers of separate accounts offer several basic portfolios that investors can then customize with the help of their advisors. When the work is done, they know exactly what stocks they hold. This is usually a manageable number, anywhere from 20 to 80. This short list of "names" (as the companies are called) is in sharp contrast to the long lists of holdings in most mutual funds, which are published periodically but may change considerably between announcements.

Generally, the average separate account investor has at least $100,000 in assets to invest, although some separate account programs offer account minimums per asset class in the $25,000 to $50,000 range. In addition, a new batch of Internet-based financial companies offers lower minimums and lower fees on a monthly basis for low-end separate accounts (called "folios"), though usually without the additional advice of investment consultants.

By and large, financial services companies are cutting account minimums to attract the burgeoning middle-class separate account customer base and to compete better against online providers. One reason is to help clients avoid big capital-gains taxes. Another is to attract customers who now turn to mutual funds for professional money management. Offering managed accounts with smaller minimums also allows customers with larger accounts to split their accounts to diversify. Or families might be able to set up separate accounts for each family member.

No matter what your account size, in contrast to mutual funds, your separate account program should allow you to make direct investments in stocks. One advantage here is that you can avoid particular stocks that you may already hold in other accounts. Another is that you can give a "thumbs-up" or a "thumbs-down" to stocks you don't want for philosophical, religious, moral, or economic reasons.

With separate accounts, you should also be able to take defensive measures, such as selling losing positions in one account to offset gains in others, thus reducing tax bills. For example, about 10 to 15 percent of Merrill Lynch managed account clients order their money managers to take tax-related actions during the year. Its clients seem to approve as Merrill's separate account business has more than doubled to $52.6 billion at the end of March 2000 from $27.3 billion at the end of 1998. By comparison, the firm's fund unit has suffered nearly $2.8 billion in net withdrawals in just the first 4 months of 2000.

WHERE TO FIND SEPARATE ACCOUNTS

By and large, the brokerage industry, especially the big wirehouses, offer the most separate account packages, with the mutual fund and banking industries struggling to catch up. The top five firms offering managed accounts are all brokerage firms: Merrill Lynch, Morgan Stanley Dean Witter, Paine Webber, Prudential, and Salomon Smith Barney. Collectively, they lead the managed account industry and had a 78 percent share of the overall market at the end of 2000.

Of the top five firms, Salomon Smith Barney rules the roost, with a 29 percent market share. Merrill Lynch is beginning to nip at the leader's heels, with a 22 percent market share, up from 20 percent in 1998. A distant third is Morgan Stanley Dean Witter (with about 10 percent of the market). Morgan is followed by Paine Webber (9 percent) and Prudential (8 percent). National full service brokerages like A.G. Edwards, regional players like DB Alex Brown, and third-party vendors like Lockwood control another 14 percent of the industry. A scattershot mix of financial services firms comprise the remaining 8 percent.

Although the big wirehouse firms still dominate separate account assets, other financial services sectors are coming on strong. Wirehouse separate account assets dropped from 87 percent in 1993 to 78 percent in 2000. Over the same period, third-party vendors like Lockwood Financial saw their market share rise from 0.6 percent to 4.5 percent. That growth spurt was driven primarily by demand from registered investment advisors, both independent and those associated with independent broker dealers.

Big players in the regional brokerage industry include Raymond James, Wheat First Union, Everen, A.G. Edwards, and Deutsche Alex Brown. Independent broker/dealers, like American Express and Financial Services Corporation, and major banks, like Wells Fargo and Chase Manhattan, lead their respective sectors.

FIGURE 3.1

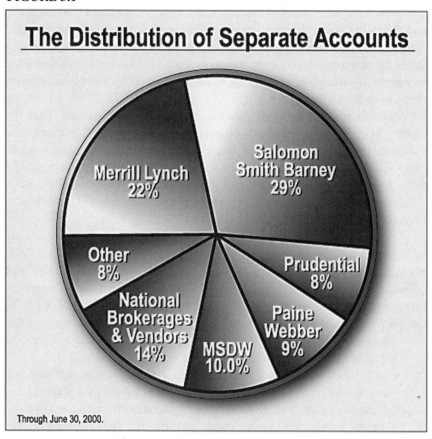

The Distribution of Separate Accounts

Salomon Smith Barney 29%

Merrill Lynch 22%

Other 8%

National Brokerages & Vendors 14%

MSDW 10.0%

Paine Webber 9%

Prudential 8%

Through June 30, 2000.

THE MUTUAL FUND INDUSTRY

The brokerage firms aren't alone. The mutual fund sector is just as eager to crash the separate account party. We mentioned earlier that fund giants like Oppenheimer, Fidelity, and MFS are gearing up big managed account efforts. MFS is offering six or seven accounts that involve equities, including large-cap, small-cap, mid-cap, and international portfolios. MFS, like most fund companies, allows (and even encourages) its fund managers to handle much of the stock selection for the company's separate accounts.

Oppenheimer took a different tack by lowering its number of separate accounts to three through 2000. These include a large-cap value portfolio, an international portfolio, and a global portfolio that combines the two styles.

Others, like Dreyfus, are building up their separate accounts gradually. The New York-based fund giant only had a handful of separate accounts by mid-2000. But down the road, Dreyfus envisions a separate account portfolio that would fill Morningstar's popular fund "boxes." The company also splits the management of its separate accounts between its stable of fund managers, by subadvisors to the Dreyfus funds, and by asset management firms with ties to Dreyfus.

Still others are going the acquisition, or outsourcing, route. Take the Chicago-based John Nuveen Group, which purchased Rittenhouse Financial Services, which had been offering separate accounts since 1989. The arrangement worked out so well for Nuveen that it spun off a mutual fund that was managed by Rittenhouse. Other outsourcers include Alliance Capital Management, which purchased separate account Regent Investor Services in 1995.

Perhaps the fund company with the longest track record in the separate account sector is Franklin-Templeton of San Francisco. Since 1991, Frankin-Templeton has been offering separate accounts (truth be told, the co author of this book, Kevin Freeman, was tapped by Sir John Templeton himself to run the company's first separate account program). Today, the company's separate accounts group has about $4 billion under management, with a brokerage network that may be unsurpassed in the fund industry.

One route that many fund companies are taking nowadays is to go online and launch separate account efforts and, in some cases, partnerships. Make no mistake, fund companies see separate accounts as a way to keep wealthy investors aboard ship. With so many affluent investors participating in the online revolution, going cyber has its benefits for fund firms. Already fund firms are jockeying for position to forge alliances with existing online wrap account providers who charge lower wrap fees than their offline brethren. That trend should only increase in the next few years.

A last word on fund companies and separate accounts. Again, don't confuse separate accounts with mutual fund wraps. In light of their apparent cost advantage, mutual fund wraps might seem like a safe and cost-conscious choice. But with them, you're paying not only a wrap fee, but also many of the expenses (though not the sales loads) associated with the underlying funds. Netted out, mutual fund wraps can be just as expensive as—and in some cases, more expensive than—separate accounts.

Finally, also remember that separate accounts are good for money invested in a taxable account because your managers can keep your accounts separate from those of other investors and take your tax situation into consideration when buying and selling securities. That's a luxury you'll give up in most mutual fund wraps.

ADVISORY ROLES

It's no secret that the popularity of separate accounts goes hand in hand with the growth of fee-based investment advice, which has expanded sharply in the past few years. According to Cerulli Associates, nearly 25 percent of the net new cash going into mutual funds in 2000's first quarter came from fee-based RIAs and mutual fund wrap programs (10.3 and 13.5 percent, respectively), instead of from sales commissions. Back in 1996, fee-based money accounted for just under 14 percent of new mutual fund cash (8.5 percent from RIAs and 5 percent from MF wrap).

These fee-based advisors include brokers at the big Wall Street firms who are making the switch from charging investors trading commissions on each market transaction. They also include independent financial advisors who use discount brokers for their clients' trading.

As financial advisors have moved to the fee-based arrangement, they want to show that they are doing substantial work to earn their fees, which range around 1 percent of assets. As a result, many advisors think they need to do more for clients than just help with the selection of mutual funds.

To establish a separate account, a financial advisor generally hires a professional money manager to create a customized portfolio of stocks for the client.

As we mentioned in Chapter 1, many fund companies are getting into the act. Among the fund companies providing separate accounts are Invesco, a unit of Amvescap PLC, Lord Abbett & Co. and TCW Group Inc. The four biggest names in the industry are Fidelity Investments, Vanguard Group, American Funds Distributors Inc., and Putnam Investments.

As Cerulli Associates points out in its 1999 report, "The State of the Wrap and Managed Account Industry," money managers are not typically affiliated with the sponsoring brokerage firm or separate account provider. "In most cases," the report states, "money managers are available across a wide range of asset classes for ultimate selection by the client, in conjunction with their financial consultant."

SUBADVISOR PROGRAMS

Usually, the separate accounts industry is segmented into two categories: subadvisor and open architecture. As Cerulli states, understanding the nuances of each is critical for everybody involved in the separate accounts process—investors, financial advisors, and money managers alike.

Cerulli defines the separate account subadvisory program as one where clients' assets are invested among a sanctioned roster of money managers, in a separate account, as determined by the sponsoring brokerage firm. Some current examples include Legg Mason, Salomon Smith Barney, and Janney Montgomery Scott.

Sidebar I: Wrap Accounts and Other Strangers

While you're conducting your separate accounts due diligence, you'll surely run into different types of wrap accounts and other fee-based programs. Don't become confused.Here's an explanation for the ones you're likely to bump into:

Mutual Fund Wrap: Programs are designed to systematically allocate investors' assets across a wide range of mutual funds. Services include client profiling, monitoring, and rebalancing. Asset-based fees are charged (e.g., 1.25 percent) instead of commissions. Minimums are typically between $10,000 to $50,000 plus the cost of the funds used.

Consultant Wraps: Often referred to as separate accounts, consultant wraps typically have unaffiliated institutional money managers manage investors' assets in separate accounts. High net worth investors are targeted by financial services firms, with minimums of $100,000 to $250,000 and up. A bundled asset-based fee (often 2.5 percent before discounts from negotiation) covers money management, trading, and custody.

Offshore/Overseas Mutual Fund Wrap: This is a mutual fund or consultant wrap program designed for non-U.S. investors. Sales take place outside the United States.

Rep as Portfolio Manager: In this case, a registered investment advisor (RIA) acts as money manager for the client by taking full responsibility for selecting a portfolio of securities.

Fee-based Brokerage: These programs allow active traders to pay asset-based fees (around 1 percent) for all trading activity instead of commissions for each individual trade. Historically, there has been no advisory element to these programs. This could change as online advisory programs continue to proliferate. Programs include both mutual funds and individual securities.

Minimums to access each asset manager typically range between $100,000 and $250,000. The investor usually pays one bundled asset fee for all managed account services, including trading, custody, clearing, money management, and investment consulting.

Under subadvisory program processes, separate account investors have a single contract with a brokerage firm that covers the scope of the program, including the brokerage firm's arrangement with the money manager. That program is discretionary, but it is the investment manager that has the discretion, not the sponsoring broker-dealer, Cerulli says. Most often, it is the broker-dealer's responsibility to pick the money manager for the client, though sometimes it remains the client's decision (more on this in Chapter 4).

OPEN ARCHITECTURE PROGRAMS

Like separate account subadvisory programs, open architecture separate accounts are invested in a separate account run by an asset manager. There are, however, several crucial differences between the two.

First, the investor, in conjunction with a financial advisor, can select virtually any money manager to manage his or her separate account portfolio rather than be limited to a smaller approved list of 35 to 80 managers usually offered by subadvisory programs. "In these types of programs," the Cerulli report states, "triangular contractual relationships typically exists where an investor has a contract directly with the money management firm, that has advisory responsibility, in addition to a contract with the sponsoring broker-age firm." In Cerulli's definition, that constitutes an "unbundled" program.

Most separate account providers offer versions of both the separate account subadvisory and open architecture models. Janney Montgomery Scott, for example, has between 50 to 60 money managers in its subadvisory program, but also includes as many as 1500 institutional money managers in an open architecture version of its separate account.

Another major difference between subadvisory and open architecture separate accounts is in pricing. Unlike a subadvisory program, which bundles together all pricing components such as trading, clearing, or manage-ment, investors in most open architecture separate account programs have more options to pay for their services. "Generally," continues the Cerulli report, "there is an arrangement where they can elect to pay some sort of directed brokerage commissions or fee plus ticket charges instead of straight asset-based fees."

Translated, this means clients in an open architecture program can pay for money management through either fees or commissions. While with both fee structures investors still get a separate account, they do have the option of how they want to pay for it. Investors will find that some open architecture programs, like A.G. Edwards Private Advisory Services Program, allow multiple pricing options; others, like Merrill Lynch, do not.

Another attribute of open architecture separate accounts that offers some appeal is that the money manager involved is likely to have more direct contact with you, the "end user." This is fueled by the fact that you have a separate account contract arrangement directly with the money manager. "This generally translates into a greater investment in systems and technologies for participating money management firms since investor account information must be maintained on their systems," adds Cerulli.

Of the 38 programs tracked by the Cerulli Report, 26 are classified as subadvisory. "Though the open architecture structure is the older of the two program designs, there are now more subadvisory separate accounts arrangements within the broker/dealer community," says the report.

The "beauty part," as Ross Perot might say, is that with subadvisors there is a set number of money managers to choose from and pricing structures are more streamlined. And not only are there more subadvisory than open architecture programs, but they also dominate in terms of assets. Of the separate account industry's roughly $275 billion in assets under management (through 2000), 70 percent are housed in programs where the separate accounts' sponsor orchestrates all aspects of money management, pricing, research, and due diligence. That consolidation has drawn great interest from the registered investment advisor (RIA) community who appreciate having those tasks handled for them, leaving them more time to devote to you and your separate accounts portfolio.

ONLINE "FOLIOS"

Perhaps the fastest growing market for separate accounts online is that of folios stock baskets that can be customized and bought and traded in one step by individual or professional investors. Folios were introduced in spring 2000 by FOLIOfn (www.foliofn.com).

These sites do a good job combining simplicity with the low-cost feature so often linked to financial services Web sites. Most of these sites offer ready-made customizable portfolios that you can make your own with a simple point and click. Some of these sites can buy one-hundredth or even one-thousandth of a share of IBM or Berkshire Hathaway. Or if you want to buy $1000 worth of 30 stocks, the online separate account programs can arrange things so you wind up with $33 of each stock. A potential downside is that some don't offer any investment advisory services at all. Typically, fees start at about 1.25 percent annually, and account minimums begin at $50,000, although minimums of $25,000 are beginning to see the light of day.

Still, most online separate account sites do offer financial advice and some form of unlimited trading. In some cases, you can enjoy "unlimited" trades but only if you do so at a designated time each trading day. In other words, you can log in as many trades as you want, but your cyber separate account provider may only log them in at 2:45 each day, for example.

Costwise, the cyber separate account sites are a penny-pincher's dream. To buy 50 stocks at discount Web broker Datek totals $499.50, at $9.99 per trade. At Foliofn, it costs $1000 less. Better yet, when you sell the stocks, you don't have to pay a commission at Foliofn. Try that at a discount Web broker.

Come to think of it, some big Web trading discounters are wading into the separate accounts business. In late 2000, E*TRADE purchased PrivateAccounts.com, in part to reach a mass investment audience that seems to appreciate investment-supported services as it does rock-bottom commission prices. Only months earlier, E*TRADE acquired closely held folio vendor Electronic Investing Corp., known as eInvesting.

There's much more about online folios in Chapter 11.

BANKS AND SEPARATE ACCOUNTS

When it comes to selling mutual funds, bank reps have been slow to promote fee-based investment products to their clients, preferring to book individual transactions and reap the benefits of upfront loads and fees. Providers of separate account programs have long argued, predictably, that this approach to profitability is short-sighted on the rep's part.

Wrapping all costs, from advisory to transactional fees, into one asset-based fee has not always been popular with investors. But in the past few years, even bank clients have started to value an individually managed program. Moving from a transaction-based to a fee-based relationship is the key to success in the separate accounts game for banks, although there are indications that banks are still stuck in neutral while the brokerage and fund industries are in overdrive.

"Banks have been slow to pick up on wrap programs because they have not understood that the high-net-worth individual wants choice," says Lee Dolan, a senior vice president at SEI Investments. "They keep trying to sell their own portfolio management services at a time when they are losing market share."

Until now, the separate account market has been dominated by major Wall Street stand-alone brokerages. But bank-owned brokerages appear to be at their heels. Mellon Financial's Dreyfus Corp. was one of the first big bank/brokerage operations to offer the accounts when it rolled out a product with a $100,000 minimum investment.

Wells Fargo Securities Inc., a wholly owned subsidiary of Wells Fargo Bank, followed suit with a separate accounts program that provided clients with access to more than 30 of the nation's top money managers, making it among the first bank-affiliated brokerage firms to offer a consultant wrap fee account. The WellsSelect account gave clients with at least $100,000 to invest access to independent money managers that typically required clients to have at least $1 million to invest. After completing an investment questionnaire, the client works with a Wells Fargo Securities Inc. financial consultant to select investment advisor candidates who best serve the client's investment objectives, risk tolerance, and other investment preferences. The Wells' separate account allows the client to work with his or her financial consultant to select one or more outside advisors. Clients can establish equity, fixed income, balanced (including municipal and global balanced), international, and global accounts. Like most programs, the financial consultant meets with the client regularly to discuss the advisors' performance results.

THE 401(K) MARKET

Your 401(k) plan might go the separate account route, too. Whether you realize it or not, some of your retirement money may be going into brokerage accounts that choose individual stocks. While technically not separate accounts per se, these brokerage accounts offer many of the same benefits and advantages of separate accounts, such as better tax structures and lower fees. In fact, a rising number of large 401(k) plan sponsors are paying mutual fund companies, insurers, banks, and other money managers to create new separate account-type programs. In some cases, they're even self-managed. But don't be fooled—they're still very much pooled investments.

CONCLUSION

You must comparison shop to get the best separate account. Separate accounts are available from a wide array of vendors, including banks, broker/dealers who sell through armies of independent investment advisors, insurance companies, regional brokers, mutual fund companies, and of course, national wirehouses such as Merrill Lynch. Minimum account sizes and fees vary quite a bit.

As we said at the beginning of the chapter, don't be reluctant to look for companies that are doing innovative things with their separate account programs. Whether that means better prices, more choices, or more control over your separate accounts, note that there is a difference between separate account programs. Whether you're going it alone or working with a financial advisor, make sure to conduct a complete due diligence program so you know and understand what those differences are.

CASE STUDY 3

Should I Go It Alone or Get an Advisor?

As an emergency room doctor at a big city hospital, Dave Joy was used to taking matters into his own hands. His split-second decisions had sometimes resulted in hospital staffers saving a life when it looked like all was lost.

Although the 34-year-old bachelor made sure he didn't take his work home with him, he did take his "can do" attitude and apply it to his growing personal financial investments portfolio. Tired of the lack of control over his mutual funds, Joy decided to invest in a separate account where he could call the shots. But should he take that step on his own or hire a financial advisor to make sure the decisions he'd be making were the right ones?

"I knew that my portfolio had grown into the mid-six figures," recalls Joy. At that point, I'd been pretty much on my own. But I felt my funds were stagnating, and I didn't have a say in how they could be fixed. So I went to a separate accounts firm and the first thing they asked me was whether I'd be using a financial advisor. I had to admit I hadn't even considered it."

Joy soon found that deciding to use an advisor was a pretty big decision. On the one hand, a separate account advisor would assess Joy's risk tolerance and investment goals. An advisor would also help Joy assemble a good asset allocation blueprint to work and recommend one or more investment managers to implement it. Plus, the advisor would track his portfolio and suggest adjustments when needed.

On the other hand, Joy liked making his own calls when it came to his portfolio. After all, why invest in an investment tool that gave you more ability to make your own decisions and not take advantage of that flexibility?

"In the end, I decided that even with a financial advisor I'd have the last call," says Joy. "Just like in the E.R., there'd be consulting and advice given, but I'd have the last decision. With my busy schedule, the benefits of having someone in my corner watching my portfolio was an attractive option—but only if I had the last word."

Joy advocates asking some tough questions when interviewing potential financial advisors. "Make sure that before recommending anything, a planner should review your financial picture, goals, risk tolerance, and the time horizon for the money being invested," he says, recalling his own due diligence process. "The advisor should also provide specific reasons for recommending a particular stock or money manager and spend time educating you on alternatives." In addition, Joy says, ask consultants whether they are registered investment advisors with the Securities and Exchange Commission and the state. Have they taken the National Association of Securities Dealers Series 65 exam? Are they a certified financial planner, a certified financial analyst, or a chartered financial consultant?

WORKING WITH THE PROS: CHOOSING SEPARATE ACCOUNT MANAGERS

Progress is impossible without change, and those who cannot change their minds cannot change anything.

GEORGE BERNARD SHAW

A big benefit of separate account programs is that they provide investors with access to money managers that might not otherwise be available. Another key feature of managed accounts is professional portfolio management. Portfolios are usually managed by institutional investment advisors (commonly referred to as money managers) on a discretionary basis. This means that investors delegate the day-to-day investment decisions to their managers. It is important to note that although investors assign the daily decision-making responsibility to their money managers, they do not in any way relinquish control over their portfolios.

With a separate account, your financial advisor assumes the role of a true consultant, assisting you in developing long-term investment plans and determining asset allocation strategies for your portfolio. If you decide to do without an advisor, the consultant's role falls on your shoulders.

But for now, let's assume that you want to work with a financial advisor. To appreciate the real value of this unique approach to investing, it is important to understand the role of your financial advisor. Once the portfolio managers have been selected, consultants are then responsible for monitoring their clients' portfolios and meeting with them on a regular basis to ensure that their long-term goals and objectives are being met.

Another important responsibility of your financial advisor/consultant is to coordinate the activities of each of the parties involved in the investment program. These include the program sponsor (brokerage firm or other financial institution), money managers, the investor, and the financial advisor.

If you don't have a stockbroker or financial planner who possesses a good understanding of separate accounts and how they work, don't fret. If you regularly work with a broker or financial planner, start there. Ask about separate accounts and see if they demonstrate a command of the issues. If you don't work with a broker or planner, or if you believe the one you do work with isn't up to speed on separate accounts, start looking for one who has a good understanding. When you do, think logically about it. Most of the issues that matter when choosing a separate account advisor apply to choosing a lawyer, a banker, an insurance agent, or a doctor. You'll want professionalism, experience, a steady hand at the wheel, and a comfortable personality you can work with. In short, you want a relationship with your financial advisor.

That's important. Unlike a stock brokerage firm, a discount trading firm, or even an old, entrenched mutual fund company, where impulse and inflexibility rule, separate accounts fairly demand the idea of lasting relationships between advisor and client.

Relationships are especially critical to newcomers to the separate accounts market. Unsure of their footing, virtually all a new customer has in his or her corner is an advisor with the expertise and experience needed to grow assets. As we said in Chapter 1, the whole idea of separate accounts is to give individuals and smaller investors the opportunity to have the same professional money management as institutional investors. That's job one for your financial advisor, who can probably expect to have some degree of hand-holding in the early months of the relationship, even if the client is market savvy.

They don't mind doing that. Advisors using separate account managers often position their own role as that of an architect and an old-fashioned country lawyer. "We explain that our role is to construct the portfolio and select the best separate account managers," says one advisor. "Then we work with those managers to meet the client's financial goals."

Also remember that financial advisors—especially the best ones— want your business. According to a 1999 survey by the Money Management Institute (MMI), the interest in advisors looking to offer separate accounts tripled from 1995 through 1999.

"All indications are that investors will continue to aggressively seek out the benefits of individual managed accounts," says Christopher L. Davis, executive director at the MMI. "We think the industry is on track to experience ongoing robust expansion well into the future."

According to the MMI study, interest among the industry's most successful advisors—those earning more than $150,000 annually—in offering separate accounts grew from 13.2 percent in 1996 to 34.6 percent in 1999. "It's clear that, going forward, the advisor community will be seeking more and more opportunities to deliver individual managed accounts," adds Davis.

Interest in Separate Accounts by Financial Advisors

	Most Successful Advisors ($150K and up)	Middle Tier Advisors ($75 to $150K)	Bottom Tier Advisors (Under $75K)
1996	13.2%	7.6%	3.1%
1997	18.6%	7.3%	3.5%
1998	28.6%	8.8%	3.0%
1999	34.6%	13.2%	3.7%

Source: Money Management Institute.

The next step is to decide how you will fund your new account. Most programs allow you to fund an account with cash and/or existing securities. If you are planning to use existing securities, you should check to see if your financial advisor will sell your current holdings under the managed account pricing structure. This may save you a substantial amount in commissions. In addition, you should examine the tax consequences of selling existing securities before proceeding.

Questions to Review with Your Financial Advisor

Investment Planning

What are my investment objectives?
What is my investment time frame?
What rate of return do I need to achieve from my portfolio?
What is my risk tolerance?

Asset Allocation

What is the importance of asset allocation?
What is the proper asset allocation for my portfolio?

Manager Selection

Given my personal goals and objectives, which money managers, or funds, are best suited for me?
Is their investment philosophy consistent with my goals and objectives?
How can I take advantage of different manager styles to reduce risk in my portfolio?

Portfolio Review (for Established Accounts)

How is my overall portfolio doing relative to my investment policy?
How does the period being measured compare with my investment time frame, as stipulated in my investment policy?

Are my money managers, or funds, managing my portfolio the way they said they would?

Is this consistent with my overall investment goal and time frame?

Should I have reason to believe that my long-term investment goals will be met by pursuing the current investment strategy?

If the answer to any one of these questions is "no," changes to the current investment strategy may be in order. If not, you should "stay the course" with your current plan.

Source: Institute for Certified Investment Management, Inc. (ICIM).

WHAT DOES A SEPARATE ACCOUNTS ADVISOR DO FOR YOU?

Remember that participating in the separate account revolution not only increases your chances of becoming wealthier, but it also makes you a better investor. Think about it. If you own a mutual fund, you own shares of funds, but you won't learn much from the experience. You'll either make money or lose money, but you won't learn anything. When you have a separate account portfolio, you receive frequent reports from your money manager that will keep you up to speed regarding current market activities. More frequent personal interaction with your separate account manager will also help you build a better relationship with your money manager and, by extension, your financial life.

The key is in control and access, which are the advantages traditionally associated with institutional investors. When you hire a no-load fund, you are basically hiring a 1-800 phone number. When you hire a separate account advisor, you're not only hiring an investment consultant, but you are hiring a manager with whom you can interact.

Most important, your separate accounts advisor should also monitor your portfolio's performance, help you change or add managers, and change asset allocation strategies. Additionally, your separate account advisor should help you stay focused on the long term. Many investors get too emotionally involved with their money, and this is certainly an understandable occurrence given the high stakes involved. But a good separate account advisor will stop you from buying high and selling low or making unsure, emotional decisions based on short-term results.

The Separate Accounts Process

Once you select an advisor, here's a snapshot of what the separate account management process looks like:

Client Profiling: The advisor conducts a thorough assessment of your financial status, investment objectives, time horizon, and risk tolerance.

Asset Allocation: Investment advisors evaluate profiles and, with your approval, allocate the dollars to the appropriate investment managers.

Monitoring: Money managers track portfolio performance, reporting to advisor and client on a regular basis, usually quarterly. Allocation may be shifted depending on your needs or market conditions.

Asset-Based Fees: Your cost is an all-in-one fee that covers all the services. The fee can be as high as 3 percent but drops with the size of the account and through rampant discounting.

Source: Cerulli Associates.

MORE QUESTIONS TO ASK YOUR SEPARATE ACCOUNTS ADVISOR

Not all separate account packages are alike. When considering a financial planner or a broker to handle your separate accounts program, a couple of issues need to be addressed first.

Before recommending anything, a planner should review the client's financial picture, goals, risk tolerance, and the time horizon for the money being invested. The advisor should also provide specific reasons for recommending a fund or money manager and spend time educating the client on alternatives.

In addition, ask consultants whether they are registered investment advisors with the Securities and Exchange Commission and the state. Have they taken the National Association of Securities Dealers Series 65 exam? Are they a certified financial planner (CFP), a chartered financial analyst (CFA), or a chartered financial consultant (CFC)? Many advisors are simply brokers with little asset management experience, according to a study by Cerulli Associates Inc. And although some firms provide their brokers with adequate tools to perform risk tolerance analysis and investment selection, others leave them free to rely on intuition and personal experience.

In short, what kind of certification and experience does the advisor have? In some states, there are no standard certification procedures or licensing requirements for financial planners. Anyone can call himself or herself a planner.

Ask advisors how many years of experience they have. Get references. Call the state securities division and the National Association of Securities Dealers to see if any complaints have been filed against them.

Make sure you know all the costs. Although it's not the only factor, you should shop around and negotiate.

In addition, how does your advisor select and monitor managers and funds? This may be the most important question of all. The money managers will be choosing your investments, and the level of ongoing performance evaluation is an important value brought to the program. Managers are selected to follow different investment styles such as value, growth, or international. Most programs provide a selection of managers for different investment disciplines.

> ### Sidebar I: Straightforward Questions
> Ernst & Young offer these tips on choosing a money manager to help with your investments. Ask questions such as: What's your client load? How do you get paid? What's a profile of your typical client? What's your benchmark for reporting whether the portfolio is doing what it is supposed to be doing? In evaluating your manager, compare your portfolio's performance to the appropriate benchmark (e.g., as the Standard & Poor's 500 Index for large companies or the Russell 2000 index for smaller companies). Get reports, quarterly or semiannually, on how well you've done, from beginning to end, after expenses.
>
> It's also a good idea to clearly outline the criteria by which your manager will be replaced.

Experts tell consumers to stay away from advisors who sell money managers and mutual funds based solely on performance history. That performance is unlikely to be repeated.

Ask how often the firm evaluates its money managers' performance. How do they evaluate the managers? Get the latest report. Have they ever fired any managers? How many? Why?

If you are investing in a mutual fund wrap program, ask if the fund family is in-house or a third-party fund. How closely does the firm manage the fund managers' investments to ensure consistency with the fund's objective? What indexes do they measure against to determine performance?

Don't forget to ask what kind of reporting the separate account offers. The level of detail in account reporting varies considerably. Some separate account programs offer a one-page overview, whereas others provide a detailed analysis that includes benchmarked performance, trading activity, and a review from the manager on how the portfolio fared.

Finally, ask the advisor whether the performance is reported gross or net of fees. Most separate account programs report performance quarterly. Your broker or advisor should call to discuss the performance and be able to answer your questions.

SHOPPING FOR A MONEY MANAGER

As we saw in Chapter 3, the good news for separate account investors is that there's plenty of good money management help out there. One of the benefits of separate accounts is that investors can choose from a host of talented money managers, sometimes as many as 150 within one separate accounts program.

You must comparison-shop to get the best separate account. As we pointed out in Chapter 3, separate accounts are available from a wide array of vendors, including banks, broker/dealers who sell through armies of independent investment advisors, insurance companies, regional brokers, mutual fund companies, and of course, national wirehouses such as Salomon Smith Barney and Merrill Lynch. Minimum account sizes and fees vary quite a bit.

Many investors make the mistake of choosing a money manager based on performance alone. They fail to investigate the investment style, the organization, the portfolio manager, the mechanics of the account, and finally, the fees.

Organization longevity alone does not mean the company has good investment managers, but it does show that the organization is committed to the business. Look for evidence of an efficiently run, profitable organization with an attention to client servicing. Make sure you examine how much insurance coverage the firm has for the fraudulent acts of employees. Also find out if your securities can be lent or used as collateral for the firm's trading account.

Know what resources support the manager's investment decisions. Ask how the company develops its economic outlook and investment strategy, where its investment research comes from, and how the information is transferred to the individual portfolio managers. Again, your financial advisor can help you get these answers.

Sidebar II: Six Ways to Shoot Yourself in the Foot
If you're committed to working with a registered investment advisor (RIA) and not a stockbroker, be prepared. With more than 20,000 registered investment advisors in the United States, investors seeking the services of a professional money manager face an overwhelming list of choices. Not only is the number of advisors daunting, but the evaluation of advisors can be complex and time-consuming. Unfortunately, most individuals don't know what key questions to ask. According to AdvisorLink, an investment advisor search and monitoring service, there are six common mistakes that individuals make when evaluating investment advisors. If you can avoid these errors, the odds of finding a good advisor and a satisfying relationship are much higher.

1. Believing Everything You See and Hear: Most advisors are honest, hardworking people and would never misrepresent their performance history. However, some advisors prominently display in their advertising carefully selected periods of high performance to attract investers. When inspecting performance figures, be sure to inspect the advisor's entire track record and pay particular attention to the footnotes (fine print) that accompany the advisor's track record.
    Tip: Always read the fine print.

2. Failing to Check an Advisor's Compliance Record: Every advisor is required to submit a document called Form ADV, Parts I and II to the SEC. Advisors rarely give out Part I unless you ask for it. Part I is important since it contains information about past bankruptcies, regulatory sanctions, legal judgments, and criminal records. "While a clean ADV doesn't guarantee an honest Advisor, it can certainly tell you if the Advisor has a checkered past," says Gary Halbert, president of ProFutures Capital Management, sponsor of AdvisorLink.
    Tip: For $39, the National Financial Fraud Exchange will conduct a background check on an advisor. Call 800-822-0416.

3. Paying Too Much Attention to Profits and Not Enough to Risks: Bull markets have a way of making investors forget about downside risk. It is very easy to become intoxicated with spectacular returns. Individuals should always consider an advisor's losing periods as well as performance in declining

markets. While volatility isn't necessarily bad, you should understand the level of risk an advisor takes. Tip: Look at the advisor's maximum drawdown and worst month.

4.   Choosing an Incompatible Advisor: There are definitely some excellent advisors out there, but the best performer may not be compatible with your objectives, time horizon, tax situation, or tolerance for risk. Some advisors swing for the fences. Others try to hit a lot of singles. Like a good marriage, the two parties must be of a like mind and share the same objectives and ambitions. Tip: Ask your advisor to describe his or her typical client. If he or she doesn't describe you, consider a different advisor.

5.   Ignoring an Advisor's Administrative Skills: Dissatisfaction with an advisor is as often a function of sloppy administration as it is poor performance. Missing statements, late tax forms, uncredited dividends, inaccurate trade confirmations, and other administrative blunders are serious mistakes that can cost individuals thousands of dollars. Also, you want to make sure all clients are treated the same so that everyone gets the same trade execution. Sloppy administration is often a red flag of other management problems. Tip: The only way you can be sure their operation is top-notch is to make a visit in person.

6.   Assuming Your Work Is Done When You've Invested Your Money: Because past performance is no guarantee of future performance, placing your money with an advisor is just the first step. You should regularly compare your advisor's performance and risk management against popular indexes like the S&P 500. "Too many investors think that their work is over once they selected an advisor. The reality is that their work has just begun," says Halbert. Tip: Make your advisor requalify for your business annually.

Source: ProFutures Capital Management, Inc.

Try to target a firm with a well-structured decision-making process for asset allocation, stock selection, and implementation. Ask if they have a "sell" discipline. What will prompt a sale and is there sensitivity to an investor's tax situation? Look for an organization whose portfolio managers have superior access to investment research and technology. Does the company encourage and provide ongoing training for employees? What is the average tenure of the employees and the turnover ratio? Does the company provide employee ownership opportunities that create rewards for effort as well as provide continuity and tenure?

Portfolio manager experience is always a crucial factor. Know the manager's overall industry experience, years managing with the current organization, and educational background. Find out if the manager is certified or working toward an industry designation. For example, the chartered financial analyst (CFA) 3-year process designation requires rigorous testing on portfolio management and security selection. Certified financial planner, registered investment advisor, certified trust and financial advisor, and certified public accountant are other designations to consider. Ask how the manager communicates investment changes and what factors he or she considers when structuring a portfolio. How long will it take the manager to structure the portfolio to meet your specific goals? Will your account be a "model portfolio" or will your manager structure your account specifically to your individual needs and objectives? A good money manager should be concerned with asset allocation and appreciate the advantage of broad diversification. Ask how many relationships the manager is responsible for managing.

Understand how the manager is compensated. A manager who is evaluated at year's end by how well he or she met your investment objective and goals will have your best interests at heart. Finally and most important, are you comfortable with your manager and can you trust his or her people with your assets?

FIGURE 4-1

Advisors Say More Investors Are Using Managed Accounts

% of clients investing less in managed accounts: 12%

% of clients investing the same amount in managed accounts: 27%

% of clients investing more in managed accounts: 40%

Source: Yankelovich Partners

CALCULATING THE HUMAN FACTOR

There are also some more specific indicators that need to be addressed when choosing a separate account manager. A key one is the "human" factor.

Yes, even a money management firm has a personality, both good and bad. For instance, determine whether your investment representatives provide you with the best information possible or simply try to hold on to your business at any cost. Do they report the same performance numbers over the same time periods consistently, or do these performance indicators change to put the manager in the best possible light during a challenging market?

Do they answer your questions about alternative investment strategies in a straightforward manner, or is everything a sales pitch? Are they direct about addressing their mistakes, or is there always a defensive twist to their explanations intended to convey that they are beyond reproach?

In addition, find out about the turnover rate in the organization. Is it a positive working environment? This means more than most people realize in terms of investment returns. If turnover is low, is it simply because they pay top dollar for individuals willing to do anything to get rich, or is it because this is the type of organization people want to be associated with for a significant portion of their careers?

Perhaps more important, how much access to information concerning the decision-making process is disseminated throughout the firm? Remember, the more information client service people have, the more information they can provide their clients.

Since information is power, an organization's failure to invite open debate concerning the investment process is a signal that power is jealously

---

Sidebar III: Rules of Thumb

As we mentioned in Chapter 3, most investment firms that offer separate accounts do so through intermediaries such as financial advisors. When talking about separate accounts with your investment advisor or shopping for a new one, your manager should provide:

- Active account management tailored to your specific investment goals, risk tolerance, and time horizon

- Day-to-day portfolio monitoring and refinement as market conditions change

- Regular performance reporting and record keeping

guarded in the hands of an elite few. This is one of the classic red flags for potentially poor organizational morale.

When the market is volatile, it's harder to make money. That means it's now more important than ever to pick a good money manager. But when shopping for someone to oversee your assets, it's not enough just to follow the performance numbers in the paper.

Remember the importance of the human element as well.

EVALUATING YOUR MONEY MANAGER

Finally, one of the most important parts of your program is the ongoing monitoring of your money manager's performance to determine if your investment objectives are being met. Performance monitoring should include quarterly reports that give you and your investment executive an objective statistical analysis of your investment manager's performance.

The report should list all your account holdings and compare your rate of return with appropriate market indices, as well as other professionally managed portfolios with similar investment objectives. And because performance is based not only on return but also on the level of risk incurred to achieve that return, the report should clearly assess the volatility of your portfolio during specific time periods.

Without any broad industry standard to measure performance, evaluating money managers becomes more of an art than a science. Most of the major wirehouses have an entire department dedicated to analyzing money managers, watching for things like style drift or manager changes and anything else that could signal a change in performance. But the analysis focuses more on methodology than performance, with firms looking for each manager to fit into a specific niche of the asset allocation chart: top-down versus bottom-up, level of expertise, depth of knowledge and background in a certain area, such as managing large-cap stocks in a bear market.

Measuring performance, though, becomes a little more complicated because none of these money managers has a specific target to hit, as do their counterparts at the mutual funds. "The benchmark for the separate account is the investment objective set between the financial advisor and the client," one financial advisor says. "When you buy a mutual fund you are buying a product, so a product should have an easily understandable performance reference, but the managed account comes with a consultant. The managed account industry is not going to live and die being pegged against a benchmark."

But since a broker's client relationships will live and die by overall performance, managed money accounts require a high level of client contact and communication. As we mentioned earlier, the first relationship is between the client and the advisor.

The broker not only has to explain how each money manager chosen for a portfolio invests for clients weaned on Morningstar reports; they also have to explain each manager's performance within the context of the overall portfolio. Technology has helped. Using e-mail and blast faxes, the managers are staying in close contact with the client's separate account firms.

> ### Sidebar IV: Ranking Investor Concerns
> If there was any doubt on what investors considered the most important criteria in hiring a financial advisor, there isn't any more. Of 4300 people surveyed by Boston-based Dalbar, Inc., a whopping 83 percent cited investment education as the key service that a financial advisor can provide a client. Of poll respondents, 80 percent also said they expected their financial advisor to maximize after tax returns. The top priority of 70 percent was getting high returns.

Overall, it is the role of the financial advisor to explain to the investor how the managed account is performing. Still, sometimes advisors themselves can be far removed from the process, usually putting together a client proposal and shipping it off to the main office. The main office comes back with a handful of recommendations that the broker then gives to the client.

"The client is well served because the firms have an army of analysts who are poring over the data and focusing on the money managers," explains Jim Galbreath, a financial advisor at Denver-based NWQ Investment Management, a $5 billion investment advisory firm. "Their sole job is to make sure the money managers are performing as expected, in the style expected by the people."

HOW MUCH WILL YOU PAY FOR YOUR SEPARATE ACCOUNT MANAGEMENT?

Pricewise, the total cost for a separate account service averages between 2 and 3 percent of assets managed on an annual basis. This fee often drops with the size of the account and through discounting.

For example, if you have an initial investment of $250,000, you might pay a slightly higher rate than the person who's bringing $500,000 to the table. Separate account investors can often expect to see discounts of up to 25 percent for simply meeting the investment advisor's minimum asset range. So in a program with a 3-percent maximum fee on a $100,000 minimum account, the investor may actually pay only 2.25 percent after receiving a discount of 25 percent (0.25 of 3 percent). These discounts usually get better with the more money you toss into the asset pot.

Separate account pricing schedules may include trading, money management, custody, and financial consultation. Separate accounts are also available for an advisory fee plus trading commissions.

GOING IT ALONE

Ah, America. The land of the rugged individualist. Like Lewis and Clark exploring the prairies, plains, and pristine Rocky Mountains on their way to the Pacific Ocean or Humphrey Bogart squaring raw deals with his fists on the silver screen, Americans like going it alone.

But is that a wise choice in the often-comprehensive world of investing? Possibly, especially if you have some experience trading stocks and can appreciate saving a few bucks on a financial advisor. If, for instance, you already know you want to allocate 50 percent of your assets to domestic growth stocks, 30 percent to international stocks, and 20 percent to Treasury bonds—and if you're comfortable with your ability to make that determination—there may be little reason to pay someone to make those allocations for you. Of course, if you're uncomfortable doing that on your own, a financial advisor can come in handy. Either way, let's look at the issues you face by flying solo.

Before you choose between teaming up with a financial advisor broker or going it alone, take some personal inventory. After all, emotions do play a major role in any investment plan, and separate accounts are no different. So ask yourself if you have qualms about the financial market. Do you shrink at the thought of crunching numbers, or are you pumped up over diving headlong into stock analysis? Do you eagerly tear through the newspaper's business pages to see how certain companies are faring? Just how much time are you willing to put into investing? If the answer to any of these questions is no, then you'd better begin ringing up some financial advisors.

In the go-go information age, time is a big factor as well. Essentially, what you're buying from a financial advisor—apart from his or her expertise—is time. In other words, your financial advisor has the time to scour the world for the best separate accounts and the best money managers.

Maybe you don't. If so, hiring a financial advisor to take the time to make the right decisions for you and your family is well worth doing.

If you are going it alone and are interviewing brokerage firms or mutual fund companies to see what kinds of deals their separate account divisions are offering, make sure they can answer the following questions to your satisfaction

- How much is the annual separate account fee? Is it negotiable? (Remember that the industry average is 2.3 percent annually.)

- Are all transaction costs included?

- What specific services does the special account provide? (For example, this could mean monthly, instead of quarterly, statements or more liberal trading rules.)

- What investment choices are available?

- How and when are changes in allocations made?

- How are performance numbers calculated and what was the amount of risk taken to achieve those numbers?

- How will the account function? Do you like the way the reports are structured and are you pleased with the frequency of the statements? Is monitoring the tax cost information included in the fee? If not, try to determine the additional time and cost and add that to the fee if you are comparing institutions where this service is included. How is dividend income and interest collected?

- If the relationship doesn't work, is there a fee for terminating the account?

- Can you see a sample of the firm's quarterly financial statement?

Some other services you should expect from the separate accounts manager you choose include:

- Regular consultation with a broker to help you plan your investment strategy.

- A good selection and description of the managers who will invest your money. Heck, even ask to meet the manager(s).

- Ongoing management of your portfolio in line with your investment objectives (buying and selling stocks, bonds, mutual funds, or other financial instruments) and regular reporting on the status of your account.

GOING ONLINE

If you opt for one of the burgeoning online separate account firms, there are some additional services you're going to want. At the top of that list are access to the company's investment advisory team and free annual portfolio rebalancing. You should also expect some help filling out the separate account application forms and easy access to customer service staffers if something goes awry while you're working on your online portfolio. In the online world, face-to-face encounters are rare, but you still should expect—even demand—quality customer service.

MORE PROS AND CONS OF FLYING SOLO

Financial writer Mary Rowland, writing on Microsoft's Money Central Web site, has some good ideas on how to evaluate whether investing in a separate account on your own is a good idea or not. She lists five reasons to invest on your own and five not to. Let's have a look.

Cons

1. **You don't know how to design a portfolio:** When investment advisors—the best of them—design portfolios, they talk about the "efficient frontier," or a string of portfolios stretching along a line of increasing risk. In other words, there is a portfolio that most efficiently matches your level of risk. A person with a high level of risk would have a much different "efficient frontier" than a person who can't stomach the idea of losing money, even for a few days in exchange for the possibility of higher returns in the long run. Each efficient portfolio on the frontier provides the greatest possible return for the risk it's taking. Designing them is part science and part art. It's not work for a novice. Rowland says that a financial advisor's job is to assess your level of risk and then design a portfolio that provides the highest possible return for the risk you're willing or able to take.

2. **You are emotional about your investments:** We mentioned this earlier. Rowland's point is that economists and psychologists who study investing identify all kinds of ways that we are irrational about our money. We second-guess ourselves. We fear regretting a bad decision. We hate to lose more than we love to win. All of these things can cause us to make bad investment decisions.

Sidebar V: A Tale of Two Investment Tools
While conducting your due diligence, make sure you know the difference between separate accounts and mutual fund "wrap" accounts. The latter may seem like the safe and cost-conscious choice. But with them, you're paying not only a wrap fee but also many of the expenses (though not the sales loads) associated with the underlying funds. Netted out, mutual fund wraps can be more expensive than separate accounts (which in some circles are also called "consultant" wraps).

Remember, separate accounts are good for money invested in a taxable account because your managers can keep your accounts separate from those of other investors and take your tax situation into consideration when buying and selling securities. That's a luxury you'll give up in most mutual fund wraps.

3. **You don't have the time:** As we mentioned earlier, creating and monitoring an investment portfolio can be time-consuming. It's difficult, too, to figure out your own investment performance as opposed to that of the funds you invested in. "Look at what happened to the Beardstown Ladies, who sold 80,000 books by claiming an average annual return of more than 22% when they actually got just over 9%," says Rowland.

4. **You lack discipline:** Among other things, a financial advisor will tell you exactly how much you must invest in your separate account to meet your goals. An advisor will even arrange for the money to be automatically withdrawn from your bank account or paycheck. So you'll be saving and investing whether you want to or not. You'll reach your goals, too. On your own, you might not even get started.

5. **You lack staying power.** When the going gets rough in the market, do you get going—out of the market? Studies show that most individual investors do much worse performancewise than professional money managers. That's because they trade in and out rather than sticking with their investments.

Pros

1. **You save a lot money:** According to Cerulli Associates, a typical annual fee for a separate account(s) is roughly 2.3 percent of your

assets. Knocking off the advisor's cut could bring your annual fee down to around 1 percent of your separate account assets.

2. **You're in control:** With you calling the shots, you're the boss. If you can do without the hand-holding and second-guessing, making your own investment decisions is the way to go.

3. **Investing can be satisfying:** Rowland cites the growing number of Internet investors who have grown accustomed to making their own investment decisions in recent years. Like the husband who paints his own house to save some money or the wife who sews her own quilts for the same reason, the self-satisfaction of handling your own affairs is tough to beat.

4. **The Internet:** Yep, the Web has become a big factor in American's self-sufficiency during the last few years. There's no shortage of investment-oriented Web sites geared to helping individual investors choose stocks. Meanwhile, thousands of corporations and mutual funds post their annual reports and prospectuses on the Internet. Several low-cost online brokerages also have emerged that give background and earnings data on specific companies, as well as executing trades. All this has made investing easier and less intimidating; hence, more people are trying their hand. And with Internet-based investment sites, you can easily track your investments and stay abreast of the market's ups and downs.

5. **Potential performance is higher:** Perhaps you don't know how to design a portfolio. Well, maybe you don't have to. If you do it yourself, you can take on a risk profile that an investment advisor would never set up for you. After all, you know yourself the best.

If the question over investing on your own rests on what your current financial advisor is already doing for you, concentrate on a few key issues. According to Maggie Craddock, a two-time Lipper award-winner as a lead portfolio manager at Scudder, Stevens & Clark and current consultant with Focus Partners LLC, the first thing to do is determine whether your investment representatives provide you with the best information possible or simply try to hold on to your business at any cost.

Craddock also advises potential do-it-yourselfers to ask if an advisor reports the same performance numbers over the same time periods consistently, or do these performance indicators change to put the manager in the best possible light during a challenging market?

"Do they answer your questions about alternative investment strategies in a straightforward manner, or is everything a sales pitch?" Craddock asks. "Are

Sidebar VI: What You Should Get from Your Separate Account Management

Between your financial advisor and your money manager, there's a list of services and benefits that you should expect from your separate account experience. Some primary examples of these services are:

- Access to top-rated money managers.

- Access to higher after-tax returns.

- Portfolios custom tailored to meet individual goals.

- A separate account that gives you more control over your assets.

- A separate account portfolio that's structured to meet your personal objectives and risk levels.

- Regular interaction between the investment manager, the relationship manager (i.e., a financial planner or), and you (thus the emphasis on good relationships).

- If your objectives change, the manager should easily be able to reallocate your portfolio.

- Separate accounts by nature have fewer holdings than mutual funds. So your money manager should be able to concentrate your investments in their best ideas.

- You should be able to maximize after-tax returns by controlling the timing of realized capital gains.

- For separate account investors with social or faith-based concerns, money managers should be able to accommodate those concerns. For example, a desire to avoid tobacco or oil companies in a portfolio on the part of investors should be graciously heeded.

they direct about addressing their mistakes, or is there always a defensive twist to their explanations intended to convey that they are beyond reproach?"

Perhaps most important, she adds, how much access to information concerning the decision-making process is disseminated throughout the firm? Remember, the more information client service people have, the more information they can provide their clients.

IT'S UP TO YOU

Ultimately, the best way to decide if you want to handle your own separate accounts investments is the sleep factor. Simply stated, can you sleep comfortably knowing that you're handling your own investment portfolio? Or will you toss and turn all night and wake up in the morning haggard and bleary-eyed? If you think there's a good chance that the latter scenario will occur, start talking to financial advisors. But if you were daydreaming while reading this passage, then rest assured you'll be fine on your own.

CASE STUDY 4

Finding the Right Separate Account

To get the right wrap for you, be sure to comparison-shop. That's the advice Geraldine Durkin offers. Based on her experience, it's advice well taken. Tired of trying to make sense of what strategy the mutual fund manager was implementing and not sure she was getting the same bang for the buck that she used to get from her fund portfolio, Durkin decided to make the switch over to separate accounts.

"I think it was the day I realized my value fund manager was investing in some emerging market stocks that just weren't compatible with the fund's mission statement and certainly not right for my risk profile," says the 35-year-old medical software technician. "When I heard about the increased control I'd get with separate accounts, I thought that was for me. The only problem was finding out in particular which one was for me."

The point is well taken. Separate accounts are available from a wide array of vendors, including banks, broker/dealers who sell through armies of independent investment advisors, insurance companies, regional brokers, mutual fund companies, and national wirehouses like Merrill Lynch and USB PaineWebber. Minimum account sizes and fees vary quite a bit. So how did Durkin select and then monitor her separate account managers?

"I chose the managers based on their ability to follow different investment styles, for example, value, growth, or international," she says. "I found that most programs provide a broad selection of managers for different investment disciplines. I also asked a lot of questions, like had the manager ever been fired before and, if so, for what reason. I really did my homework."

Durkin also wanted to know what kind of reporting the separate account offered?

"I found that the level of detail in account reporting varies considerably. Some offer a one-page overview, while others provide a detailed analysis that includes benchmarked performance, trading activity, and a review from the manager on how the portfolio fared."

She also advises getting the straight skinny on numbers, asking money managers whether their separate account performance is reported gross or net of fees and how often performance is reported.

"Once I had those answers, making my decision was easy," Durkin says. "Like I said, you've got to do your homework."

CREATING AN INVESTMENT POLICY STATEMENT

It's no secret that creating goals is the most fundamental component of investment success or any other endeavor, for that matter. Goals help us take action; they make the process more fun; they give us determination and a vision that keeps us going. In short, goals give us a much-needed sense of purpose along with a road map for success.

People who sell goals short do so at their own risk. Without goals, they tend to drift along toward failure. Rest assured they'll get there eventually. But a person who instills goals into his or her life understands that, although mistakes may be made along the way, failure is not an option—and won't be if one's goals are met.

Consider advertising industry legend David Ogilvy, who had two goals: establish the world's largest ad agency within 12 years and, by that time, have a list of clients that included his favorite companies, including

Bristol-Meyers, Campbell Soup, General Foods, Lever Brothers, and Shell Oil. He reached both goals with plenty of room to spare.

Or how about the famous explorer John Goddard? When Goddard was a boy of 15, he made a list of all the things he wanted to do in life. Ultimately, the list had 127 goals, including explore the Nile, climb Mt. Everest, run a 5-minute mile, play the piano, and circumnavigate the globe. By middle age, he'd met more than 100 of these goals and was well on his way to meeting the rest.

THE INVESTMENT POLICY STATEMENT

There's a lot of Ogilvy and Goddard in serious investors: the risk taking, the motivation, and the commitment to succeed. But both men would be the first to say that those attributes, while to be admired, won't mean much without a blueprint on how you're going to get from here to there.

That's where an investment policy statement comes in. An investment policy statement pours the concrete and lays the foundation for all future investment decisions that will be made concerning your separate accounts portfolio. Although separate accounts are a breed apart from mutual fund or brokerage accounts, investment policy statements are basically the same no matter which investment vehicle you choose. They act as a sort of security system for your portfolio, first identifying goals and then creating a vigilant and thorough review process to make sure your separate account portfolio stays on the right track and never deviates from its mission, be it capital accumulation, capital preservation, or a combination of both.

For investors, investment policy statements keep you focused on your objectives during short-term swings in the market while providing a baseline from which to monitor investment performance of the overall portfolio, as well as the performance of individual money managers. For separate account investors, investment policy statements also outline the ground rules of the relationship between you and your investment advisor. How? Because by having an investment policy statement, you can expect to have information prepared that will clearly show you whether or not your investment portfolios are achieving their stated goals and objectives.

STATEMENT STAGES

An investment policy statement is usually developed by you and your investment advisor, acting with your best interests in mind. A good plan outlines portfolio goals, the types of investments your separate account portfolio will allow, the types it won't, the criteria for admitting stocks, bonds, or mutual funds into the plan, and the criteria for ejecting securities from it.

By implementing a set of standards by which the plan operates, you're less likely to manage your separate account by emotion instead of logic. When you see a stock or group of stocks plummet, it's only natural to want to pull the trigger and oust the underperforming stocks from your portfolio. That could be a mistake because stocks fall all the time for myriad reasons, including cyclical sector activity, a delay in the release of a product, or a less than rosy forecast from a lone Wall Street securities analyst. All of these reasons for a stock's decline are likely to be short-term in nature. A sector may indeed be underperforming, for example, but that doesn't mean a well-managed, profitable company within that sector can't see its stock price rise. Or a single analyst can easily misread a company's progress if he or she hasn't done necessary homework. Consequently, your investment policy statement can be a helpful and objective reminder that longer term performance is more important than short-term volatility.

Of course, your policy statement can work both ways. If, in the bull market of 1999, you loaded up on technology stocks, a good investment policy statement would have warned you that your portfolio wasn't sufficiently diverse. Sure enough, overloaded in dubious dot.com stocks, many investors who either didn't have investment policy statements or had them but ignored them were hammered by the technology sector meltdown of 2000.

There, language in a policy statement can act as a brake by stating that a plan will only include diversified stocks, for example. And if your portfolio is underperforming, an investment policy statement gives you and your advisor guidelines with which to replace it.

An investor policy statement also helps identify the minimum performance level required from a given stock to remain in the plan and how poorly a stock can perform before it's jettisoned from your separate account portfolio. Your investment policy statement can, for example, evaluate how your portfolio should rank against its peers or its benchmark, and it also can specify which benchmark should be used. A large-cap-oriented portfolio might look weak when compared with one index but strong when compared with another. Risk-adjusted return should also be addressed. It may not be enough to outperform the benchmark if the portfolio's level of risk increases disproportionately.

WHERE AN INVESTMENT POLICY STATEMENT FALLS INTO YOUR SEPARATE ACCOUNT PROCESS

Your investment policy statement will be prepared by you or your investment advisor after an initial client interview. If you plan on preparing your own investment statement, it's a good idea to at least bring an investment advisor aboard as a consultant when preparing your statement. Unless you're George Soros or Warren Buffet, you could probably use the help.

If you do meet with an investment advisor or with the investment firm managing your separate account portfolio, make sure that the following ground is covered:

Acceptable types of securities
Asset allocation ranges
Legal constraints
Regulatory constraints
Return requirements
Risk tolerance
Tax considerations
Time horizon

Sidebar I: Elements of a Good Investment Policy Statement

What should your investment policy statement cover? An investment policy statement is a written document containing:

- Your plan's goals

- The parameters to be followed by investment managers in realizing those goals

- Target rates of return

- Minimum life of funds

- Risk parameters

- Other restrictions

With respect to participant-directed defined contribution plans—typically 401(k) plans—the investment policy statement should contain the types of investments that meet the "broad range of investment alternatives" requirements of section 404(c), which allow participants to:

- Affect potential returns materially

- Control risk in their accounts

- Diversify their investments

- Minimize the risk of large losses through asset allocation

Your investment policy statement should also identify the appropriate benchmarks for measuring investment performance for each type of investment. For example, a fund whose investment objective is growth and current income should be measured against industry growth and income fund averages.

Other important components of an investment policy statement include:

- Investment manager selection and termination procedures

- Participant control parameters

- Employee communication and education policies

Once your investment policy is agreed on, it is formalized in an investor policy statement and an invester advisory agreement by an investment advisor and the separate account manager. You should have a copy on hand, as will both your investment advisor and your separate accounts manager. Keep it with your other financial documents in your home office, preferably in a secure, fireproof location like a safe or copied onto your computer as a backup file.

MECHANICS OF AN INVESTMENT POLICY STATEMENT

When you meet with your investment advisor and possibly the investment company managing your separate account, know some basics before you sit down. A well-crafted policy statement, a standard with pension and endowment accounts that frequently have to answer to others, will:

- Summarize your large-scale financial goals, your feelings about risk, your expectations.

- Document fairly specific comments on the purpose of certain investments and the rationale behind them.

- Outline general policies and procedures for managing the portfolio over the long term.

- Establish who calls the shots when picking securities that comprise your separate accounts portfolio.

Establishing Realistic Objectives

Your separate account portfolio should be guided by a rational, consistent policy suited to your unique circumstances. To establish clear and definable expectations, your statement should include your investment objectives and goals in a concise manner. It should also establish risk tolerance, return requirements, income needs, liquidity requirements, investing time horizon, tax considerations, legal and regulatory concerns, and unique needs and circumstances.

Let's say you want to retire at age 55 with about $100,000 per year as your postretirement annual income. You also want to finish off your kids' college tuition and set something up for them to inherit when you've slipped the surly bonds of earth, as they say. What's your advisor going to take into consideration? Your age, your current financial condition, the impact of inflation on your portfolio's progress, your specific financial goals, and your risk tolerance level, which will ultimately materialize after all of the foregoing factors are taken into consideration.

While we engage in a more detailed conversation on risk tolerance in Chapter 8, your investment policy statement sets the table in terms of how much risk you can afford to take with your separate accounts portfolio. You need to establish how much risk you are willing to take to achieve those investment returns. After all, the higher the desired return, generally the higher the risk you must take. Are you willing to accept losses within certain categories as long as the overall portfolio does not lose principal over a 12-month period? Would you accept an overall portfolio loss of 5 or 10 percent for 2 years running but not for 3? Write your stipulations into the policy statement. One common result of individual investors building their own investment portfolios is that your risk tolerance may prove to be out of step with your investment return objectives. Consequently, you may need to adjust either your anticipated returns because you'll need to be more conservative in your investments, or you will have to stomach higher risk, which isn't a good idea if it leaves you edgy. That's when panic decisions are made.

You'll also want to use your statement to determine the duration of your separate account portfolio. Unlike a pension fund or mutual fund, which typically is designed to go on forever, your separate account portfolio will have a defined life, which typically is your life expectancy, but perhaps shorter. How much time you have is important in determining what assets and investment strategies you use for the portfolio.

Some investment plans are more realistic than others, but a good investment policy statement reflects what you want to accomplish with your long-term separate account portfolio.

Defining Your Asset Allocation Strategy

Once investment objectives are established, your investment policy statement should establish an asset allocation strategy that you can live with by specifying an acceptable long-term asset allocation mix between the asset classes you plan to use. Your investment policy statement should explain how your advisor evaluates the stocks or other securities used to implement the long-term asset allocation strategy. Again, your investment policy statement will force your advisor—or force you if you're not using one—to keep your investment goals in mind when considering any potential investment opportunities.

When you establish your asset allocation strategy, ask yourself what classes of assets you want to put into your portfolio that will give you the return you want and what classes you want to keep out. Do you want to include stocks, bonds, cash, and real estate investment trusts (REITs) but not junk bonds, gold, or limited partnerships? How much, if any, foreign exposure do you want to take? What portion of the portfolio will you allocate to stocks? Bonds? Cash? Will you invest in mutual funds at all or stick to individual securities? What benchmarks will you measure investment returns against? These are the questions you'll face when preparing your investment policy statement.

Your investment policy statement should also emphasize procedures for keeping things running smoothly. It might include a commitment to rebalancing your portfolio every other year or when it drifts from the approved asset mix by more than 10 percent. This will keep your asset mix—the largest driver of returns—steady, no matter how the different funds might perform.(See Chapter 9 on asset allocation for a deeper discussion on how to implement an asset allocation plan.)

Who's the Boss?

Your statement should also clearly state who is the final arbiter when it comes to making investment portfolio decisions. Chances are with a separate account it will be either you or your investment advisor (the investment firm managing your separate account may offer or recommend certain securities for your portfolio, but you won't want them picking stocks for you–that's what a separate account is for). After all, things can get hot between you and your advisor if the market is tanking. So having approved decision-making and implementation procedures in place is critical to your portfolio's success.

Your agreement with an investment advisor to manage your separate accounts may also include language in the statement that limits the amount that may be allocated to any one security or industry (to ensure proper diversification). Language may also be included to earmark securities or investment practices that are not acceptable (e.g., aggressive growth stocks or socially irresponsible investing).

If you want, you can shape your investment policy statement by yourself or with an advisor to include a component that helps you select a good separate accounts portfolio manager. The guidelines for doing so should set specific qualitative and quantitative requirements such as conformity to a specific asset class and style, a minimum tenure of the current manager, historical performance standard relative to a representative index or peer group, and/or fund expense standards relative to a peer group.

MAKE A STATEMENT

Remember, your investment policy statement is not etched in marble. Your personal financial circumstances may change, requiring more or less cash needs, or as you age in retirement, you may want to be more conservative. So feel free to amend elements of your policy statement to reflect these changes.

Even if you're investing in separate accounts on your own, you shouldn't be without an investment policy statement. Besides defining your financial objectives, ascertaining the funds available for investment, and establishing the investment methodology and strategy that will be used to reach those objectives, the statement will act as a road map for your long-term investment plan. Furthermore, if you don't use an investment advisor, putting together an investment policy statement can be even more helpful because it forces you to spell out your investment strategy. This should help you avoid panicky decisions when the market declines, as it invariably will.

But an investment policy statement goes beyond the merely strategic and functional. Emotionally, having an investment policy statement can help you remove much of the emotion, anxiety, and second-guessing from investment decisions. The key is to develop the right statement for you—and to trust it.

C H A P T E R

PUTTING YOUR SEPARATE ACCOUNT PLAN INTO ACTION

You miss 100 percent of the shots you never take.

WAYNE GRETZKY

It's been said of our creator that He gave us two ends on purpose: one to sit on and one to think with. He knew that the success or failure of any individual has been dependent on the one he or she uses most.

Consider Colonel Sanders, who looked at the prospect of retirement with contempt. Instead, he used his first social security check to help open a small fried chicken restaurant. Or the great Babe Ruth, whose strategy for hitting a baseball was easy. "Keep swinging," the Bambino once said. "You'll never hit a home run by waiting."

Swinging into action, whether you're simply out to dig your garden or launch a rocket to Mars, is the key. The same holds true for getting started with your separate account plan. You've done your homework, you know where to find the best separate accounts, you know where to find the best investment advisors, or you've decided to go it alone. Now all that's left is opening an account, formulating an investment plan, and putting that plan into action. Here's how to get that process rolling.

OPENING A SEPARATE ACCOUNT

First things first. Meet with your investment advisor and open a separate account. If you're a lone wolf, contact the separate account manager and ask for a separate account form to fill out. If there's an office nearby, go down there and fill it out. Ask for help if you need it.

Go to that initial meeting prepared. Bring current account statements or other financial records to refer to while you meet with your separate account advisor. Be prepared to discuss your financial goals such as early retirement, college funds, money for a new home, money to start a small business, and/or vacation and travel funds.

If you use an advisor, he or she should help you complete the necessary paperwork, which allows you to open an account at the brokerage firm servicing your separate account. If your advisor doesn't help you, insist that he or she do. After your paperwork is completed, your advisor will forward the appropriate paperwork to the brokerage house along with your deposit. Your advisor should also monitor the flow of the paperwork to ensure it is not "lost in the mail" or left on the desk of a vacationing worker.

Generally, the brokerage house will open your account and make your deposit within 24 hours of receipt of your paperwork. The account will be in your name with your advisor authorized as your financial advisor. Note that transferring assets from other banks, brokerage houses, or mutual funds usually takes 2 to 4 weeks depending on various factors. Once your account is established, your advisor, with the help of the money manager, immediately begins monitoring your holdings as well as making trades and investment decisions in line with your financial situation and goals.

Your advisor will issue quarterly reports showing you the performance of your separate account. The brokerage house provides you with monthly statements as well. Usually, any questions you have regarding the services

> ### Sidebar I: Here's What to Expect from Your Investment When You Open Your Separate Account
>
> Potential advantages you receive from the consulting process include:
>
> - Personal attention and advice from a dedicated investment professional.
>
> - Written investment objectives that help establish your goals and risk tolerance.
>
> - A clearly defined investment strategy you can follow with confidence.
>
> - A choice of professionally managed investment solutions suited for investors who haven't the time, knowledge, or objectivity to direct their own investments.
>
> - Assistance with investment manager or mutual fund selection to help you make knowledgeable decisions about who should manage your assets.
>
> - A quarterly portfolio review that helps you understand how your portfolio is performing and establish whether your investment objectives are being met.
>
> - One point of access to hundreds of investment options.
>
> - One consolidated monthly account statement.
>
> Source: UBS PaineWebber

of your separate account should be directed to your financial advisor, not the brokerage firm handling your account.

Remember, you'll also be charged a total "wrap fee" of up to 3 percent of assets in your account (note that companies like Separate Account Solutions are bringing those costs down considerably). This fee may be broken down and billed quarterly or monthly to your account. The fee is typically all inclusive and incorporates the manager's fee, trading and transaction costs, custody and clearing, Internet access to your account, monthly reports, comprehensive quarterly performance reports, confirmations on all transactions within the account, and many other benefits.

FUNDING YOUR SEPARATE ACCOUNT

You can fund your account either by sending a check to your investment advisor or by transferring over an existing account or partial assets from an existing account directly to the separate account money manager. If you'll be transferring an account or a partial account from another brokerage firm, you need to send your advisor a copy of your most recent statement(s) from the transferring firm along with any accompanying documents.

Most programs allow you to fund an account with cash and/or existing securities. If you are planning to use existing securities, you should check to see if your financial advisor will sell your current holdings under the managed account pricing structure. This may save you a substantial amount in commissions. In addition, you should examine the tax consequences of selling existing securities before proceeding.

If you have an existing account, such as an IRA, some other form of retirement plan, or a general brokerage account and you would like to transfer that account to fund your managed account, you'll need only fill out the appropriate documentation from your financial advisor. Again, your advisor should assist you in this process. Most securities are acceptable for transfer into a managed account; however, certain securities will cause delays in placing the account under management.

According to the New Jersey-based Investment Center, Inc., a wrap-fee advisory firm, the following is a list of unacceptable securities that may not be transferred to a separate account:

- Annuities

- CDs

- Illiquid foreign securities

- Limited partnerships

- Nonnegotiable positions

- Options

- Precious metals

- Safekeeping positions and unit trusts

Note that international and fixed-income holdings could delay acceptance if the positions do not meet minimum denominations. Your advisor can tell you which securities cannot be held in your account.

If you need to withdraw money from your account, you'll need to contact your separate account money manager directly or your financial advisor (who'll contact your money manager for you). If securities need to be sold in the account, then, generally speaking, it will take 3 or 4 business days for the securities to settle. If the assets to be distributed are in a retirement account, you'll have to sign and forward to your advisor a distribution form. At that point, a check to you by regular mail should be expedited by the separate account money manager that can take approximately 5 business days following the 3 days in which your funds need to settle. An overnight check to you should be received by the fourth or fifth business day after the initial request. Count on paying about $15 or $20 for overnight delivery.

OUTLINING YOUR OBJECTIVES

Developing a separate account plan is a process that has several components. But they needn't be complicated.

First you open an account. Then you talk with your investment advisor to determine your financial objectives or conduct your own research and lay out your own financial blueprint. Next you weigh your risk-tolerance options to determine your comfort zone within the market. Then you examine your current holdings. After all this information is gathered, you (or you and your investment advisor), with the help of a seasoned money manager your advisor has chosen for you, undertake an asset allocation analysis that indicates what percentage of your portfolio is to be put into equities and what percentage is to be put into fixed-income securities. Afterward, on an ongoing basis, you should review how your portfolio is performing and whether it's meeting your risk, time horizon, and asset management goals.

Remember, determining the correct asset allocation, identifying the appropriate investment vehicles, tracking their performance, and keeping abreast of relevant investment manager developments can be both difficult and time-consuming, especially if you try to tackle it all by yourself. A financial advisor will help you avoid that fate.

Regardless of whether you're calling the shots or your advisor is on board, your investment program should be thoroughly planned. As stated earlier, included in your plan should be return expectations, time horizon, and risk tolerance. As you probably already know, higher return expectations require that an investor have the ability to accept higher levels of risk.

You also know that investments carry different levels of risk and expected return. Moderate return goals may be secured with a portfolio of fixed-income securities, whereas aggressive goals may require a portfolio containing all stocks. If your goal falls somewhere in between, your portfolio might contain a balance of different types of financial instruments.

The degree of risk an investor is willing to take is a key element in the separate account selection process. Most investors can count on their advisors and their money managers to point out the levels of risk that are part and parcel of a given investment. If you're 70 years old and your money manager advises that 100 percent of your assets go into his firm's growth-oriented separate accounts, that's a red flag. You can help your manager by filling out the investor questionnaire we alluded to earlier in this chapter.

Another area to which your money manager contributes is the time horizon for such investing. The shortest time frame should probably be no less than 3 to 5 years, although this varies by the amount and type of stock and risk you take. Shorter time frames may encounter poor economic conditions where the stock values drag down the overall account value. Longer-term strategies invariably provide the greater return through stock appreciation. Your broker should also help you determine your investment objectives (growth, income, speculative, etc.). Part of this determination is through a review of age, health condition, marital status, income, other assets, net worth, estate plans, and other considerations. Such a review should be more encompassing (as already addressed) than a simple stock account if for no other reason than the size of the account is usually fairly large, as is the liability if something goes wrong.

Based on your risk comfort levels and your financial objectives, your financial advisor will work with your separate accounts money manager to create an asset allocation strategy that works for you. We'll delve more deeply into asset management strategies in Chapters 7, 8, and 9.

REVISITING YOUR PLAN

After you've completed your asset allocation plan, you'll want to go back and revisit your separate account at least once every quarter. Your separate accounts money manager will provide you with an offline quarterly performance statement every 3 months and may offer you more current updates via a secured Internet Web site.

> ### Sidebar II: A Blueprint for Success
> Confused about your separate account investment process? Don't be. Here's a snapshot of what you'll need to do to get your investment plan rolling:
>
> 1. Investment objectives, asset allocation guidelines, risk parameters, and performance benchmarks are established with the creation of a customized investment policy statement. This document serves as a set of guidelines and instructions for the investment advisor describing precisely how you wish to have the money managed and what results you expect. Your advisor can help you complete it.
>
> 2. Work with your money manager to generate investment ideas for possible placement in your separate account portfolios.
>
> 3. Your money manager will provide continuous tracking and performance monitoring of all of your separate account investments.
>
> 4. You or your advisor must apply various combinations of strategies provided by the model portfolios to actively manage your account in keeping with your predefined investment policy statement.
>
> 5. Your account is maintained with ongoing evaluation and regular portfolio reviews provided on a quarterly basis.

Each update should include a detailed multipage activity and performance report on your portfolio. Your report should provide information on market values, performance and benchmark comparisons, investment dividends and interest, and securities sales and purchases activity. Additional features of your separate accounts performance statement might include economic and market commentary, a summary of investment gains and losses for tax reporting and planning, and a breakdown of what percentage of the portfolio is allocated to different securities.

Although individual separate accounts investors have to examine their own situation and come to their own conclusions, there are some clues to successful rebalancing strategies that might come in handy for you. At the top of that list is the natural ebb and flow of the financial market, which, quarter to quarter, may knock your carefully planned asset allocation plan out of whack, taking your risk profile and time horizon calculations with it. For example, suppose that your original plan called for 30 percent short-term bond, and 70 percent equities. Left unattended, your equities will likely outgrow the bonds over the long haul. As the percentage of stocks rises, the character of the portfolio changes. While a higher loading in equities may be good for long-term performance, it will place the portfolio at increasingly higher risk. At that point, it might be wise to add some more cautious stocks, such as utility or manufacturing company stocks, or even U.S. Treasury bonds, to the mix.

A side benefit of rebalancing is that it forces you to buy low and sell high. Over time, you should expect a small but measurable profit as a result of this "diversification benefit." This is particularly effective in well-diversified multiasset class portfolios, notes David Armstrong, a financial planner and investment columnist. "You should also look at both taxes and transaction costs before you decide on your rebalancing strategy," advises Armstrong. "Hyperactive trading is unlikely to add value. Benefits of an absolutely 'perfect' asset allocation could easily be consumed by additional costs."

Armstrong promotes a basic strategy for separate account beginners. "Once a year check to see if any asset class varies from its target weight by more than 3%," he says. "If so, consider rebalancing to meet your original asset allocation needs."

KEEPING IT SIMPLE

Overall, it pays to keep your separate accounts process fairly uncomplicated. Now that you're taking more responsibility for your investments, you don't want to gum up the works by weaving options straddles and Portuguese debentures into your separate accounts plan.

Many experts agree with that sentiment. In a recent report published by Standard & Poor's on separate account management, the emphasis on a sound separate account plan is placed on two pillars: common sense and sound judgment. All points to a successful separate accounts experience originate from there, leading Standard & Poor's to note that "a clear, concise investment philosophy embodying these traits should follow, articulating the manner in which investments are selected, purchased and ultimately sold."

The Standard & Poor's report centers on how asset management companies are handling separate accounts for their customers. At Carnegie Capital Asset Management Company, the investment process begins by examining the "big picture": Is the economy expanding or contracting? Are we in a bull or bear market? Answering these questions as well as identifying trends that are giving force to our world are critical because the answers provide the base of the overall investment landscape.

> ### Sidebar III: Your First Meeting
>
> When you meet your separate accounts advisor or your separate accounts money manager to open a new account and develop a plan for your investments, be prepared to address the following issues:
>
> - Your current financial situation: assets, debts, income, expenses
>
> - Any anticipated changes to your current financial situation: retirement, inheritance, illness
>
> - Your risk/reward comfort level
>
> If you work with a financial advisor, take time to learn more about how your separate accounts advisor works. Before you leave, you should be aware of your advisor's
>
> - Investment philosophy
>
> - Fee structure
>
> - Procedures used in selecting assets
>
> - Performance results from accounts similar to yours
>
> - Differences from full-service brokers and mutual funds

Once these questions are answered, Carnegie Capital hones in on the microview of your investment objectives and drills down to find long-term results. "We seek growth companies in dynamic industries whose stocks are well-capitalized and attractively priced," says Carnegie in the Standard & Poor's report. "In our research, we seek to maintain a long-term perspective because, in our view, attempting to exploit short-term gyrations is generally a futile exercise. Our efforts, rather, are focused on the prospects of individual companies and whether their common stocks are under-or over-valued relative to their intrinsic net worth."

Carnegie adds that employing a long-term approach usually requires patience as well as a degree of contrariness; for example, the firm is often buying when others are selling. This approach attempts to minimize the portfolio's investment risks, thereby enhancing its potential investment return.

The company notes that in addition to carefully evaluating a company before investing, it also attempts to recognize specific sell indicators. Such signals could include changes in the prospects of an industry, loss of competitive advantage by a company, highly overpriced stock, or impairment of the company's fundamentals. "Should such developments become apparent, we believe our clients' money would be better invested elsewhere," Carnegie says.

Carnegie, like most separate account money managers, will work with you from the outset in determining and defining your investor profile. Your separate accounts money manager will also help you develop a mutual understanding of your investment goals, financial objectives, risk tolerance, and time frame. As your financial and personal circumstances change, they'll also ensure that your investor profile should be updated to keep pace with those changes.

That said, it's about time that you receive the same high-level service that the Vanderbilts and DuPonts have received from their money managers for years. That's the beauty of the separate account: top-shelf management at bottom-shelf costs.

CASE STUDY 5

Understanding Separate Account Paperwork

Bob Donaldson wanted more control. He just didn't want more paperwork. So when the 60-year-old retiree opened his new separate account, he made it a point to tell his financial advisor that he didn't want to be spending his mornings filling out forms and signing documents. "That's when I play golf," the six-handicapper says.

To his surprise, Donaldson didn't spend much time at all pushing paper. "My advisor and my money manager set it up in a way where I just had to answer a few questions up front, and that was pretty much it. I signed the papers and went on my way. No hassles and no wasted time."

Opening his separate account barely took 2 hours, he recalls. "The separate account manager had me fill out some questionnaires to find out what my financial objectives were and what my risk tolerance was. They'd already examined my current holdings and were able to put together a target portfolio quickly," he says.

Donaldson had the option of meeting with his separate account manager on site, but he did most of the contact work over the phone and by fax machine. His financial advisor had already forwarded current account statements and other financial records to the money manager ahead of time.

"All I had to finish up was mail the appropriate paperwork to the brokerage house along with my deposit," he said. "Within 24 hours, my account was opened and we were making trades."

Donaldson does note that it took a bit longer to transfer assets from his bank and from his old mutual fund house. "But that didn't mean I couldn't trade and choose my stocks," he says. "All in all, it was a user-friendly experience."

7

NOT WITH MY MONEY YOU DON'T: UNDERSTANDING SEPARATE ACCOUNT FEES

He who pays the fiddler, calls the tunes.

MARGARET L. CLEMENT

A wise prophet once noted that timing is everything. Such is the case with separate accounts, which fit quite snugly into the trend away from financial service transaction fees and toward fee-based accounts. Simply stated, with fee-based accounts, both investors and advisors benefit from increased assets. With transaction-based brokerage accounts, the broker is the primary beneficiary of increased trading in the account.

Thankfully, it's the investor who benefits from separate accounts, especially when it comes to fees. As we stated earlier, the average annual separate account fee is 2.11 percent, according to Cerulli Associates. Theoretically, separate account fees can be as high as 3 percent.

That's good news for investors, who don't like paying high fees for parking garages or dental appointments, let alone portfolio management. In one survey by Stratford, Connecticut-based Prince & Associates, 52 percent of respondents cited fees as a chief reason for using separate accounts.

But who is charging the high fees and who is charging the low fees? And how do you figure out which is, in the end game, a better deal for you? One way to answer these questions is to identify who's charging what in the separate accounts world.

Typically, it's the wirehouses like Salomon Smith Barney and Merrill Lynch that are charging around 2 percent for their separate account programs. According to Cerulli research, wirehouse separate account fees dropped from 2.42 percent in 1999 to 2.15 percent in 2000. Banks, which are just beginning to ramp up their separate account efforts, are charging the lowest rates in the financial services industry at 1.97 percent (down from 2.95 percent in 1999). The insurance industry (2.0 percent) and regional brokerages (2.26 percent) check in slightly higher. The highest rates (see Figure 7.1) come from the third-party sector (3.0 percent).

But even these prices aren't what they seem. According to Cerulli, the price paid by investors for separate account programs can be much lower than the advertised price, sometimes 25 to 30 percent lower. That's because investors can negotiate lower fees, which is something they can't do with

Sidebar I: Separate Accounts and Taxes
Separate accounts are good for money invested in a taxable account, because money managers can keep your accounts separate from those of other investors and take your tax situation into consideration when buying and selling securities. That's a luxury you'll give up in most mutual fund wraps. (There's a lot more on separate accounts and taxes in Chapter 9.)

FIGURE 7.1

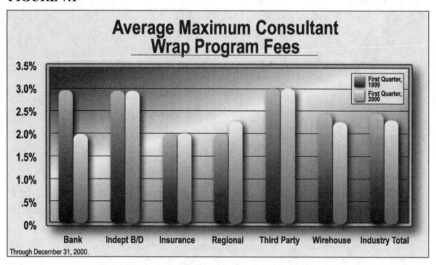

the arbitrary fee structures charged by mutual fund firms (more on this in a moment). In addition, online separate account programs, which are easier to administer and don't require added costs like printing and phone rep services on top of administrative and trading costs, are helping to lower separate account fees further.

Remember the cost example we cited in Chapter 5? We said that in a program with a minimum investment of $100,000 and an initial fee of 2.5 percent, a client investing $600,000 might pay 2.5 percent for the first $500,000 but only 2 percent for the last $100,000. On average, investors receive discounts of 25 percent in separate account programs, according to Cerulli Associates. This means an investor in a separate account program with a 3 percent maximum account fee on a $100,000 minimum account might actually pay 2.25 percent after receiving the 25 percent discount. Note also that these discounts increase exponentially as assets rise.

In addition, costs can be reduced further by cutting out the intermediary, so to speak, and eliminating the financial advisor, or registered investment advisor (RIA), from the picture. Separate account investors who go it alone can cut about 1 percent from their management fees. That's right. About one-third to one-half of your fee goes to the investment advisor.

In some instances, both investment advisors and money managers don't want to discuss separate account fees and how they're broken down. And brokers don't really want you to know that you can negotiate fees and lop 25 percent or more off the advertised fee, unless you're the type of investor who has assets in the $500,000 and higher range. But if you speak up, chances are you can get a healthy price break, too.

One more piece of good news: We anticipate that separate account fees should diminish even further as more financial services companies enter the marketplace.

MUTUALLY EXCLUSIVE

Although separate account fees aren't necessarily perfect, they can't help but look brighter and shinier when sharing a spotlight with mutual fund fees. This is because the mutual fund industry has been making hay by charging fees for service that don't necessarily differentiate between a $10,000 account and a $1 million account. According to the September 11, 2000, edition of *Forbes* magazine, it costs fund companies roughly the same to service the $1 million account as it does the $10,000 account. Interestingly, *Forbes* calls that the "dirty little secret" of the fund industry. Here's a look at how your money works under both scenarios.

Separate Account Fees

We've said all along that investors are shifting to privately managed accounts for tax efficiency, control over fees, and influence in portfolio construction. One reason for the interest in separate accounts is that advice is rapidly becoming a commodity, a trend accelerated by technology-driven advice engines. Another is that, from a financial perspective, they're a lot easier to swallow than mutual funds.

That's especially true when it comes to investors cracking open their piggy banks, as separate accounts also offer unprecedented control over fees. As we noted earlier, in some cases, advisors can negotiate fees with the investment manager. And fees are typically tiered to the asset level of the investments. All in all, the fees are at least competitive with mutual funds and in many cases are lower, before advisor fees are added. Plus, separate account fee structures are more easily understood than fund fees. In the separate account world, everything's up front.

One financial advisor who has been moving several of his clients into separate accounts says that his customers don't even know they're paying more for mutual funds than they are for separate accounts. He had a client

Sidebar II: It's the Communications, Stupid
A survey conducted for CapTrust Financial Advisors found that frequent updates are most important to investors—more so than whether they pay fees or commissions, or whether they use individual managed accounts or mutual funds. The study attempted to gauge investors' perceptions of the fee-based consulting style of business.

Most important to investors is an update that goes beyond simply receiving a monthly statement. More than 90 percent of investors who received a regular update said it enhanced the broker's credibility. Regular updates was "one of the blow away areas" in terms of a positive response, states Bobby Lamy, a Wake Forest business school professor who directed the study. In fact, the more assets invested, the higher the value investors placed on frequent updates.

Use of money managers was a wash—clients don't see the difference between a broker handling the money versus a money manager. "There were a lot of 'don't knows' and 'not sures' on this one," says Lamy. Satisfaction with a fee arrangement seems to be somewhat higher—93 percent of respondents indicated a high level of satisfaction under a fee structure versus 83 percent under a commission arrangement.

The survey also indicated it is important for advisors to separate the process of setting goals and objectives from an analysis of risk tolerance and an investor's time horizon. Investors tend to see these areas separately. The results are based on interviews of 250 investors with at least $250,000 in investable assets. The survey was conducted by Wake Forest representatives last July–August 2000.

who had been in a mutual fund wrap fee program with fees at around 2 percent. The advisor reallocated everything into separate accounts with a fee of about 2.35 percent. When the client complained that he had raised her fees, the advisor replied, yes, the fees had gone up, but her overall costs had gone down. With the internal cost of the mutual fund, she was paying at least 3 percent in fees.

That's a point well worth considering. After all, one of the primary features of separate accounts is to allay the fears of stock and bond purchasers that a single broker would merely be trying to sell products solely for the commission. As differentiated, separate accounts charge the overall account an annual fee irrespective of how often the stocks within the account are bought or sold. As we've stated, commissions are not charged to the investor. As we've also noted, separate account fees are usually based on a sliding scale similar to that of break points on mutual funds: the larger the account, the lower the overall fees. Brokers may also discount the fees to better customers or when they simply want to gather additional accounts. The fees are split between the broker offering the account to the client, the money manager, and the wrap account provider. Such splits may provide that one-third goes to each party, or perhaps 50 percent goes to the broker-dealer and the other 50 percent is split between the money manager and the provider.

Investors who open individually managed accounts often do so with a minimum investment of at least $100,000. A new industry trend has lowered minimum asset levels to $25,000. No matter what level you come in at, the money in the account—less the initial quarter's fees, which typically equal 0.75 percent or less of the opening balance—is invested by the portfolio manager. Fees can range from as low as hundreds of dollars per year to 3 percent of assets on an annual basis, but count on paying somewhere in the middle, at about 2.3 percent of your separate account assets each year.

In addition to covering transactions, these fees encompass reporting, custody, and the services of a financial advisor (but only if you choose to use one). There are no additional charges.

Unlike mutual fund investors, managed account investors do not pool their money. Rather, they own the securities in their account directly. Managed account investors can specify certain selection parameters to customize the account according to their needs, thereby enjoying greater flexibility and control than with a mutual fund.

Sidebar III: Going Online? It Could Cost You Less

Are you ready for a separate minimum asset base of $10,000? One company thinks you are, and no surprise here, it's on the Web. According to the November 13, 2000, edition of *Web Finance*, a new company called BridgePortfolio is targeting lower-net-worth investors, those with between $10,000 and $250,000, and partnering with financial planners and advisors who want to expand their client base. Created by two University of Chicago Graduate School of Business students, BridgePortfolio launched its Web site recently. Thury Foster, co-CEO with Chad Meyer, worked at Safeco Mutual Funds for 5 years, and he became interested in how to provide advice to investors who lacked the assets to qualify as clients of planners. At the same time, he saw increased attention being paid to separately managed accounts as an alternative to mutual funds. The Internet seemed to have the potential to marry the two trends in the formation of a profitable business.

BridgePortfolio is a nationally registered investment advisor. Trading services are provided by Charles Schwab & Co. The minimum initial deposit to open an account is $10,000, qualifying an investor for the mutual fund advisory service or BridgePortfolio's stock portfolio accounts. The mutual fund advisory service fee is 1 percent, which Foster says is comparable to a financial advisor's fee.

The fee for stock portfolio accounts starts at 1.95 percent when assets are between $10,000 and $50,000, and it declines to 1.45 percent when assets reach $1 million. The stock portfolio accounts fee includes the advisory service, portfolio management, and all trading costs.

BridgePortfolio pays advisors a referral fee of 50 basis points the first year a client opens an account and 25 basis points for each year the account is open. A portfolio subadvisor receives 45 basis points annually for assets under management.

Unlike some online separate account firms that recommend stock portfolios based on historical data and adjust portfolios only once or twice annually, BridgePortfolio's portfolios are actively managed, although most follow a buy-and-hold approach. The annual turnover rate ranges from 5 to 25 percent.

One concern regarding such lower minimums is whether or not clients will actually receive attention and advice. Most observers believe that it is simply not profitable to manage less than $100,000 in a separate account.

In addition, it is often tempting to dismiss the advantages of one investment strategy over another based purely on the fact that one seems to cost more than the other. The recent popularity of no-load mutual funds is proof that many investors, particularly those who like a no-frills "hands-on" approach to investing, are doing just that.

Mutual Fund Fees

Imagine being an investor who has placed $100,000 in a mutual fund. Then imagine at the end of the year getting a bill for $1500. Now imagine how you'd feel if the fund lost money.

At the end of 2000, many investors shared that feeling. Still, few people bother to take the time and figure out just how much they're paying in fund fees. Let's face it, calculating the actual dollar amount paid in fees requires some math. An investor has to take the net asset value of fund shares and multiply that by the fund's annual expense ratio to calculate an annual expense. For example, a $100,000 investment in a fund with a 1.5 percent expense ratio means the investor is paying the fund company $1500 in annual fees.

Simply stated, mutual fund fees are based on a percentage of a fund's assets, so the dollar amount you pay grows as your account grows. In addition, the percentage of assets that funds charge as fees has been rising for years, even though it's supposed to fall as funds get larger. And some funds are still charging fees for distribution and marketing, even though they take no new investments and aren't doing any marketing.

All mutual funds charge fees to cover expenses, and most also need to make a profit for the management company. The biggest expense is the management fee, which pays the fund's advisor—the company that buys and sells securities for the fund. Many funds also charge 12b-1 fees, named after the Securities and Exchange Commission (SEC) rule that established them. A 12b-1 fee helps cover marketing and distribution costs, such as advertising or brokers' commissions.

To make sure investors can compare fund costs, the SEC requires funds to disclose their expense ratios, which show how much of a fund's assets they take every year for management, 12b-1, and other fees. According to an article in the May 2, 1997, edition of *Florida Today* entitled "Mutual Fund Fees Are Rising," at the end of 1996, for example, the average stock fund has a 1.54 percent expense ratio. The average bond fund's ratio is 1.07 percent, and the average stock-and-bond fund's ratio is 1.31 percent.

That may not sound like much, but consider this: Suppose you invested $10,000 in a government securities fund last year. The average government securities fund earned only 1.7 percent, or $170. If it had an average expense ratio of 1.07 percent, you would have paid $107 (1.07 percent of $10,000) to the fund, which is a substantial portion of all you earned. After inflation and taxes, your fund fared better than you did.

Thanks to a roaring bull market, stock fund investors fared better. A typical stock fund investor paid $154 on a $10,000 investment in 1996. That year, stock funds on average gained 19.5 percent, or $1950 in value. Adding back that $154 would have boosted the fund's 1996 return to 21 percent—a nice bump.

What's more, the expense ratio doesn't include all the fees and expenses a fund racks up. It omits upfront sales fees, or loads, and it doesn't cover the commissions a fund pays when it buys and sells stocks. Trading costs, which can average another 0.3 percentage points to expenses, are deducted directly from your fund's total return.

Sidebar IV: Digging Deep on Fund Fees

Why do similar funds charge different service fees? Good question. According to an article in the July 25, 2000, edition of *The Buffalo News* entitled "Watch Your Mutual Fund Fees," you have to dig deeply into the numbers. Here's how they did it.

Mutual fund A, also known as the Technology I fund, has an annual expense ratio of 1.74 percent. This means investors pay 1.74 percent of the value of their accounts to cover expenses for managing the fund. Fund B, the Technology II fund, has an expense ratio of 1.10 percent.

According to the story, the investor who put $10,000 in fund A would have $48,905 after 20 years at a 10 percent annual return. With the same market performance, the less expensive Technology II fund would net $55,024 in 20 years.

That extra $6119 over a 20-year period could help pay a decent chunk of a child's college education or help pay off a mortgage. And it's certainly more advantageous for you to have the money in your pocket than in the mutual fund firm's pockets.

The good news for fund investors is that they're pretty much open to everybody. Mutual funds have lower minimum investment requirements than separate accounts, often $1000 or less. The bad news is that it's difficult to figure out exactly how much you're being charged. Here's why. Normally, with a no-load mutual fund bought directly from the fund company, the entire investment is placed in the fund at the time of initial purchase. With a front-end load fund, on the other hand, the investor's money is placed in the fund only after deducting a sales charge. In the case of a 3.5 percent load fund, the fund would invest $965 of the investor's initial $1000.

Beyond the initial sales charge or lack thereof, the difference in fee structure between load and no-load mutual funds virtually disappears. Management fees, transaction costs, custody fees, and distribution and marketing costs (known as 12b-1 fees) are deducted automatically from the fund's assets. These fees are usually not seen directly by investors but instead are specified in the fund's prospectus and statements of additional information.

Mutual fund expenses for stock-based portfolios typically range from 1.5 to 2 percent per year for no-load funds and from 2 to 3 percent per year for load funds. But that's just for starters. According to Morningstar Mutual Funds, the average diversified domestic equities fund incurs about 1.63 percent

> ***Sidebar V: Here's Where Your Money Goes***
> Following the fee trail on a separate account isn't difficult. For
> example, on a 2.95 percent fee on a $100,000 account, $750 goes
> to the money manager, $750 goes to the broker, $600 goes to the
> brokerage firm, $400 pays for the manager selection, and $450
> goes to cover custody of securities and clearing charges.

in annual costs, including a 1.32 percent expense ratio and 0.31 percent in
transaction costs. Tack on an additional 0.94 percent annual sales charge on
average for load funds or an estimated 1 percent annual charge for no-load
funds purchased through a financial advisor (again, if you use one), and that
annual cost figure rises to approximately 2.6 percent.

Investors should note that transaction costs tend to vary depending on
the type of securities in the fund. Trading foreign securities, for instance,
can cost almost twice as much as trading domestic securities.

As we noted earlier, your mutual fund expense ratio also may include a
12b-1 fee, which by law must be disclosed separately. That's a number well
worth looking for because it can take an annual bite of up to 1 percent of
your investment, Donald Topkis says. Named for a rule added by the SEC
to the Investment Company Act of 1940, the 12b-1 was originally supposed
to be used only to offset marketing costs. But today, almost anything goes.
A big part of 12b-1s, for example, often gets funneled back to brokers and
financial planners as a "service fee" for as long as you hold the fund.

Struggling with Load Fund Fees

Perhaps the most onerous costs associated with mutual funds come from
the load fund sector. Load funds offer advisory services, whereas no-load
funds don't, but charge a higher fee to do so.

All funds have annual expenses, which differ from sales and redemption
charges, also called loads. A front-end load is a fee charged to the investor
when purchasing a fund. The load typically helps pay the commission to the
broker selling the fund.

A back-end load, or redemption fee, is assessed when an investor sells
a fund. Redemption fees are still assessed when switching between funds in
the same fund family because the switch involves selling shares in one fund
and buying shares in another.

Because of the stigma associated with load funds, full service brokerage
companies have come up with new gimmicks; they have hidden their loads

by moving them from the front (paid on purchase) to the back (paid on exit from the fund). The result is the same. You will end up paying a large sales or maintenance fee in some fashion, and it will reduce your return.

> ### Sidebar VI: Fund Fee Facts
> The average annual expenses charged by stock funds has doubled in the last 40 years and increased 65 percent in the last 20 years. In 1999, the average mutual fund fee was 1.58 percent. This may not seem like much, but expenses compound just like returns. With the impact of fund expenses, if you invested in an average stock fund, you would have accumulated only 73 percent of what you could have earned had you been invested in the Standard & Poor's 500 Index for 20 years.

Back-end loads usually disappear in 5 or 6 years, but during those years, your annual expense for the fund will be 1.5 to 2 times the annual expense for the exact same fund with a front-end load; in other words, the load is spread out over several years, but it doesn't stop. Year after year, you continue to pay a much higher fee on the fund. And if the fund does poorly and you want to get out early, you will end up paying twice: the much higher annual expense while you were in the fund and the sales fee to exit.

NEW SHERIFF IN TOWN

When you consider the costs, both front end and back end, of mutual funds and how much they can cut into your investment returns from year to year, separate accounts look better all the time. And as more financial services firms enter the market, fee prices should fall even lower in the next year or two. When it comes to fees, mutual funds may have the numbers right now, but separate accounts have all the momentum.

CASE STUDY 6

Mutual Funds and Separate Accounts: The Fee Picture

Charlie Connors couldn't believe what he was reading. Thumbing through the Sunday newspapers, he ran into an article detailing how mutual fund fees are rising even as fund performance is sliding backward.

According to Morningstar Inc., the average shareholder in a U.S. stock fund today is paying 10 percent more annually in fees than in 1986. "When I read that, I felt like I was getting fleeced by the fund companies. Further down in the article, I read where separate accounts fared better than funds in terms of fees and performance. I thought that separate accounts deserved a closer look."

Soon enough, the 37-year-old construction company executive found a separate account program that required a minimum of $10,000. His fee for stock portfolio accounts started at 1.95 percent when assets are between $10,000 and $50,000, and it declines to 1.45 percent when assets reach $1 million. "My stock portfolio account fee includes the advisory service, portfolio management, and all trading costs," says Connors. "When you add up all the hidden fees of mutual funds, like 12b-1 fees and so on, I was paying over 2 percent. It was, in my mind, a big difference, especially considering the fact that I had more control over my separate accounts than my funds, and the tax picture was better, too."

BLUEPRINT FOR SUCCESS: DEVELOPING SEPARATE ACCOUNTS INVESTMENT STRATEGY

*Long range planning does not deal with future decisions,
with the future of present decisions.*

PETER DRUCKER

It's one thing to have all the ingredients for success but quite another to have the recipe. In the chaotic maelstrom of Wall Street, investors go bust when they have the former but not the latter. That's why having a solid investment plan is so critical to the success of your separate account strategy. Here, in Chapter 8, we'll cover the critical ingredients necessary for your portfolio's success. Then, in Chapter 9, we'll explain how to put those ingredients to use and build a blueprint for your separate account campaign that will be the envy of one and all.

Some of what you'll be reading in Chapters 8 and 9 are investment terms and descriptions you've seen before and some you haven't. We think that only by covering all the basics and merging some interesting new issues and strategies into the mix will you become a superior separate account investor. This is important now that you're taking on more responsibility for your investment fortunes and making a lot more decisions than you would if you'd stayed in the mutual fund world, or even if you relied on the services of a full-service stockbroker. That's a fact of life for separate account investors who value control and flexibility in their financial lives.

So, you're the expert now. Whether you're working with a financial advisor or a brokerage firm on your separate account, chances are that you'll be required to make more of your own calls on what goes into your investment portfolio. The good news is that you'll still have help, because most separate account programs have portfolios in place for investors of all stripes, and all you'll have to do is pick and choose one that's right for you. The bad news is that you won't be able to pick up a phone and rail against a fund manager or stockbroker for their dubious investment decisions. Now, you'll only have to walk a short distance to your bathroom mirror to finger the culprit if things don't go to your liking.

That's okay, though. One reason you opted for separate accounts was to have more control over your investments, and that's exactly what you're going to get. Consequently, you'll be responsible for more than just making investment decisions; you'll also have to conduct some more independent research, some more due diligence on companies in which you're considering parking some of your investment dollars, and some more portfolio tracking and performance monitoring to keep your investment portfolio chugging along in the right direction. Let's examine some of these issues in greater detail. By chapter's end, you'll have a better grip on what it takes to build a world-class portfolio. Then, in Chapter 9, we'll explain how to put your gleaming new portfolio into play and how to keep it performing solidly in the years to come.

BUILDING BLOCKS

Before we delve into the tools and techniques you'll be using as a separate accounts investor, a few reminders are in order first, particularly on the process of investing in separate accounts.

After helping you clarify your financial goals and determining your risk tolerance level, your broker or financial advisor will provide you with a list of one or more money managers who specialize in the investment objectives that best fit your profile. For example, your account may be split among three managers, one handling the small-cap portion of the portfolio, another handling large-cap stocks, and the third investing in foreign stocks. As we noted earlier, expect to pay about 2 percent of assets annually for management and transaction fees, including compensation for the financial advisor or broker.

Before you decide on a separate account, keep taxes in mind, too. Since you control turnover in your portfolio, you can better control the tax implications of your investments. With actively managed funds, portfolio managers buy and sell stocks as they need to, sometimes creating large capital-gains distributions on which shareholders must pay taxes regardless of how long they have owned the fund—or even if the fund ends the year in the red.

GETTING HELP

Aside from control, fee and tax benefits, and trading flexibility, it's important to remember that with most separate accounts, you will be gaining some sort of financial advisor assistance.

> ### Sidebar I: Why Would I Want More Than One Separate Account Portfolio?
>
> Hey, just because you're investing in a brand new financial tool doesn't mean you can't enjoy some old-style benefits. With separate accounts, for example, you might create one separate account for retirement, another for your child's college education, and another for your riskiest of stocks. You may also want different portfolios for your individual, IRAs, joint, or custodial accounts for children. To be fully diversified, you may want to own portfolios that represent different investment strategies, sectors, countries, or types of companies.

One of the primary motivations for a separate account is the supposedly added expertise and objectivity of a professional money manager. Unlike a mutual fund manager or a registered stockbroker, your money manager isn't tied down by tax issues or by having to sell a brokerage company's favorite stocks above all others. Your separate account money manager can decide what to do solely on the movement of the market and the individual stock selections of the industries he or she understands or analyzes. Having an independent money manager on your side is a big advantage right off the bat.

The key for most separate account investors is to work closely with either their financial advisor, who will in turn work with the money manager, or work with their money managers directly if they decide to bypass the investment advisor. Your money manager has to know certain things about you before recommending any separate accounts investment programs or asset classes.

That means not only filling out applications and forms that include your risk comfort levels, your investment time horizon, and your financial goals, but your trading and investing history as well. Also included in this preliminary information gathering process is a thorough review of age, health condition, marital status, income, other assets, net worth, estate plans, and other considerations. Such a review should be more encompassing (as already addressed) than a simple stock or mutual fund account if for no other reason than the size of your separate account is usually fairly large— and so is the liability if something goes wrong.

With separate accounts, investors not only must understand their own financial capabilities but (as we pointed out in Chapter 4) their money manager's financial capabilities. Some separate account programs, particularly the independent broker-dealers, want you to use their in-house managers. Smaller firms, particularly the independent broker-dealers, might allow you to select from several outside managers the broker-dealer firm has reviewed. This kind of due diligence of asset managers, conducted on your own or with the help of your investment advisor, should consider the returns the manager has posted for his or her type of fund (income, growth, international) against a benchmark index known by most investors. The Standard & Poors (S&P) 500 Index, the Solomon Bond Index, and the Morgan Stanley Capital Europe, Australia, Far East (EAFE) Index for international funds are just a few.

The review must also consider the time frame—2-, 5-, 10-year periods— assuming the manager has conducted fund/asset management for such a time. In some cases, the review could utilize a hypothetical evaluation based on the manager's investment formula and strategies for a previous time frame if the manager has a short or nonexistent track record. Additionally, figures can be distorted. Some firms may use indices more favorable (lower) than their returns (Wilshire 5000, Russell 2000, Dow Jones, S&P 400, S&P 100). Further, the returns for the 1980s and 1990s reflected one of the strongest growth periods for decades, and there's some legitimate doubt whether the first decade of the new century will be as strong.

Of course, in such a volatile investing environment, choosing the right asset classes is paramount, as is choosing the money manager who'll handle your separate account. As we mentioned earlier, due diligence in choosing your money manager is critical. So hands-on attention on your part is equally critical.

Some Wall Street money managers don't like individual investors who come calling in person, but considering the healthy chunk of money you'll be investing in your separate account, it might be worth your while to visit potential money managers on site. Let them know you've whittled down your money manager selection list to a few choices; then stand tall and start asking pertinent questions. Such personal reviews should determine more than just the return background of the advisor. How long this individual has been there has already been addressed as a major concern, but how long he or she might remain is certainly another concern. Has he or she skipped

Sidebar II: Investment Preparation Resources

Here are some good investment resources, recommended by Frank Armstrong, author of *Investment Strategies for the 21st Century*.

The Wealthy Barber (Updated Third Edition) by David Chilton, Prima Publishing. Chilton's classic take on investing and the average American. User-friendly with sage advice for the investing public.

A Random Walk Down Wall Street (Fifth Edition) by Burton G. Malkiel, W.W. Norton & Co. Burton G. Malkiel, the father of *The Wall Street Journal's* dartboard contest and one of the primary forces behind the move toward indexing, asks, "Why can't the experts beat the monkey consistently? How efficient is the market? Can managers add value?" The answers may change the way you think about the stock market and how you go about investing.

Capital Ideas by Peter L. Bernstein, Simon and Schuster. An enjoyable history of the advances in modern finance and the sometimes unlikely folks who brought them to us.

Portfolio Selection (Second Edition) by Harry M. Markowitz, Blackwell. Based on Markowitz's doctoral thesis written at the University of Chicago in 1952. The ideas in the book became the basis for Modern Portfolio Theory, which revolutionized the art of investment management and provides investors with a rational approach to measure, monitor, and control risk. Markowitz single-handedly dragged finance out of the Dark Ages. He won the Nobel Prize in economics in 1990 for this work.

Fundamentals of Investments (Second Edition) by Gordon J. Alexander, William F. Sharpe, and Jeffrey Bailey, Prentice Hall. A college textbook coauthored by Nobel Prize winner William F. Sharpe.

from one firm to another frequently? Or perhaps the firm itself has a tendency to fire managers at a whim. Does the manager actually conduct day-to-day operations or leave them to underlings? How many hours does he or she work? How many days per month or year are spent on company sites interviewing chairpeople and presidents and visiting plant sites? In addition to these requirements, your separate accounts money manager should also provide a system to collect custodial fees, allow for trading of stocks (again, for small broker-dealers, the trading and commissions may have to go through their account), provide for client reports (at least quarterly for good reporting), and monitor the performance of the manager.

DEVELOPING A BLUEPRINT

Once you've hired a money manager, it's time to sit down and go to work building your investment portfolio. A major benefit of separate accounts is that you get to choose the exact investment portfolio you want. If you lean conservatively, there's no shortage of blue-chip stocks and Treasury bond offerings to choose from. Likewise, aggressive investors can choose from a wide array of growth stock classes to fill their portfolios. But when you start looking for the right portfolio, keep things simple at first.

Most investment portfolios are comprised of five or so components. Usually, they include some combination of the following:

1. Liquid assets (cash and equivalents)
2. Fixed income (bonds and annuities)

3. Equities (stocks)

4. Real estate

5. Precious metals and other investments

Most separate account programs will only include stocks and bonds, although some that include money-market instruments or real estate investment trusts are out there. For the purposes of this book, we're concentrating only on stocks and bonds, which are the cornerstones of the separate account portfolio.

Figuring out which stocks and bonds will comprise your portfolio isn't a difficult process, as long as you apply the old investment tenets such as knowing your risk levels, having a fixed time horizon, using some form of investment diversification, and having fixed investment goals (e.g., retirement, college, opening your own business, etc.). Here's a brief look at the two of the more important factors in the separate account decision-making process: risk and diversification.

Risk and Reward

The trade-off between risk and reward cannot be overemphasized. The more uncertain the investment, the greater the investment risk. The greater the investment risk, the greater the opportunity for hefty investment returns. If you're uncomfortable with too much risk and seek to minimize it, then you'll be penalized with lower investment returns. One thing's for sure: You can't completely eliminate risk. And if you don't take any risk, you surely won't make any money, as shown by Figure 8-1.

Investment risk is perpetually tied to market volatility—the fluctuations in the financial markets that constantly appear over time. The sources of this volatility are many: Interest rate changes, inflation, political consequences, and economic trends all can create combustible market conditions that can change a portfolio's performance results in a hurry. Ironically, it is the very nature of this volatility that creates the opportunities for economic benefit in our separate account portfolios. Volatility often works in the investor's favor, as it did during the bull market of the 1990s.

WHAT'S YOUR TOLERANCE FOR RISK?

How much risk you can take depends on many factors such as your age, your financial needs, your comfort level, and how many dependents you

FIGURE 8-1

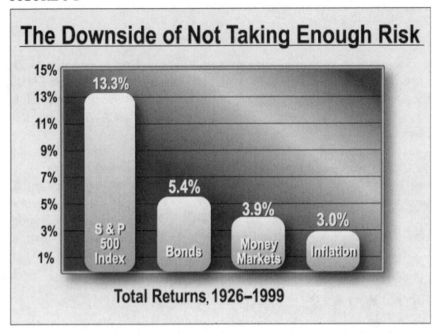

have. If you're 25 years old, single, childless, and debt-free, you obviously have more tolerance for risk than a 55-year-old nearing retirement with two kids in college.

Trying to pin down your tolerance for risk is akin to chasing ghosts: It's an uncertain process that's forever susceptible to second-guessing. You can never be quite sure what your tolerance for risk will be from year to year. But this test, developed by Lincoln Benefit Life, a subsidiary of Allstate Life Group, can help clear things up:

1. If someone made me an offer to invest 15 percent of my net worth in a deal he said had an 80 percent chance of being profitable, I'd say:

   A. No level of profit would be worth that kind of risk.
   B. The level of profit would have to be seven times the amount I invested.
   C. The level of profit would have to be three times the amount I invested.
   D. The level of profit would have to be at least as much as my original investment.

2. How comfortable would I be assuming a $10,000 debt in the hope of achieving a $20,000 gain over the next few months?

   A. Totally uncomfortable. I'd never do it.
   B. Somewhat uncomfortable. I'd probably never do it.
   C. Somewhat uncomfortable. But I might do it.
   D. Very comfortable. I'd definitely do it.

3. I am holding a lottery ticket that's gotten me to the finals, where I have a 1 in 4 chance of winning the $100,000 jackpot. I'd be willing to sell my ticket before the drawing, but for nothing less than:

   A. $15,000
   B. $20,000
   C. $35,000
   D. $60,000

4. How often do I bet more than $150 on one or more of these activities: professional sports gambling, casino gambling, or lottery tickets?

   A. Never.
   B. Only a few times in my life.
   C. Just in one of these activities in the past year.
   D. In two or more of these activities in the past year.

5. If a stock I bought doubled in the year after I bought it, I'd:

   A. Sell all my shares.
   B. Sell half my shares.
   C. Not sell any shares.
   D. Buy more shares.

6. I have a high-yielding certificate of deposit that is about to mature, and interest rates have dropped so much that I feel compelled to invest in something with a higher yield. The most likely place I'd invest the money is:

   A. U.S. savings bonds.
   B. A short-term bond fund.
   C. A long-term bond fund.
   D. A stock fund.

7. Whenever I have to decide where to invest a large amount of money, I:

   A. Delay the decision.
   B. Get someone else, like my broker, to decide for me.
   C. Share the decision with my advisors.
   D. Decide on my own.

8. Which of the following describes how I make my investment decisions?

   A. Never on my own.
   B. Sometimes on my own.
   C. Often on my own.
   D. Totally on my own.

9. My luck in investing is:

   A. Terrible.
   B. Average.
   C. Better than average.
   D. Fantastic.

10. My investments are successful mainly because:

   A. Fate is always on my side.
   B. I was in the right place at the right time.
   C. When opportunities arose, I took advantage of them.
   D. I carefully planned them to work out that way.

Grading: Give yourself one point for each answer A, two points for each answer B, three points for each answer C, and four points for each answer D.

Results

- **19 points or fewer:** You're a conservative investor who feels uncomfortable taking risks. You probably realize that you will have to take some calculated risks to attain your financial goals, but this doesn't mean you will be comfortable doing so.

- **20 to 29 points:** You're a moderate investor who feels comfortable taking moderate risks. You are probably willing to take reasonable risks without a great deal of discomfort.

- **30 points or more:** You're an aggressive investor who is willing to take high risks in search of high returns. You are not greatly stressed by taking significant risks.

THE DIFFERENT TYPES OF RISK

There's no shortage of risk classes. Some are more complicated than others, and not all of the more complex ones are listed here. That said, the ones you see here are the primary forms of risk you'll likely run into when investing in your separate account plan.

Stock-Specific Risk

Remember the dot.com meltdown of 2000? Many investors loaded up on highfliers like Amazon.com and Priceline.com only to see their values plummet. Separate accounts, by their diversified nature, severely diminish your chances of losing a lot of money. Whereas an investor dabbling in one or two stocks can see his or her investment wiped out, the chances of that happening in a separate account are remote, if not extinct. As we've said, separate accounts normally invest in up to 50 companies. The chances of all 50 companies going broke at the same time are slim indeed.

Risk of Passivity

We know some perfectly reasonable people who don't trust the financial markets and who feel more comfortable sticking their money in a bank savings account. It's a big mistake. Here's why: By sticking $10,000 in your bank savings account and being "passive" with your money (i.e., not accepting the risks and rewards that go with investing in the stock market), you're going to wind up losing money. Passbook savings account interest currently amounts to about 2.5 percent, not even enough to keep up with the 3.4 percent rate of inflation. So your initial $10,000 actually decreases its purchasing power the longer it stays in your savings account.

Inflation Rate Risk

A blood brother of passivity risk, inflation rate risk is based on the purchasing power of a dollar down the road. What we can purchase for $10,000 today will cost us $13,440 in the year 2008, based on 3 percent annual growth in inflation. Typically, stocks are the best investment when looking to outpace inflation, and money-market funds are the least effective in combating inflation.

Market Risk

Market risk is pretty much what it sounds like. Every time you invest money in the financial markets, even via a conservative money-market mutual fund, you're subjecting your money to risk. With market risk, uncertainty due to changes in the overall stock market is caused by political, social, or economic events and the mood of the investing public.

Perhaps the biggest investment risk of all, though, is not subjecting your money to market risk. If you don't put your money to work in the stock market, you're unable to benefit from the stock market's consistent growth over the years.

> ### Sidebar III: Understanding Investor Behavior
> What behavioral patterns impact an individual's investment making decisions? A lot, according to a working paper, "Trading Is Hazardous to Your Wealth: The Common Stock Investment Performance of Individual Investors," published by the *Journal of Finance*. The paper examines the trading activity of 66,465 household accounts from 1991 to 1996 at a major discount brokerage. The study observes trading patterns, compares results, and attempts to find a psychological reason for investor behavior.
>
> The paper's authors, Brad Barber and Terrance Odean, both of the University of California's Davis School of Management (Finance), explore how three behaviors—overconfidence, regret avoidance, and attention—contribute to investors' underperformance.
>
> **Overconfidence**: Overconfidence manifests itself in several ways. Sometimes people take too much credit for their success, confusing a bull market with stock-picking brilliance. Or they overestimate the precision of their knowledge. Several years ago, a large insurance company found that among its own employees who rated themselves as very sophisticated in financial matters, the majority thought that money-market funds held common stock. Or investors choose inappropriate benchmarks. If they held a stock that doubled they'd be satisfied, even if the market had tripled over that same time.
>
> **Regret Avoidance**: Regret avoidance drives investors to hold losers and sell winners. Investors hate to sell losers, and

understandably so: Selling a loser means confronting a failure that the investor may not care to recognize. It feels so much better to sell a winner; that's only confirming a good purchase.

Attention (or Chasing the Action): Barber and Odean found that the investors in their study purchased stocks that performed worse than the stocks they sold. The investors are therefore underperforming their own benchmarks—the portfolios that they started with. The study documents that the difference in performance between stocks sold and stocks purchased (excluding trades for nonspeculative reasons) was minus 5.07 percent, on average, 1 year later and minus 8.61 percent two years later. That's right: The stocks that are sold do much better, on average, than the stocks that replace them.

Source: Frank Armstrong, author of *Investment Strategies for the 21st Century*, president of Investor Solutions, Inc, a fee-only advisor specializing in global asset allocation strategies utilizing no-load mutual funds, and chief investment strategist for DirectAdvice.com.

That's the good news. The most formidable element of risk you face as an investor is the risk of losing some or all of your money. That was the case in October 1987 when the stock market fell 500 points—losing 22.5 percent of its value in a single day. On that day, a $10,000 investment in the stock market would have fallen to $7750.

Credit Risk

Usually associated with bond investments, credit risk is the possibility that a company, agency, or municipality might not be able to make interest or principal payments on its notes or bonds. The greatest risk of default is usually with corporate debt because companies go out of business all the time. There's no credit risk with Treasury-related securities because they're backed by the full faith and credit of the U.S. government. To measure the financial health of bonds, credit agencies like Moody's and Standard & Poor's assign them investment grades. A-rated bonds are considered solid, whereas C-rated bonds are considered unstable.

Currency Risk

Normally related to international or emerging-market investing, currency risk is due to currency fluctuations that may affect the value of foreign investments or profits.

Interest Rate Risk

When bond interest rates rise, the price of the bonds falls, and vice versa. Fluctuating interest rates impact stocks and bonds in significant ways. Typically, the longer the maturity of the bond, the larger the impact of interest rate risk. But long-term bonds normally pay higher yields to compensate for the greater risk.

Economic Risk

When the economy slows, corporate profits—and thus stocks—could be hurt. For example, political instability in the Middle East makes investing there a dicey deal at best, even though much of the region is flush with oil, arguably the world's most in-demand commodity. A war there, such as the Gulf War of 1990–1991, can negatively impact the fortunes of companies that do business with countries like Saudi Arabia, Israel, or Syria.

Sure, that's a lot to digest on one investment issue. But selling the impact of investment risk short is one of the biggest mistakes an investor— separate account or not—can ever make. Spend some time thinking about your tolerance for risk and then invest accordingly. And if you're working with a personal financial advisor, make sure you discuss risk before deciding on the securities that will comprise your separate account portfolio.

Diversification

Diversification simply means dividing your investments into more than one type. It's one of the best ways, if not the best way, to protect your portfolio from the pendulum swings of the economy and the financial markets. Since a separate account portfolio may invest in many different securities, a decline in the value of one security may be offset by a rise in the value of another.

Diversification can take other forms as well. For example, you could diversify your common stock holdings by purchasing stocks representing many different industries. That would be safer than concentrating in a single sector. Or you could diversify your bond holdings by buying a mixture of high-quality bonds and some lower-rated bonds. The high-quality bonds would tend to reduce the overall risk associated with the bond portfolio.

Another important form of diversification is obtained when you invest in different types of securities such as stocks, bonds, real estate, and money-market instruments, to name the major investment types.

A Closer Look at Diversification

To illustrate how powerful the principle of diversification is, consider the following alternative scenarios:

A.   A $100,000 investment with a guaranteed fixed rate of return of 8 percent will grow to $684,850 after 25 years.

B.   The same $100,000 could be evenly diversified between five separate investments each with a different degree of risk, as follows[*]

$20,000 at Total Loss—0
$20,000 at 0%—20,000
$20,000 at 5%—67,730
$20,000 at 10%—216,690
$20,000 at 15%—658,380
Total—$962,800

The net result would be an accumulation value of $962,800 after 25 years, or $277,950 more than the guaranteed investment. Although three of the five investments performed less than the guaranteed investment, the diversification into other assets that did perform well provided a greater long-term total return.

Prior to the evolution of separate accounts, if you attempted to build your own diversified investment portfolio of 50 stocks, you'd likely wind up paying tens of thousands of dollars in trading commission charges for the privilege. A separate account, however, enables you to get that kind of diversified investment but with a reasonable management fee.

[*]Source: Syverson, Strege, Sandager & Company

MARKET CONDITIONS

Above and beyond your own tolerance for risk and your own time horizon, a good separate accounts investor will evaluates current financial market conditions before deciding on an investment portfolio. That's especially true considering the wild and wooly ride investors have taken with the stock markets, particularly the NASDAQ, in 2000 and 2001. For those who thought the NASDAQ was bulletproof, they were reminded in a period of 18 months or so that even Superman is vulnerable to kryptonite. Fears about inflation, interest rate hikes, and even government's involvement in business (i.e., the Microsoft ruling) sank the NASDAQ, a symbol of bravado in an ever-increasingly high-tech world. That market lost more than 50 percent of its value in 2000, or about $3.5 trillion, its worst loss in an admittedly brief history.

Consequently, managing your own expectations is a big part of your separate account investment planning process. We've all heard about "buy-and-hold" investing and why it doesn't really matter what the market's doing when you get in, as long as you stay in. Sure, there's a great deal of truth to that line of thinking. Studies show that stocks can grow (on average) up to 10 to 12 percent annually, and bonds can grown at a rate of up to 6 to 8 percent per year for longer term Treasuries. Combined with the miracle of compound interest (your accumulated investment returns rolled over year after year), a long-term outlook coupled with a solid, disciplined investment strategy can yield big bucks over 20, 30, and especially 40+ years.

The trick is in staying in the market and not missing its sharp upticks. Market timers—those Wall Street daredevils who try to get in and out of the stock market at the most optimal moments—risk missing those market spikes by weaving in and out of the financial markets. And that money is hard to make back.

Market timers also generally experience higher transaction costs compared to a buy-and-hold strategy. Every time an investor sells or buys securities, a transaction fee is incurred. Even if the market timer achieves above average returns, the transaction costs could negate the superior performance. Trying to time the market can create additional risk. Using the time period of 1962 to 1991, an investor buying common stocks in 1962 would have had a return of 10.3 percent with a buy-and-hold strategy. If that same investor tried to time the market and missed just 12 of the best performing months (out of a total of 348 months), the return would have been only 5.4 percent.

One additional negative aspect of using market-timing techniques is the tax reporting complications. Going in and out of the market several times in one tax year (sometimes several times in a month) generates numerous taxable gain and loss transactions that all must be accounted for on the investor's income tax return.

CASE STUDY 7

Putting a Separate Account Plan into Action

Dan Flaherty could barely contain himself. He's just opened his first separate account, and the 28-year-old sales executive couldn't wait to put his investment plan into action.

A keen observer of Wall Street, Flaherty was one of the smart ones who began investing for his retirement right out of college. "I put $2259 away each year and netted on average about 10 percent on my investments. I figure by the time I turn 62 I'll be a millionaire if I stay the course. And I will stay the course."

Satisfied that the cornerstone of his long-term investment plan was in place, Flaherty wanted to use his separate account portfolio to augment his retirement fund. "I have a daughter and two sons, and I know they'll need help paying college bills. And my wife and I want to build an addition on our home next year. So I was looking for other ways to save some money that could grow with us and meet our shorter term needs."

Being a relative youngster, Flaherty loaded up his initial separate account with growth stocks and some value stocks for balance. "No dot.coms and no chasing IPOs," he says. "Like Joe Friday said on *Dragnet*, 'Just the facts, ma'am.'"

Flaherty figures he's still young enough to take more risk with growth stocks in his separate account portfolio. Over time, he'll grow a bit more conservative. "But that's a long way off," he says. "Right now, I'm willing to take some chances on the stock market."

9

TRACKING SEPARATE ACCOUNT PERFORMANCE: PORTFOLIO REBALANCING AND ASSET ALLOCATION STRATEGIES

Suppose you were on a nonstop flight from Los Angeles to Bombay and heard the following announcement: "Ladies and Gentlemen, this is your captain speaking. We're now traveling west across the Pacific Ocean. In a few hours, you'll be able to look down and see land. When that happens, we're going to start looking for a big city with an airport. If we find one before our fuel runs out, we'll land. Then we'll figure out where we are and decide where we go next. In the meantime, folks, just sit back and enjoy the trip." Well, would you? No, probably not.

Remember in Chapter 7 when we pointed out that having the ingredients of a successful plan is useless without having a recipe to use those ingredients? That's kind of like the airplane captain flying to Bombay without a clue. Sure, he has a plane, a flight crew, and some fuel and provisions for his crew and passengers—everything he'll need to get across the Pacific Ocean and to his destination. But without a flight plan, all that equipment and all those tools will be meaningless because, in the end, he really doesn't know how he's going to reach his destination.

Investors often make the same mistake. They go out and buy the most sophisticated personal computers with the most advanced trading and analytical software available. They study *The Wall Street Journal* and subscribe to the hot Internet investment sites. They smugly point to their Web-enhanced mobile phones with their stock tickers and access to the their online trading firms. But without a blueprint, a recipe, a formula for putting these tools to good use for their investment portfolio, they're as vulnerable and clueless as the airplane pilot trying to get from L.A. to the Orient without a flight plan.

It doesn't have to be so. With a good asset allocation program and a good portfolio rebalancing system, any investor can get where he or she needs to go without breaking a sweat. This is especially true in the world of separate accounts, where investors have a bigger say in what stocks they own and more control over selling them and replacing them with new ones.

BUILDING THE PERFECT PORTFOLIO

Most separate account customers are savvy investors who have some experience in pulling together an asset allocation plan, whether through a mutual fund program, a 401(k) or individual retirement account (IRA), or through a stock investment portfolio. Consequently, separate account investors more or less know the score and have some idea of how to proceed in building a solid investment portfolio. Primarily, it means taking the following steps:

1. Deciding which asset categories will be represented in the portfolio.
2. Determining the long-term "target" percentage of the portfolio to allocate to each of these asset categories.
3. Specifying for each asset category the range within which the allocation can be altered in an attempt to exploit better performance possibilities from one asset category versus another.
4. Selecting securities within each of the asset categories.

The first two steps form the foundation for the portfolio's risk-return characteristics and are often referred to as investment policy decisions. Traditionally, a diversified portfolio was built with three asset categories: cash equivalents, bonds, and common stocks. Other asset categories, however, may be considered, although not as often in an individually managed investment account. Among them, for example, are international bonds, international common stocks, real estate, and precious metals. To the extent to which these various asset categories are affected differently by changing economic events, each will have its own unique pattern of returns.

Let's have a look at the primary asset classes that you'll be choosing from and see how they shape up.

Growth Stocks

These stocks, which can be volatile, seek maximum earnings potential and high share prices from the hard-charging companies they invest in. Growth stock portfolios invest in fast-growing, well-established companies where the company itself and the industry in which it operates are thought to have good long-term growth potential. A good example of a growth mutual fund is Fidelity's Magellan Fund, which for years was the highest-returning mutual fund in the industry.

Aggressive Growth Stocks

These are similar to growth stocks, but even more aggressive; they tend to be the most volatile of all asset classes. Aggressive growth portfolios seek to provide maximum growth of capital with secondary emphasis on dividend or interest income. Here, your money managers will help you choose common stocks with a high potential for rapid growth and capital appreciation. But it comes at no small risk: Aggressive growth stocks, because they bet on the fortunes of small up-and-coming companies with little or no track record, are riskier than most stocks. A good example of an aggressive growth mutual fund is American Century's Ultra Fund, which blew away the competition in the early to mid-1990s. In the last few years, though, Ultra has struggled because of its sustained exposure to so many high-risk companies.

Both traditional growth funds and aggressive growth funds are okay if you have a long time horizon before retiring. If you have 80 percent of your separate account assets in an aggressive growth fund at age 55 and the stock market tanks, you could lose a lot of your retirement money. But at age 25, 35, or even 45, aggressive growth stocks are a good investment because their returns typically outpace most other funds' performance.

Growth and Income Stocks

These stocks seek both long-term growth and a reasonable amount of income. Although management strategies vary among separate account managers, two management strategies usually apply with growth and income stocks: The money managers invest in a dual portfolio consisting of growth stocks and income stocks or a combination of growth stocks, stocks paying high dividends, preferred stocks, convertible securities, or fixed-income securities such as corporate bonds and money-market instruments.

Sidebar I: Getting Started
When establishing an asset allocation strategy, try these simple steps:

- Think about how long you'll be investing.

- Decide how much risk you can take.

- Pick a target mix that's right for you.

- Select investments that will help you achieve that mix.

- Adjust your investments gradually. Start with your future deferrals to match your asset mix and gradually redirect existing balances to fit into your overall plan. The more money you are moving, the more time it should take to complete your asset allocation strategy.

Growth and income stocks are popular with separate account investors because they offer good opportunity for growth and also offer some protection against excessive risk.

International Stocks

We love international funds, if only because our money gets to travel to more interesting places than we do. International portfolios focus on stocks of companies outside the United States. International portfolios are not to be confused with global portfolios, which seek growth by investing in securities around the world, including the United States. Both provide investors with another opportunity to diversify their separate accounts portfolio, because foreign markets do not always move in the same direction as the United States.

Fixed-Income Portfolios

More informally known as bonds, fixed-income securities attempt to provide high current income while preserving investors' money. Growth of capital, the hallmark of most stock portfolios, is of secondary importance to bond portfolios. Unlike stocks, bonds invest in securities that offer "fixed" rates of return. This means that you pretty much know what you're going to get on the return from your investment.

The chief variable in a bond is its price. Since bond prices fluctuate with changing interest rates, there is some risk involved despite a bond's conservative nature. When interest rates rise, the market price of fixed-income securities declines and so will the value of the income portfolio's investments. Conversely, in periods of declining interest rates, the value of fixed-income products will rise and investors will enjoy capital appreciation as well as income. That's because in a declining interest rate environment, existing bonds that offer higher fixed rates of return are in greater demand. When rates rise, bonds that lock returns in at lower interest rates are in lower demand.

Some fixed-income portfolios seek to minimize risk by investing exclusively in securities whose timely payment of interest and principal is backed by the full faith and credit of the U.S. government. These include securities issued by the U.S. Treasury, the Government National Mortgage Association (Ginnie Mae securities), the Federal National Mortgage Association (Fannie Maes), and Federal Home Loan Mortgage Corporation

(Freddie Macs). Government bond portfolios invest only in national government or government agency debt. They have slightly lower credit risk than regular bond classes. Treasury portfolios invest only in direct obligations of the national government. U.S. Treasury bond portfolios offer investors the lowest credit risk, and dividend distributions are exempt from state income taxes in most states. They are great investments for separate account investors who are drawing near to retirement.

Municipal Bonds

Municipal bonds invest only in the debt of state or local governments, which use the bonds to raise money for civic projects, such as new roads and bridges. For most individuals, dividend distributions from municipals are also exempt from national income taxes, and some are exempt from state and local taxes as well.

Money-Market Portfolios

The safest of all fixed-income securities, money-market investments try to maintain a constant (usually $1) NAV per share, while yielding dividends from their investments in short-term debt securities. They invest in highly liquid, virtually risk-free, short-term debt securities of agencies of the U.S. government, banks and corporations, and U.S. Treasury bills. They have no potential for growth. Their market value is also not insured by the FDIC or other government agency. Enough defaults in a money-market portfolio's securities can cause it to be unable to maintain its constant NAV.

GETTING SPECIFIC

Make no mistake about it, separate account asset classes can get a bit more complicated than the portfolio sectors just identified. Take James P. O'Shaughnessy, a money manager who sold his mutual fund business to open NetFolio, another online separate accounts provider. For about $200 annually, NetFolio offered investors "baskets" of stocks numbering anywhere from 5 to 50. On the company's Web site, investors could find numerous asset classes that included these stocks. The site offered a good description of various asset classes. However, NetFolio closed in 2001.

Here's a snapshot of some of the separate account asset classes—or "baskets," as O'Shaughnessy calls them—that his firm offers, along with a brief description:

Concentrated Growth: A 20-stock portfolio that combines the top 10 stocks from the company's Market Leaders Growth and Cornerstone Growth strategies. When growth stocks are performing well, this strategy takes advantage of both large- and small-cap growth stocks.

Growth Blend: A 30-stock strategy that combines the 10 lowest price-to-sales ratio (PSR) stocks from the company's Market Leaders Universe and the top 10 stocks from both the Market Leaders Growth and Cornerstone Growth strategies. Two-thirds of the resulting portfolio is made up of small- and large-cap growth stocks, and one-third consists of large-cap value stocks.

Cornerstone Growth: A 25-stock strategy for those who want to focus on small-cap investing. It is comprised of companies with a minimum market cap of $172 million, price to sales less than 1.5, earnings higher than in the previous year, and good trading liquidity.

Model Portfolio: A 40-stock strategy suited to investors who want a blend of styles. The portfolio is a 50-50 mix of growth and value; 75 percent are large stocks and 25 percent are small stocks.

Value Blend: A 30-stock large-cap blend strategy, with two-thirds of the portfolio invested in value stocks and one-third in growth stocks. The value component includes the 10 highest dividend-yielding stocks and the 10 lowest PSR stocks from the company's domestic Market Leaders Universe.

Concentrated Value: A 20-stock portfolio to be used as the value component in a larger portfolio.

Index Plus: A strategy designed to be highly correlated to the S&P 500 while still seeking to outperform it over the long term. The 30-stock portfolio contains the 10 largest stocks from the S&P 500, the top 10 stocks by price appreciation from Market Leaders Growth, and the 10 lowest PSR stocks from the domestic Market Leaders Universe.

Value: A 25-stock portfolio for investors desiring a higher current income through dividend yield. It consists of the 25 companies from the Market Leaders Universe with the highest dividend yields.

Capital Preservation: A conservative strategy designed to preserve capital while taking advantage of the company's Value Blend strategy's potential for growth. The strategy is a 50-50 blend of Treasury bills and the 30-stock Value Blend strategy.

Sidebar II: Sample Investor Profile

This brief questionnaire can help you determine your Investor Profile and an asset allocation model appropriate for your objectives. To give you an idea of how it works, we've answered the questions ourselves to see where we fit in the asset allocation world:

1. What do you consider most important when investing for retirement?

   Protecting the value of my investments.

   Increasing the value of my investments, but with little risk.

   Significantly increasing the value of my investments, with moderate risk.

   ✓ Maximizing the value of my investments, accepting relatively high risk.

2. Do you maintain separate savings and investment accounts outside of your retirement plan to protect you in the event of an emergency?

   No.

   Yes, enough to cover my expenses for 2 months or less.

   Yes, enough to cover my expenses for between 2 and 6 months.

   ✓ Yes, I have an adequate emergency fund that will cover my expenses for more than 6 months.

3. In approximately how many years do you expect to retire?

   Fewer than 5 years.

   5 to 9 years.

   10 to 20 years.

   ✓ More than 20 years.

4. Most investments fluctuate over the short term. If you had a long-term investment of $10,000 and it lost value during the first year, when would you move to a more stable investment?

When the investment lost $1000 (a 10 percent loss).
When the investment lost $2000 (a 20 percent loss).
When the investment lost $5000 (a 50 percent loss).
✓ Would not move my investment within the first year.

5. Which of the following statements reflects how you invest?

I must feel that I will not be putting my investments at risk.
I want to feel secure about the safety of the majority of my investments but am willing to risk a small portion for the possibility of greater returns.
I want a balanced portfolio with some low-risk investments and some providing higher risk and potentially greater returns.
✓ I want to invest aggressively, emphasizing investments with a higher degree of risk and higher potential returns, while limiting low-risk investments.

6. Approximately what portion of your monthly take-home income goes toward predictable installment-type payments (e.g., as auto loans, credit cards, home equity loans, and child support), not including a home mortgage?

Less than 10 percent.
Between 10 percent and 25 percent.
Between 25 percent and 50 percent.
✓ More than 50 percent.

7. How do you expect to use your retirement savings?

I expect to need my retirement savings within the next 5 years to make a major purchase or to cover a major nonretirement expense.
I expect that I will not need my retirement savings for at least 6 to 9 years, but know that a shorter-term need could arise.

I expect that I will not need my retirement savings for 10 to 20 years, but expect that a shorter-term need could arise.

✓ I don't plan to touch my retirement savings for at least 20 years.

8. Which one of these types of investments have you used the most in the past?

Savings accounts, savings bonds, and certificates of deposit.

Bonds and/or bond mutual funds.

Stocks and/or stock mutual funds.

✓ Aggressive investments such as international mutual funds or funds investing in small, emerging companies.

9. What retirement savings vehicles are you currently counting on or, if appropriate, contributing to?

Only social security.

My employer's pension plan and social security.

My 401(k) or other voluntary retirement plan, a pension, social security, and/ or an individual savings plan (such as an IRA or CD).

✓ My spouse's voluntary retirement plan, my own voluntary retirement plan, a pension, social security, and/or an individual savings account.

10. How often do you tend to monitor your investments?

Daily.

Monthly.

Quarterly.

✓ Annually.

Conclusion

According to BARRA RogersCasey, investment consultant to Allmerica Financial, we're aggressive investors based on our responses to their questions. Based on our asset allocation worksheet responses, the following model is recommended.

Recommended Portfolio by Asset Class

- Aggressive growth: 25%

- International: 15%

- Income: 20%

- Growth and income: 15%

- Growth: 15%

More Aggressive Investor Profile

- Objective is to accumulate wealth to meet long-term financial goals.

- Willing to accept greater fluctuations to maximize the potential for long-term asset growth.

ASSET ALLOCATION FOR THE SEPARATE ACCOUNT INVESTOR: A BACKGROUNDER

The concept of asset allocation is simple. You take investment capital and, depending on variables like net worth, time frame, risk acceptance, and other assets the investor owns, decide the appropriate places where it should go. Asset allocation operates on several levels. The top is strategy— how much of each dollar goes to stocks, bonds, liquid savings accounts, and so on, usually based on a pyramid or a baskets approach to the degree of risk inherent in each asset class. Then come tactics—the deployment of the money within these divisions. For example, in stocks, there are growth, blue-chip, micro-cap, and so forth, whereas in bonds, there is range of duration and credit quality. Then comes the issue of whether to put some money in assets classed with a low correlation to stocks and bonds to counter the effects of sudden losses. If you've ever worked with a financial advisor or stockbroker, chances are you've heard of asset allocation.

Asset allocation works on the principle that not all investments behave the same way at the same time. Some, such as equities or equity mutual funds, have greater short-term price fluctuations; others, such as guaranteed investment certificates (GICs) and money-market mutual funds, are generally more stable. More volatile investments, however, offer the potential for greater long-term gains. Financial markets also vary in performance cycles. If North American stock markets are on the rise, those in other areas of the world may be in decline. In times of dropping interest rates, shorter-term bonds generally outperform longer-term bonds. Moreover, when stock markets are strong, bond markets may be weak.

Generally, properly allocating your investment dollars means assembling a portfolio from the three major asset categories: cash, fixed-income, and equities. Cash includes money in the bank, short-term investments such as Treasury bills, and money-market mutual funds. Fixed-income investments include bonds, guaranteed investment certificates, and other interest-generating securities. Equities are stock market investments, amd they can be further subdivided into different styles, such as "value" and "growth."

Through asset allocation, you can use these variations in the performance of securities and financial markets to your advantage. Asset allocation ensures that your portfolio is diversified, so you reduce the degree of short-term fluctuations while maintaining the potential for long-term returns. You can also reduce the risks associated with putting all your eggs in one basket.

Once you've devised an asset allocation strategy, you can adjust it to meet your changing financial goals as you move through life. For example, when you're younger, you may want to concentrate more on equities to build wealth. When you approach retirement, you may wish to preserve the wealth you've accumulated through a greater concentration of lower-risk fixed-income assets.

Jeffrey R. Kosnett, writing in the August 1999 edition of *Life Association News* ("Asset Allocation: Thinking & Consulting About All That Money"), aptly points out that asset allocation is seemingly everywhere:

> It is the subject of countless books, software programs, academic papers, Web sites, off-the-cuff commentaries, and, make no mistake, shoddy short-cuts. The Internet and financial magazines and newsletters are bursting with commentary that tells readers to be X percent in stocks, Y in bonds and Z in cash—a premise that suffers from the misconception that all investors are alike. Stockbrokers, insurance companies, mutual fund firms, financial planners and consultants try to differentiate investors by questionnaires and by installing on Web sites free, interactive asset allocation screens.

The truth of the matter is that, while indeed everywhere, asset allocation strategies for separate account investors don't differ all that much from traditional stock portfolios or even from mutual fund portfolios. The cornerstones are all the same: selecting certain types of investments and then determining how much to invest. Anywhere on Wall Street, or Main Street for that matter, the goal of asset allocation is to achieve the best possible return while reducing the risk.

There's no shortage of reasons why asset allocation is the heart and soul of your separate accounts program, and one of the most compelling ones is in a recent study by Ibbotson Associates that concluded over 90 percent of investment success is determined by being in the best performing sectors of the market. In other words, it is not so important that you own Ford or General Motors common stock, but that you were participating in the automotive sector.

The Ibbotson study is just the latest in a string of similar research papers on the impact of asset allocation on investment portfolios that began 15 years ago. In 1986, Gary Brinson, along with collaborators L. Randolph Hood and Gilbert Beebower, published a study about asset allocation in the *Financial Analysts Journal*. Based on analysis of a decade of data from 91 pension funds, Brinson and colleagues concluded that more than 90 percent of an investor's return is attributable to how you weight assets among stocks, bonds, and cash. In other words, how much money you put into stocks as a group matters a lot more than which specific stocks you own.

The ripples from the Brinson study are still felt on Wall Street today. Financial advisors, stockbrokers, and even mutual fund companies have positioned themselves as the ultimate practitioners of allocation strategy, encouraging an ever more refined slicing and dicing of the investment landscape into specialized asset classes that supposedly help individual investors build ever better portfolios. This has dramatically changed how people choose their investments and how financial services companies sell them their investments. The U.S. equity market alone is now often split into as many as a dozen subcategories, and asset allocation software designed for planners routinely divides the investment world into more than 20 different groups. (One program reportedly designates 1000 asset classes, including Turkish utilities and lard futures.)

Sidebar III: Where Do You Fit in Riskwise?
The following lists can help you classify your attitudes as an investor. Do you see your own portfolio here?

Ultra-Aggressive Portfolio

35% Small-cap stocks
20% International stocks
20% Sector funds
15% Large-cap stocks
10% Emerging-market stocks

Aggressive Growth Portfolio

30% International stocks
35% Large-cap fund stocks
35% Small-cap stocks

Growth Portfolio

40% Large-cap stocks
25% International stocks
30% Small-cap stocks
 5% International bonds

Growth and Income Portfolio

40% Large-cap growth and income stocks
20% Large-cap growth stocks
15% International stock stocks
15% Small-cap stocks
10% Intermediate-term bonds

Conservative Income Portfolio

25% Large-cap growth and income stocks
25% Long-term bonds
20% Intermediate-term bonds
15% International bonds
10% International stocks
 5% Small-cap stocks

Conservative Portfolio

40% Money-market and short-term bonds
25% Intermediate-term bonds
10% International bonds
10% Large-cap stocks
10% International stocks
 5% Small-cap stocks

The Brinson study may have been too generic for some. It didn't account for emerging markets or microcaps, didn't separate growth stocks from value stocks, and didn't examine large caps and small caps (in fact, the study primarily looked at the three most basic asset classes: stocks, bonds, and cash). However, it did establish some pioneering points.

First, it demonstrated that the single largest driving force behind investment results was the policy decision allocating among stocks, bonds, and cash. Study leaders found that if they knew the percentage allocated to each class, they could account for the vast majority, 94 percent, of the variations in returns between large domestic pension plans. More recent studies have concluded that when the size and style characteristics of the portfolio are factored in, you can account for over 98 percent of the plan results.

Second, Brinson and colleagues found that the factors that most investors had assumed contributed the most to investment returns, individual stock selection and market timing, contributed less than 6 percent to the results. Worse yet for active managers, on average the contribution was negative.

But that's not all. The Brinson study also demonstrated that—and this is very important to separate account investors—exposing your investment to additional opportunities can help enhance your returns and help reduce your overall investment risk. Not a bad trifecta.

POINTS OF DETERMINATION

Unfortunately, the Brinson study opened up another whole can of worms. Sure, it's great to know that allocation was more important than old-fashioned stock picking. But how do you determine what the best-performing sectors are and what your asset allocation mix should be?

Many financial advisors say, quite sensibly, that your asset allocation plan depends on where you are in life. If you're just starting out, a long-term strategy that emphasizes stocks is advised. This strategy tends to emphasize growth to build assets by investing in more aggressive stocks. It may also include a commitment to income investments such as bonds to moderate risk. An example of a portfolio that employs a long-term strategy may include 70 percent equities, 25 percent bonds, and 5 percent short-term instruments or cash.

If you're middle-aged, maybe in your late 30s to early 50s (your peak earning years), you're often advised to adopt a midrange strategy that provides a balanced approach with investments in both equities and bonds to provide some growth potential along with current income. An example of a portfolio that employs a midrange strategy may include 50 percent equities, 40 percent bonds, and 10 percent short-term instruments or cash.

If you're nearing or in retirement, advisors often advocate a short-term strategy that places more emphasis on capital preservation (using bonds). This strategy is designed to emphasize current income, capital preservation, and liquidity, while maintaining a smaller portion of the portfolio in stocks for growth potential. An example of a portfolio that employs a short-term strategy may include 50 percent bonds, 20 percent equities, and 30 percent short-term instruments or cash.

Let's face it. An individual's risk tolerance and goals for returns on investments are the dominant factors influencing what percentage of his or her investment dollar should be put into each of the three investment categories and the specific types of issues that should be bought in each category. Making these choices wisely delivers the maximum return within each investor's comfort zone for risk, enabling an investor to reach realistic financial goals without losing sleep.

Sidebar IV: The Perils of Marketing Timing

The Cost of Being "Out of the Market," 1982–1987

Missing the best 10 days of a bull market is one thing. Imagine missing the best 40 days of the 1980s bull market. Note the comparison between the buy-and-hold investor who remained in the stock market during the entire period from December 21, 1981, through August 25, 1987, and the market timer who missed the top 40 days of market performance.

Investment Period	Average Annual Return	Percentage of Return Missed
Entire 1276 Trading Days	+26.3%	0.0
Less the 10 Biggest Days	+18.3	30.4
Less the 20 Biggest Days	+13.1	50.2
Less the 30 Biggest Days	+8.5	67.7
Less the 40 Biggest Days	+4.3	83.7

*Period Ended August 25, 1987.
Source: University of Michigan Study.

A last word: These asset allocation programs are simply examples and shouldn't be consider investment advice, but they do give you a broad idea of how asset allocation works. Having accomplished that, let's take a deeper look at asset allocation and some more sophisticated strategies.

THE ASSET ALLOCATION PROCESS

We mentioned earlier that mixing asset classes best suited to your risk profile, time horizon, and financial goals was critical whether you are investing in mutual funds or separate accounts. That's one reason, in the area of asset allocation, at least, you might want to bring in a financial advisor to help you make those decisions. Achieving the right mix of stock types (small-, mid-, large-caps, and internationals) and bonds (short-, medium-, and long-term) to obtain maximum return for your volatility tolerance while maintaining adequate diversification is a tricky business. Heck, even a lot of brokers and fund managers get it wrong. So considering consultation with a qualified financial planner or advisor should be at the top of your separate account asset allocation "to do" list.

Whether you work with a financial advisor or not, the purpose of the asset allocation decision is to weigh the investment's expected reward against the risk associated with that decision. This information, in conjunction with your tolerance for risk, is the primary factor necessary to determine a proper asset allocation mix.

There are two primary ways of allocating assets. The first method is to use a stable policy over time. Based on your income needs and risk tolerance, you might pursue a balanced strategy. This might require putting 25 percent of your dollars in each class of assets, such as stocks, bonds, cash, and real estate. Then, each quarter or year, you rebalance those dollars back to your original allocation of 25 percent in each class. This forces you to sell off some of the best-performing assets, while buying more of the weakest performers. This allocation system eliminates the need to make decisions on the expected return for each class and instead allows for more stable returns over long time periods.

The second means of allocating assets is through an active strategy. With this method, you first determine your tolerance for risk and your long-term goals. Then you allocate ranges of your total portfolio you will invest in each class. Thus, if you need a good mix of growth and income, you might allow your investment in stocks to range from 35 to 65 percent of your portfolio based on the market. You would develop these ranges for each asset class.

An active strategy involves making a prediction of where you expect each class of asset to go over the next year. If you believe we are in a fast-growing equities market, you would put the maximum amount of dollars into common stocks or common stock mutual funds. Therefore, you would be lowering the amount of dollars invested in other asset classes. Likewise, if you believe that we are in a period of great risk for the markets, you would put more dollars into cash as a means of protecting your portfolio.

Obviously, an active strategy requires a lot of homework and a good knowledge of the financial markets and what impacts on them. It is a higher-risk strategy because if you make the wrong decision, you put your portfolio at greater risk than if you had pursued a stable strategy. However, if you consistently make the right calls, you can make a substantially higher return than you otherwise would. Figure 9-1 presents some more sophisticated separate account asset allocation options.

Organizing your asset allocation campaign is fairly straightforward, once you get the hang of it. As Kosnett writes, asset allocation operates on several levels. The top is strategy: how much of each dollar goes to stocks, bonds, liquid savings accounts, and so on, usually based on a pyramid or a baskets approach to the degree of risk inherent in each asset class. Then comes tactics—what he describes as the deployment of the money within these divisions. "For example, in stocks, there are growth, value, blue-chip, micro-cap, international, high-dividend, etc., while in bonds there is a range of duration and credit quality," Kosnett explains. The good news is that virtually all separate account companies either produce or distribute custom asset allocation software so you can not only see the value of creating a sensible allocation, but can use the programs to suggest reasonable weightings consistent with the client's personality.

That's fortuitous because as Kosnett adds, information spreads so rapidly, and economies are so interrelated that whenever U.S. stocks tumble, European and sometimes Asian investors also sell off, and the news reports spread the idea that there is a direct connection. (The same is true with rallies; European markets have also hit record highs in recent years.) "This thinking makes sense, given how so many 'American' companies make a large part of their sales and earnings abroad and how such 'European' companies as Siemens and DaimlerChrysler are more accurately described as stateless enterprises," he writes. "If the Federal Reserve were to go forward with unexpected interest rate boosts, British, French, German, and Japanese markets would also be pounded even if their central banks didn't also tighten."

FIGURE 9-1.   Sample aggressive and conservative portfolios from Separate Account Solutions

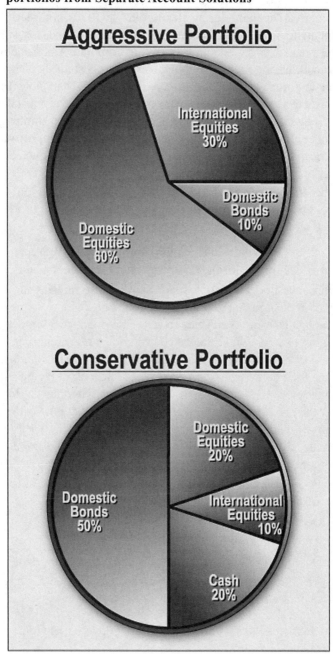

Another market trend that makes asset allocation even more critical is the prices of U.S. stocks and bonds, which once moved in opposite directions. As the American economy grew steadily in the 1950s, long-term interest rates crept higher to the point where seasoned Treasury bonds lost significant value. But stocks kept appreciating anyway as corporate America dominated the world and leading industrial companies kept boosting dividends, which were more important to investors in those days than they are now. Today, the biggest threat to stock values seems to be rising interest rates or just the expectation of rising rates. Analysts question how stocks can keep climbing if rates are no longer at or near their lows. The correlation, therefore, between blue-chip American stocks and Treasury bond prices has become much closer.

Sidebar V: Summing Up

There are four key points to consider to help you determine the right asset allocation:

1. Your investment goal: The most common are for retirement, for education, or for the down payment on your first home.

2. Your investment horizon: Once you have determined your goal(s) the time horizon is easy to calculate. If for retirement and you have 20 to 30 years to go, you can consider a more aggressive portfolio because you can ride out the highs and lows of a volatile stock market. But if your primary goal is to save for a home, you don't want to take the risk of facing a dip in the stock market just as you are ready to withdraw the funds for the home purchase. In that case, you are better off with money-market instruments. Saving for educational expenses are usually somewhere in between depending on the amount of time you have before needing the money.

3. Your risk tolerance: Here are some good questions to ask yourself.
   - Do market fluctuations keep you awake at night?
   - Are you unfamiliar with investing?
   - Do you consider yourself more a saver than an investor?
   - Are you fearful of losing 25 percent of your assets in a few days or weeks?

If you answered "yes" to these questions, you are likely to be a conservative investor.

- Are you comfortable with the ups and downs of the securities markets?
- Are you knowledgeable about investing and the securities markets?
- Are you investing for a long-term goal?
- Can you withstand considerable short-term losses?

If you answered "yes" to these questions, you are likely to be an aggressive investor. Or if you fall somewhere in between the two, you could call yourself a moderate investor.

4. Your financial resources: The amount you have to invest will also be a factor in the risk you might want to take.

CASE STUDY 8

Building an Asset Allocation Strategy

Mary McGuire knew that she had a lot to learn about investing. But as a recent widower who lost her husband in a golf cart accident, she'd taken it upon herself to learn more about the wily ways of Wall Street. And with her financial advisor's help, the more she read about separate accounts, the more interested she became.

"My husband had all of our money in mutual funds, and I guess we did all right," she says. "But when I looked at the financial statements I thought we could do better."

With her advisor's help, the 71-year-old McGuire opened a separate account with a major wirehouse. She went downtown to meet with her new money manager and with her financial advisor. Together, they mapped out a strategy that would ensure Mary that she'd have enough to live on even if she lived to be 100. "Plus there'd be some left for the kids, too," she adds.

From her studies of asset allocation programs, Mary knew that, on Wall Street at least, timing was everything. For example, an individual planning to retire in 15 years who has a high tolerance for volatility may want to have 70 percent of his or her holdings in the stock market, 28 percent in bonds, and 2 percent in money markets. If that person is planning to retire in 25 years, he or she might ratchet the securities holdings up to 80 percent.

Those retiring in 15 years but with less stomach for volatility may want to keep 50 percent in stocks and 38 percent in bonds. For equally volatility-shy people 10 years younger, the percentage in stocks could be around 65 percent.

But Mary didn't want to take those kinds of risks. She felt more akin to the person retiring in 5 years faced with the daunting task of allocating their assets for maximum return without betting the farm. In that situation, severe market decline could occur immediately before retirement, leaving the retirement kitty drastically short.

With her separate account manager and financial advisor's help, Mary crafted a separate account plan that would benefit from stocks' penchant for growth and from bonds' relative stability. "We decided to put 48 percent in bonds (principally intermediate-term bonds), 2 percent in money markets, and 50 percent in stocks—primarily large-cap stocks," she says. "I felt comfortable with that."

CHAPTER 10

TAXING MATTERS: UNCLE SAM WANTS YOU— HERE'S HOW TO ESCAPE HIS CLUTCHES

I feel very honored to pay taxes in America. The thing is, I'd feel just as honored for about half the price.

ARTHUR GODFREY

Americans have been fighting the Internal Revenue Service for years. Legendary humorist Will Rogers once overpaid his income taxes but was unable to collect the money he was owed. After endless queries that were ignored, Rogers evened the score on his next year's return by listing under deductions: "Bad debt, U.S. Government—$40,000."

Mutual fund investors can identify with that. They've been taking it on the chin from the IRS—and from their fund companies, for years. Take shareholders of Fidelity Investment's once high-flying Japan Smaller Companies fund, which recognized a capital gain of $4.65 per share through September 30, 2000—a sizable 28.3 percent of its total net asset value. Although the fund delivered a stunning 237.4 percent return in 1999, investors had lost 35 percent of their money for calendar year 2000. A capital-gains burden of $4.65 per share and a 35 percent decline in performance are usually the trigger for investors to reach for their phones or their laptops and begin canceling their fund accounts.

The tax liability can be especially galling if a fund's manager held onto shares for less than a year. If this happens, short-term capital-gains taxes are owed. And the higher your tax bracket, the worse the pain. If your fund generated $10,000 in short-term capital gains for your account and you're in the 39.6 percent bracket, you'll owe $3960 in taxes.

In the Fidelity fund example, here's how the numbers work out: An investor who put $100,000 in the fund at the start of the year would only have $65,000 on November 28 after a 35 percent decline. If that same investor stays in the fund until December 15, when the fund company pays out its distribution, he or she would be responsible for paying taxes on $5118 worth of capital gains. For someone in the 28 percent tax bracket, the tax bill generated would be $1160. Put another way, after losing $35,000 in the fund's value, the investor would have to pay $1160 out of pocket in additional taxes.

Of course, most years capital gains aren't as big an issue as they were in 2000. But market conditions that year whipped up a "perfect storm" for capital-gains liens that shocked many investors.

Several trends combined in 2000's turbulent stock market to make the tax hit especially unpleasant. Mutual funds holding technology stocks have enjoyed strong gains for the last several years. They passed on strong returns, but the stocks in their portfolios also built up huge gains. Plus, the incredible run in the NASDAQ over the last couple of years pushed valuations to the point where many managers realized it was prudent to sell. Once the stock markets corrected in the spring, many growth funds began posting negative returns, motivating some investors to cash out. To pay out those leaving, portfolio managers had to raise cash. Given a choice, most managers will sell a stock that has had good performance recently. Most portfolio managers emphasize overall returns and give less attention to the tax consequences of the stock trades they make. Investors have to take some of the responsibility, too. As long as the returns from their mutual funds were good, most investors paid little attention to the capital-gains taxes.

SOME BACKGROUND

It's no secret that investment portfolios and taxes have been closely entwined for decades. You can't swing an umbrella around Wall Street without hitting a tax accountant and you can't swing one in the IRS's Washington, D.C., office without hitting a tax agent with Series 7 credentials. Interestingly to advocates in both camps, most of the recent trends impacting on investments and taxes have occurred in the last 15 years or so.

According to the October 22, 1999, edition of *Outlook* magazine "Pumping Up After Tax Returns," by Brian Scott, a CPA with Costa Mesa, California-based Glowacki Framson Financial Advisor, the rise of tax-aware investing can be traced to two major elements.

The first is the divergence of ordinary income tax rates and long-term capital-gain tax rates. In 1989, all ordinary income and capital gains were taxed at 28 percent. Then, while capital-gains rates stayed level, ordinary income rates quickly rose to 39.6 percent, creating a noticeable differential. And in 1997, the drop in capital-gains rates made ordinary income rates double the capital-gains rate. Having one tax rate that is twice the other creates

> ### Sidebar I: Tax-Sweeping Separate Accounts
> Some separate account providers are following the fund industry's lead in offering "tax-efficient" index-type accounts. Here's how they work.
>
> Such funds can mimic the performance of an index like the S&P 500 or the Russell 2000 without buying every stock in the index. Each night, the separate account provider's computers "sweep" every account looking for losses that can be harvested. When the computer jettisons one of your stocks, it might buy a comparable one to maintain your portfolio's sector and risk characteristics. The computer might also go ahead and buy the original index back, but only after 31 days. Why? To accommodate the so-called "wash sale" rule that limits write-offs of stocks sold and then bought right back again.

a significant tax arbitrage opportunity if ordinary income can be shifted to capital gain. And the long-term capital gain can be further arbitraged by deferring it because unrealized capital appreciation has a current tax rate of zero.

The second factor is the bull market of the 1980s and 1990s, which coincided with an upward trend in the number of aging baby boomers saving for retirement. The bull market has increased the size of individual investment portfolios and their resulting income. And although managing taxes on portfolio income has long been an issue for wealthy families like the DuPonts, Rockefellers, Vanderbilts, and their multigenerational trust funds, it's now a concern for individual taxpayers as well—a concern that CPAs are eminently positioned to address.

Scott says quite accurately that most portfolio managers have plied their trade in a tax-free environment, with total return as their yardstick. In this tax-free Shangri-la, it did not matter if this return was generated from dividends, interest, short-term gains, long-term gains, or unrealized appreciation. Total return was all that mattered. But to taxable investors, maximizing after-tax return is what matters. A taxable investor with 10 percent unrealized appreciation ends up with a larger account after paying taxes than the investor with 10 percent realized long-term gain, and a much larger account that the one with 10 percent ordinary income. Compound that result over a few years and the differences are noticeable. Over 30 years, small differences in after-tax return have a huge impact.

A number of studies have indicated that the average stock fund loses 2 to 3 percent to taxes. Assuming a return of 10 percent and a 2.5 percent tax loss, the after-tax return is 7.5 percent. If tax management can save half the taxes (1.25 percent), what percentage increase in portfolio value will we have over 10, 20, and 30 years? The answer, says Scott, is 12 percent, 26 percent, and 41 percent higher portfolio values. Thus, the value of being a "tax-sensitive" separate account investor is not to minimize taxes, but to maximize after-tax return.

BROADER TAX CHALLENGES FOR FUNDS

Although 2000 was particularly odious for fund investors, mutual funds are a collector's boon in any year. Part of the problem with mutual funds and taxes, as Scott suggests, is a human one. To claim a magical five-star rating from Morningstar or to win a year-end bonus, a fund manager might ignore the tax implications of frequently trading stocks. One high-flying technology fund recently posted a whopping one-year return of 389 percent, but its shareholders could face a capital-gains distribution of around 33 percent because of the manager's trading patterns.

The strained relationship between fund companies and the IRS doesn't end there. Mutual funds aren't sensitive to the differing expectations of their investors. A couple in their 70s putting the finishing touches on their estate plans have entirely different needs than a couple in their mid-20s saving for their first home. The older couple knows their heirs get a stepped-up basis on appreciated stock, allowing them to avoid all capital-gains tax consequences. In a separate account, the older couple can hold on to their winners. In a mutual fund, by contrast, they might be forced to accept a capital-gains distribution they and their heirs would rather not have.

When you add all of the disadvantages of mutual funds and taxes together, you've got, as they say in the tabloid newspaper biz, a scoop. According to a 1995 Ibbotson Associates study, taxes and investment costs would have trimmed stock returns for a high-tax-bracket investor by nearly 3 percent annually from 1926 to 1993. The study showed that annual large-company stock returns would have dropped from 10.3 percent to 7.7 percent after taxes and transaction costs were deducted.

Uncle Sam is getting into the act on the other end as well. Looking to shed a little light on how much its fellow government agency makes from mutual fund taxes, since 1995, the Securities and Exchange Commission estimates that investors in diversified U.S. equity mutual funds saw 15 percent of their returns go to the IRS. Furthermore, in a 2000 proposal that required mutual fund firms to disclose after-tax returns, the SEC said that more than 2.5 percentage points of the average stock fund's total return are lost each year to taxes. Want more? The agency also cites a study by KPMG Peat Marwick that rates the impact of taxes on the performance of mutual funds, which varied from as little as zero for the most tax-efficient funds to 5.6 percent for the least tax-efficient funds for the 10-year period ending December 31, 1997.

Consequently, an investor's ability to use those losses both inside and outside of a portfolio is the major advantage of separate accounts. Although by law mutual funds must distribute a minimum of 90 percent of their income and realized capital gains to shareholders, losses remain locked up inside the fund, where the manager can net them against gains. Furthermore, in locking up losses an investor could use, mutual funds sometimes generate gains an investor doesn't want or need. Typically, a fund will distribute gains near the end of the year to any and all—old and new, bankrolled and bankrupt—shareholders. "Whether you bought the fund the day before or 20 years ago, you get the same dollar-per-share distribution," says one financial advisor. "[As a result,] the new investors end up paying a tax bill for the shareholders that have been there longer. So when you have an inflow of new money all the time, like mutual funds have had the last 10 years, it's easy to be tax efficient. When it flips the other way and money is leaving, it's incredibly hard to be tax efficient."

> ### Sidebar II: Mutual Funds and Taxes: A Marriage Not Made in Heaven
>
> There's little doubt that mutual fund taxes pack a poison pill for unwary investors. Many investors likely don't even realize that they're taking the full brunt of the fund industry's trouble with taxes.
>
> According to the June 26, 2000, edition of *Barron's*, the average balanced fund in the Lipper universe showed a 33.3 percent return from mid-1997 to May 31, 2000. Applying Morningstar's gauge of tax efficiency, which showed similar funds to be only 79 percent tax efficient, the expected after-tax return would only be 26.2 percent over that time frame.
>
> The problem with mutual funds, *Barron's* says, is that most funds buy stocks with an extremely long-term orientation, rarely incurring capital gains by selling big winners. Meanwhile, losses are harvested frequently to offset any gains. Unfortunately, this hurts shareholders who buy the funds after stocks have appreciated.

Fortunately, separate accounts are significantly more tax-friendly than mutual funds—even reputable tax-efficient index funds. See Figure 10-1 for a capsule summary of the value of separate accounts. Unlike investors in mutual funds who own shares of a portfolio, separate account investors own their stocks directly. Generally, this means they can direct their money managers to hold certain stocks to avoid capital-gains taxes or sell others to create a tax loss. With mutual funds, your capital-gains situation is at the mercy of your fund manager. Try calling Fidelity Investments and telling the manager of the Magellan Fund to hang on to those Cisco shares just a little longer to avoid any capital-gains taxes this year. In point of fact, mutual funds are terribly tax inefficient. According to the September 2000 edition of *Money* magazine, the average equity fund is only 80 percent tax efficient, which means that 20 percent of the return is lost every year to taxes. Ouch.

When Chris Cordaro, an investment advisor with Chatham, N.J.-based Bugen Stuart Korn & Cordaro, began steering clients away from index funds and toward separate accounts in August 1999, the results opened his

FIGURE 10-1

Tips for Using Separate Accounts to Minimize Your Taxes

- "Harvest" losses to offset realized gains in other assets
- "Harvest" gains to offset realized losses in other assets
- Give depreciated securities to charity or family members
- Turn short-term capital gains to long-term capital gains by managing the date of sale

eyes. "We generated tax losses of seven percent a year in 1999," he told Bloomberg.com in a October 10, 2000, interview. "With a $200,000 portfolio, that meant you had $14,000 in tax losses at the same time you enjoyed the return of the S&P, which was around seven or eight percent." Using the loss to offset long-term gains translated into an additional 1.75 percent to 2 percent return, assuming a state and federal capital-gains rate of 25 percent. By contrast, if a client in the 40 percent tax bracket used the losses to offset ordinary income, the losses added an additional 3 percent to his or her return.

Cordaro's experience illustrates a big difference between mutual funds and separate accounts. In a separate account, an investor pays taxes only on actual realized gains in his or her account. By contrast, a mutual fund investor buys into the fund's existing tax liability. Regardless of when the investment was made, whenever the fund sells securities and thus realizes capital gains, the investor must pay taxes on the full capital gain. That's the case whether or not the fund investor has been in the fund long enough to participate in the underlying stocks' gains. In a separate account, the client never has to pay tax on someone else's capital gains.

Former fund investors who have moved over to separate accounts are finding that separate accounts give them more control over taxable transactions. If such an investor needs to realize losses, or if it's a good time to realize gains, these transactions are easily arranged in separate accounts. But in a mutual fund, an investor must take the capital gains and losses whenever the manager chooses to make the transactions. This might not be good timing for the investor. Control over the timing and amount of taxable transactions in a separate account may be a significant advantage to certain investors.

MUTUAL FUNDS AND SEPARATE ACCOUNTS: TAX DIFFERENCES AT A GLANCE

With separate accounts, investors obtain complete tax planning flexibility. When you buy a no-load mutual fund, you are going to be given a Form 1099 at the end of the year. You will have no planning capabilities But if you have a separate account and your money manager buys 20 securities, it's realistic to expect perhaps 5 to 7 of them to decline by year's end. With separate accounts, though, you have tax planning capabilities and can easily sell those stocks and buy them again in 31 days to effect a tax swap. If you want to take your gains in a year in which you have had other losses, that's easily done with a separate account portfolio.

When you own shares in a mutual fund, whether it's a load fund or not, you may have an unrealized capital-gains tax liability built into that portfolio. For example, on the date you entered the fund, EMC Corp. was worth $70 per share. But if the fund purchased EMC Corp. for $30 per share, you'll have the unenviable burden of a $40 per share unrealized gain. That's the kind of tax liability you can do without.

SEPARATE ACCOUNTS OR MUTUAL FUNDS? TAX-RELATED FEATURES

Separately Held Securities

- *Mutual Funds*: No, the investor owns one security, the fund, which in turn owns a diversified portfolio.

- *Separate Accounts*: Yes, the investor owns securities in an account managed by the investor's money manager.

Unrealized Capital Gains

- *Mutual Funds*: Yes, the average U.S. mutual fund has a 20 percent imbedded, unrealized capital gain.

- *Separate Accounts*: No, the cost basis of each security in the portfolio is established at the time of purchase.

Customized to Control Taxes

- *Mutual Funds*: No, most funds are managed for pretax returns, and investors pay proportionate share of taxes on capital gains.

- *Separate Accounts*: Yes, investors can instruct money managers to take gains or losses as available to manage their tax liability.

Tax-Efficient Handling of Low-Cost Basis Stocks

- *Mutual Funds*: No, stocks cannot be held in an investor's mutual fund account, so there is no opportunity to manage low-cost basis stocks.

- *Separate Accounts*: Yes, the handling of low-cost basis stocks can be customized to the client's situation, liquidated in concert with offsetting losses, etc.

Gain/Loss Distribution Policies

- *Mutual Funds*: Virtually all gains must be distributed; losses cannot be distributed.

- *Separate Accounts*: Realized gains and losses are reported in the year recorded.

Source: Lockwood Financial.

This doesn't mean that separate accounts are tax dodges. They aren't. If you have a taxable account, you will get hit with a capital-gains liability if your money manager sells a security at a profit. The advantage with separate accounts is that at least the investor is paying taxes on his or her own gains rather than on someone else's.

Consider the case of one anonymous investor, we'll call him "Investor X," who got burned by a huge mutual fund tax bill. A fund investor since 1975, Investor X put aside $300 every month toward his mutual fund.

Although that doesn't seem like much at first glance, it was enough to generate a staggering $16,000 tax bill in 2000, even though he hasn't sold so much as one share of the fund in 25 years.

How did our friend Investor X get into this mess? By being in a mutual fund that changed managers, that's how. The new manager rolled in and sold a big chunk of the share's holdings, thus triggering the huge capital-gains distribution tax.

But Investor X could get into tax trouble in other ways with his mutual fund. If, for any reason, a multitude of investors decided to leave the fund all at once, the manager might have to sell shares just to pay them all off. By law, fund companies must pass along to their shareholders net capital gains. In effect, Investor X could get hit with a whopping tax bill simply because many of his fellow fund shareholders wanted out.

For example, imagine a situation where Investor X buys and holds shares in a given open-end mutual fund. Meanwhile, Investor Y comes in the next day, buys $5 million in shares in the same fund and, 6 months later, decides to cash in all of his or her investment. The manager for that fund will have to rebalance that portfolio to raise the cash to make up for the redemption increase, hence creating capital gains that our friend Investor X, who never transacted, will have to pay anyway at the end of the year.

ADVANTAGE, SEPARATE ACCOUNTS

So there's the rub. With individually managed accounts, investors pay taxes only on the capital gains they actually realize. Because they own the securities in their account directly, they can work with their tax advisor to implement tax planning strategies that mutual fund investors may not be able to duplicate. With mutual funds, investors pay taxes on their pro rata share of capital gains experienced by the fund, whether or not they benefited from the securities' sale.

Consider this hypothetical scenario. Assume that a fund purchases stock at the beginning of the year for $30 per share. Over the next several months, the stock's price rises to $60 per share. Coincidentally, an investor buys shares in the fund just as the stock's price reaches this peak. Later in the year, the stock's price falls to $58 per share, and the fund sells its position. At the end of the year, the investor is allocated a pro rata share of the fund's gain on the stock (the difference between the purchase price of $30 and the sale price of $58), even though the investor did not benefit from the gain.

In fact, the stock actually declined in value after the investor purchased shares in the fund.

Over time, managed account investors and mutual fund investors who hold their investments for the same period and whose portfolio managers follow identical strategies will report little, if any, difference in capital-gains taxes, at least on those particular investments. For the mutual fund investor, however, the point at which the gains are realized may be moved forward, and that can affect the investor's tax planning strategy. This is a hypothetical illustration and is not intended to reflect the actual perfor-mance of any particular security.

> ### Sidebar III: Taking Control
> According to the July 9, 2000, edition of *The New York Times,* about 10 to 15 percent of separate account clients at Merrill Lynch direct their money managers to take tax-related actions during each year. Is it any coincidence that Merrill's separate account business rose 50 percent in 1999 while its fund unit experienced record withdrawals?

Says David Harris, in the December 1, 2000, issue of *Financial Planning* magazine, the upshot for separate account investors is that separate accounts give them far greater control. Harris, a senior vice president of investments at Salomon Smith Barney in New York, says this is dramatically different from a mutual fund scenario where an investor cannot control the sale or purchase of stocks in the fund to minimize the tax burden he or she must bear.

In a mutual fund Harris says, "the client generally understands that decisions resulting in mutual fund capital gains—and taxes—are initiated by the fund managers. What the client may not realize, however, is that some-times these investment decisions are not really voluntary (such as when a fund manager is forced to sell to meet shareholder redemptions). It's possible for a perfectly savvy investor to end up in a mutual fund with a bunch of investors who have confused "buy low, sell high" with "buy high, sell low."

With a separate account, he adds, the investor is only subject to the impact of his or her own decisions, rather than at the mercy of other investors who are "pooled" alongside them. When implementing a strategy that maximizes tax efficiency, this autonomy is critical. "Having a separate account is not dissimilar to owning a mutual fund," Harris says, "but with the lid off so that one can see everything that is going on in the fund in real time, including all purchases and sales of securities."

PORTFOLIO ALLOCATION ISSUES

It certainly warrants mentioning that, as a separate account investor, you've got to be aware of the stocks you've moved in and out of your account. To take advantage of these capital-gain losses effectively, among other things, you have to keep track of tax lots—shares of a particular stock grouped according to the purchase date and purchase price. For newer investors, and for those separate account folks working without the aid of an investment adviser, it's a fairly comprehensive process.

Financial advisor Scott advocates a tax campaign that employs one of two basic strategies:

1. Avoid selling securities that have appreciated, and if you must sell, wait until the gain is long term.
2. Sell securities that have experienced a loss to offset realized gains.

These strategies sound like a modified buy and hold, and they basically are. Passive or index strategies are also generally tax efficient, especially the larger, less volatile indices. An index fund buys all the stocks in an index and holds them. Turnover would only occur when a stock was removed from the index. For the S&P 500 Index, most turnover would be generated by smaller companies being removed from the index (probably because they went down in value) or because of a company merger. So add index funds to the pool of tax-aware investments.

In an attempt to generate higher returns, active managers tend to trade more frequently than passive managers. To come out ahead in a nontaxable account, Scott adds, the new investment only needs to beat the old investment by transaction and research costs. In a taxable account, the return threshold for the new investment must overcome the loss of capital to taxes as well. The tax advantages of a buy-and-hold strategy might lead one to look at turnover ratio for selecting the portfolio manager. Although low turnover is generally good, it can be misleading. A separate account investor who has high turnover due to loss harvesting may actually be more tax efficient.

Whether they are employed in a mutual fund or in a separate account, a natural result of basic tax-managed strategies is a more concentrated portfolio because winners are never sold. This violates the principles of diversification and rebalancing a portfolio and may substantially increase the risk characteristics of the portfolio.

Investment manager styles impact taxes as well. Growth stocks tend to use cash flow to fund growth, and they pay little or no dividends. They have

Sidebar IV: Tax Lingo for the New Separate Account Investor

- *Tax-managed fund*: A mutual fund managed with a sensitivity to tax ramifications that tries to minimize taxable distributions.

- *Total return*: The increase in asset value over the period including the reinvestment of income and capital gains.

- *Tax-adjusted return*: After-tax total return. Normally calculated by assuming taxes are paid at the maximum applicable federal rates on all income and capital-gain distributions for the period.

- *Tax efficiency*: The tax-adjusted return for the period divided by the total return (before tax) for the period.

- *Turnover ratio*: A measure of how frequently a fund replaces existing investment holdings with new purchases. The calculation is the lesser of purchases or sales for the period divided by monthly net assets.

- *Potential capital-gain exposure*: The percentage of a fund's total assets that represents capital appreciation, both unrealized and realized but undistributed.

- *Loss harvesting*: Selling investments with unrealized losses. Realized losses can be used to offset past, current, or future realized gains and reduce gain distributions to shareholders.

- *Tax-aware investing*: A strategy for investing that addresses the comprehensive tax situation of individuals and their portfolios, including earned income, investment income, and taxation by type of account, as well as tax features of asset classes, investment styles, and individual managers.

Source: California Society of Certified Public Accountants, 1999.

high price-to-earnings and price-to-book ratios. Return is mostly capital appreciation, and therefore, growth-style managers with low turnover tend to have a high degree of tax efficiency. Since growth managers sell stocks that stop meeting growth targets, they tend to hold on to the stocks with the greatest appreciation.

On the other side, value stocks have high dividend yields or low price-to-earnings or price-to-book ratios. They generate a lot of cash flow on a regular basis. Value managers tend to end up with higher than average dividends flowing from the stocks in their portfolio and more income to distribute. Since value managers buy stocks that are out of favor with the market, they tend to sell them when the market recognizes their value and bids up the price, thereby realizing the capital gain.

According to the *Outlook* magazine article, another consideration for a tax-aware investing strategy is that of portfolio allocation to asset classes and across accounts. Typically, the investor should have an asset allocation consistent with the modern portfolio principles of diversification and risk versus reward trade-off. In developing the asset allocation, consider the tax features of various asset classes and suballocations to investment styles.

Municipal bonds generate tax-free income, but corporate bond income is taxable. Stocks generate dividends and capital gains. Small company and growth stocks generate less dividends than large value stocks.

In addition to asset class allocation, consider how the assets will be allocated across accounts of different types. Consider the impact of investing in qualified plans, IRAs, Roth IRAs, and taxable accounts for today as well as over your lifetime. Other possible account types that may come into play are charitable trusts, taxable trusts, annuities, and variable life insurance contracts.

Some administrative challenges crop up that can impact your tax burden from mutual funds as well. Moving from stocks or mutual funds into a wrap program is no simple matter. If your portfolio includes stocks or funds that have risen in value, selling them in one swoop can trigger a large capital gain, which is just what you are trying to avoid. Your advisor may work out a plan to liquidate your holdings over time so as to minimize the tax impact and shift the cash to investment managers to start anew. Some separate account firms will take a portfolio of securities or funds and do that for you.

Tax-wise, it's not always in your best interest to shed your portfolio of all its mutual funds. Funds you already have in an individual retirement account or similar plan may not need to be moved. The account is sheltered from taxes, so distributions won't swell the tax bill.

TAX-AWARE SEPARATE INVESTING

Overall, the process of tax-aware separate investing should follow the basic investment consulting process, as outlined by Brian Scott in *Outlook*, October 22, 1999:

1.   Analyze the existing situation: This includes the investment horizon, purpose of the portfolio, existing tax situations, and how the portfolio fits into the financial plan.

2.   Design an optimal portfolio to accomplish the financial objectives at the lowest risk.

3.   Formalize the plan for the asset allocation and selection of investment managers and for the most tax-efficient means of repositioning the portfolio.

4.   Implement the plan.

5.   Monitor the managers and the returns to determine if the plan is on track.

Overall, the key to successful tax-aware investing is combining expert knowledge of tax issues with expert knowledge of the investment process.

CASE STUDY 9

A Taxing Situation

Investor Michelle Stover never saw it coming. Opening her mutual fund statement, Stover never could have guessed how much she owed Uncle Sam from her mutual fund's tax distributions. She wasn't alone.

Investors across the United States were knocked for a loop as the average equity mutual fund stuck shareholders with the highest capital-gains distributions ever in 2000. In fact, more than 9 percent of the average fund's NAV was subject to capital-gains taxes in 2000, according to a report by Wiesenberger. Adding insult to injury, the average fund delivered a paltry 0.03 percent return.

The year 2000's record-setting capital gains distributions have their roots in 1999's bull market. That's because fund managers, eager to get the most out of the skyrocketing equity markets, kept little cash on hand. The average fund held just 1.01 percent in cash at the end of the first quarter of 2000, just as the NASDAQ began its plummet.

So when spooked investors started pulling out of funds, those funds had to sell their holdings to cash out the investors. Many of these holdings were highly appreciated stocks that had been held for less than 12 months.

That was bad news from a tax standpoint. Investors would have to pay the short-term capital-gains tax rate on the gains those stocks had made. Short-term capital gains are taxed at an individual's income tax rate.

"It really made me change the way I viewed mutual funds," said Stover. "Sure, they've been a big benefit to my family during the bull market years. But once the bull stopped running, we got gored."

Stover joins 58 percent of investors who say that the impact of taxes on their investments has become more of a concern since 2000, according to a separate survey by tax-managed fund leader Eaton Vance. Many of these investors have since turned their attention to separate accounts, those individually managed investment accounts that offer better tax structures than mutual funds do, at a lower price and with greater control for investors.

"I met with my advisor, who explained to me that separate accounts offered more tax-efficient mutual fundlike investments. That sounds good to me—I never want to see a tax bill like that again."

11

CUSTOMIZING YOUR SEPARATE ACCOUNT

All for one and one for all.

ALEXANDRE DUMAS, AUTHOR OF *THE THREE MUSKETEERS*

Let's face it, everyone wants to be the boss. And with separate accounts, you can. Separate account customers call their own shots, build their own portfolios, and customize their own holdings to fit their needs, be they spiritual, financial, or otherwise. Customization is a big attraction for the growing numbers of do-it-yourself investors. If an investor wants to mix and match particular stocks and particular industries, that's not a problem with separate accounts.

Take the big technology stock sell-off of early 2001. In 2000, long-favored tech stocks were hammered after a 10-year run that left many portfolios fatter than ever. But sensing a dismal year for tech stocks in 2001, many fund investors were forced to withdraw from their tech-oriented mutual funds entirely, instead of carving off a dubious stock or two.

As 2001 began, tech stocks were gasping for air and nearly half of growth stock funds experienced investor defections. Growth funds encountering investor withdrawals included such stalwarts as Fidelity Aggressive Growth Fund, American Century Growth Fund, and Janus Olympus Fund, according to Financial Research Corp., Boston. The problem with these funds? No ability for customers to customize the portfolios on their own. Instead, they were held hostage to the whims and moods of fund managers.

Handing the controls over to separate account investors is an idea that may make Wall Street skittish. After all, if investors are personalizing their own portfolios, who needs a stockbroker? But the reality is that most separate account investors work hand-in-hand with financial advisors to customize their separate account portfolios. The ones who don't by and large have educated themselves about general finance and investment topics, generally through reading the latest financial news and accessing investment market research.

Mutual fund investors, on the other hand, find their hands tied when it comes to making personal investment decisions. Ditto for fund managers who must adhere to the fund prospectus. Separate account investors and their money managers are not bound by a prospectus and can adhere to individual client investment restrictions. When you buy a fund, you have no say in the fund's holdings, nor do you own the underlying shares. There may be minimum investment requirements, and investors pay an expense ratio, which in the case of actively managed funds can total several hundred dollars a year depending on your account size, not including any one-time commissions to buy the fund.

Sidebar I: Applying Social Values to Overseas Markets
Are there studies on non-U.S. equity portfolios? You bet.

- In April 1998, Stephen Williams of the WM Company submitted a master's thesis to the University of Edinburgh illustrating various types of "ethical indices" modeled on existing *Financial Times* broad market gauges. These studies indicate performance similar to the Domini 400 against the Standard & Poor's 500.

- Frank J. Travers of Oppenheimer & Co. studied 23 screened portfolios which he described as non-U.S. His winter 1997 article in *The Journal of Investing*, "Socially Responsible Investing on a Global Basis: Mixing Money and Morality Outside the U.S.," concludes that over the periods he studied, these portfolios outperformed Morgan Stanley's EAFE Index and produced competitive returns to a universe of unrestricted portfolios.

That's not to say that separate account investors are choosing stocks in a helter-skelter fashion. Most separate accounts are of the selected variety, coming "ready-to-order" based on market indices, investment style, sector, risk, geography, and social issues.

The key is that shares in a separate account are owned by you and may be sold individually. So, for instance, if you have a problem with owning tobacco stocks or health-care companies that develop "morning-after" pills, you don't have to include them. Likewise, if you have an aversion to Netscape but want access to the rest of the Internet sector, you can buy an Internet-weighted separate account without it. That's the beauty of separate accounts: Consumers are free to delete or add stocks to suit their own objectives.

This independence and customization are manifest in myriad ways. For example, while many mutual funds, including low-cost index funds, allocate your dollars among the equities based on their market capitalization, separate account investors may choose equal weighting if it suits their strategy. Or separate account investors can manage the income tax impact by controlling the buy and sell decisions. Say you have a large profit outside your separate account. If so, you can ask your account manager to take losses to offset the gain. Likewise, if you have other losses, you can ask a portfolio manager to take selective gains.

CRAFTING PERSONALIZED PORTFOLIOS

Simply put, separate account investors like managed accounts because they can be in charge. They can have control and power over their affairs if they use separate accounts. They have the power to set strategy and be in charge of their portfolio. They can choose their own stocks, enjoy access to top managers, and have the ability to change managers easily. And these days, separate account investors are using their newly found independence to do something they couldn't do with mutual funds: engage in socially responsible investing (SRI) strategies.

It's an investment trend that's gathering more steam at the beginning of the new millennium. Buoyed by a two-decade-long bull market—with 2000–2001 a notable exception—and a renewed sense of social responsibility, Americans are more willing than ever to make personal statements with their investment portfolios. The trend affects all walks of life, from the idealistic young dot.com entrepreneur who gives generously to favorite causes, like the environment and the homeless, to the compassionate grandmother whose benevolence is felt by urban hospices and rural rehab clinics alike.

Sidebar II: Gender Differences in Values-Based Investing
Women account for 48 percent of mutual fund shareholders, but they make up about 60 percent of all socially conscious investors, reports the Social Investment Forum (www.socialinvest.org), a nonprofit group promoting socially responsible investing.

But let's give credit where credit is due. Sharing what we have with the less fortunate is a staple of the American way of life. By far the largest charitable-giving country in the world, the United States has seen its citizens ratchet up their charitable efforts in recent years and has enacted government legislation in the form of charitable tax deductions to make giving a win-win situation for committed donors and grateful donees.

Who are these socially conscious investors and why do they place such a high premium on charitable giving and values-based investing? Typically, socially responsible investors are those who seek to factor ethical and moral considerations into the investment process. By and large, they don't see social investing as a goal in itself. Rather, they are motivated to use their money to make a positive difference: to advance a fair employment system, to create a cleaner environment, or to make the world a better place in which to live.

They also do not agree on every social screen. As might be expected, many religious groups, health associations, schools, labor unions, foundations, retirement funds, environmental organizations, women's advocacy groups, and simply concerned individuals are those who are making socially responsible investing a priority investment issue.

What every values-based investor does have in common is the ability to completely customize his or her own portfolio through separate accounts. Let's see how and examine some values-based investment strategies.

A MARRIAGE MADE IN HEAVEN: SEPARATE ACCOUNTS AND VALUES-BASED INVESTING

Pointedly, the advantages of socially responsible investing are proving to be a big selling point for the separate account industry. Why? Unlike mutual funds, which lock investors into fixed portfolios of companies that are jettisoned only with the approval of the fund manager, separate account investors call their own shots and determine which stocks fit their specific needs, both financially and spiritually. Aligning one's investments with one's values is thus made significantly easier with separate accounts, giving investors yet another reason to reconsider their mutual fund portfolios and take a harder look at separate accounts.

Sidebar III: Values a Plus, Performance a Must

Some studies have indicated that investors applying social criteria not only do not negatively impact portfolio performance but can help increase performance. Some examples include:

- In 1993, S. Hamilton et al. reported in *Financial Analysts Journal* on their studies of socially screened mutual funds. They concluded: "Investors can expect to lose nothing by investing in socially responsible mutual funds [when compared to a benchmark of randomly selected mutual funds]."

- In 1995, M.A. Cohen et al. of Vanderbilt University reported that between 1987 and 1989, green investors, who typically have quite stringent screening criteria, did not seem "to pay a premium for their convictions" as compared to the S&P 500.

- In a 1997 study in *The Journal of Forecasting*, John B. Guerard, Jr., then director of quantitative research for Vantage Global Advisors, reached a similar conclusion. Guerard compared the performance of Vantage's 1300 company universe against a subset of 950 that passed four major screens: military, nuclear power, product exclusion (alcohol, tobacco, and gambling), and environment. Mr. Guerard found the Vantage Global Advisors' unscreened universe produced a 1.068 percent monthly average return during the January 1987–December 1994 period, where a $1.00 investment grew to $2.77. A corresponding investment in the socially screened universe would have grown to $2.74, representing a 1.057 percent average monthly return.

Here's how it works. Say you've opened a screened separate account, and a customized portfolio is delivered to you for the growth portion of your portfolio. Skimming the list of stocks in your separate account money manager's portfolio, you notice a big red flag. A strip-mining company that harvests precious minerals from hard-to-reach rural locations grabs your attention. An ardent environmentalist, you blanch. Reaching for the phone, you call the customer service representative at your separate account money management firm and let her know in no uncertain terms that you don't want any part of that stock. Politely you add that you are delighted with the rest of the portfolio.

"No problem," she responds in a blink. "We'll take that stock out of your portfolio and replace it with another, along with a confirmation stating we've removed that stock from your holdings." Try doing that with a mutual fund. No problem with separate accounts. So how does a socially conscious separate account investor get started? It's not very difficult. Basically, there are three ways to invest for social and ethical outcomes. The first is avoidance or exclusion, which is a resistance to invest in companies whose values are in direct conflict with those of the investor. Next is the more activist approach of investing in companies whose ethics are contrary to those of the investor and then using the investor's proxy rights to vote change (for the good) within the company. The third approach is inherent in those investors who actively invest in companies whose ethics are in sync with their own.

The most practiced method of implementing socially responsible investing for the separate account investor is through social screening. Screening is the inclusion or exclusion of securities within a universe to reflect social concerns. Social screens should rarely be the sole reason for investing but should instead be combined with financial screens.

RESOURCES TO HELP YOU BUILD SOCIALLY CONSCIOUS PORTFOLIOS

The following Web sites and other sources are especially useful:

- www.socialinvest.org shows a chart of community investing options and lists mutual funds, updated monthly.

- www.crosswalk.com is for conservative Christians who want to make sure their mutual funds don't invest in companies that profit from pornography, abortion, antifamily entertainment, or gay lifestyles.

- www.workfamily.com compiles a list of model companies with good family-friendly policies.

- www.Coopamerica.org shows how to make a financial plan and how to integrate social investing. Also check out their publication, *Real Money*, which is published quarterly and costs $10. Also available is a *Financial Planning Handbook* for $5, plus the *Social Investment Forum Directory* of products and services for $2. Call 202-872-5307.

- www.Greenpages.org   helps you look up financial planners and portfolio managers in SRI to aid you.

- Responsible Wealth, a project of United for a Fair Economy, is a new group of persons of wealth who are dedicated to social justice. Call 617-423-2148, ext. 12. Or e-mail rw@stw.org Their Web site is: www.stw.org.

- Making a Profit While Making a Difference is the annual gathering of institutional investors in SRI. Call Capital Missions at 517-876-8766.

- *Investing with Your Values: Making Money and Making a Difference* is a good book on social investing by Jack Brill, Hal Brill, and Cliff Feigenbaum, available in hardcover from Bloomberg Press. It was released in September 2000.

Some other good Web sites are http://www.goodmoney.com and http://www.SocialFunds.com.

For separate account investors, social screening actually began with exclusionary or avoidance screens. The screening process is implemented through a rating system in which a company is examined, issue by issue, for both positive and negative factors relative to a given list of concerns. According to the Social Investment Forum (Washington, DC), the major avoidance screen criteria are typically as follows:

- Abortion: Avoidance of companies that develop tools and procedures that lead to abortion.

- Antifamily Values: Avoidance of companies that fail to promote "family friendly" policies in the workplace.

> ### Sidebar IV: The Era of the Values-Based Investor Is Upon Us
> Growth of assets involved in socially responsible investment significantly outpaced the broad market. Socially responsible investment assets grew at twice the rate of all assets under professional management in the United States. Between 1997 and 1999, total assets involved in socially responsible investment grew 82 percent—from $1.185 trillion to $2.16 trillion. In the same period, according to a comparison of total assets under professional management in the United States reported annually in *Nelson's Directory of Investment Managers*, the broad market grew 42 percent (including both market appreciation and net cash inflows).
>
> Source: Social Investment Forum.

- "Sin Stocks": Avoidance of companies engaged in the production or selling of alcohol and tobacco or the promotion of gambling.

- Nuclear Power: Exclusion of corporations involved in the sale or production of nuclear power and/or the utilization of nuclear power in the fuel mix.

- Military Contracts: Exclusion of corporations involved in the production of conventional or nuclear-related military weapons or products, including parts suppliers; based on percentage of total revenue attributable to these businesses.

- Environment: Exclusion of companies that have been large polluters in the past, those that pollute today, and those making no effort to reduce their environmental pollution.

- Animal Testing: Avoidance of companies currently using animal testing, whether directly or indirectly.

- Non-U.S. Operations: Avoidance of companies with operations in certain countries because of human rights abuses or the way in which employees are treated in those countries.

Identifying these issues and merging them into your separate account portfolio are two different things. As a separate account investor, your job is to be prepared to state your social concerns and beliefs unequivocally to your money manager. Based on your definitive social concerns, you will draw up a document that delineates social concerns along with financial guidelines: asset allocation, risk tolerance, and so forth. Social screens are then applied, and you (by yourself or with your advisor) decide which companies are borderline. Screens should be refined to a point where they are neither too strict nor too loose. Only then should assets be invested. Separate account portfolios must be reviewed periodically to be certain the holdings still reflect the direction of the guidelines. An obvious and primary consideration is finding money managers who have the capability and in-house technology to manage a social portfolio.

Overall, investing according to socially responsible guidelines is no different from any other stock investment. It just means a little more research. There are two things you must consider—your financial objectives and your social objectives—and then find a way to marry them.

Sidebar V: Tracking SRI Performance

Table. Domini 400 Social Index Performance[a]

	DSI 400	S&P 500	S&P MidCap	Russell 1000
12 months ending 8/31/99	45.55%	39.90%	41.68%	39.36%
24 months ending 8/31/99	27.30%	22.98%	13.26%	21.61%
36 months ending 8/31/99	32.33%	28.60%	20.72%	27.29%
60 months ending 8/31/99	27.51%	25.11%	18.87%	24.30%

Sources: Wilshire Associates; Kinder, Lydenberg, Domini & Co., Inc.

[a]The Domini 400 is a socially screened version of the Standard & Poor's 500.

CASE STUDY 10

Feeling Good About Feeling Responsible

Mike Rush has a great life, with a rewarding career and good friends all around him. So why was he so ticked off at the world a few years ago, and what did he do to help change the world for the better?

Let's start back in 1998, when the 45-year-old corporate executive lost an uncle to lung cancer. It was the third cancer-related death in his family in 2 years, and he knew why. He came from a long line of smokers in his family.

"I'm not a smoker myself, never have been," says Rush. "But I've been around smokers my whole life, and lately, I'm seeing people I cared a lot about paying the ultimate price."

An avid investor his whole life, Rush decided to take matters into his own hands and write his mutual fund manager to urge her to stop investing in companies that made tobacco products. Receiving no answer, he sent another letter. Again, no reply.

"I began to think I didn't have enough control, let alone clout, to change my mutual fund manager's ways," he adds. "But a friend told me about separate accounts and how I could build a basket of stocks that matched my needs and goals. I saw it as a way to earn more returns and make a social statement at the same time."

Working with a financial advisor who matched him up with a good separate account money manager, Rush found out from his manager that the avoidance of tobacco companies in an socially responsible investment portfolio need not result in underperformance. He discovered that other, more appropriate stocks with better financial characteristics are often substituted, and/or the tobacco industry could simply be avoided altogether, with no attempt to replace it. His money manager also told him of the commissioned work of Kinder, Lydenberg & Domini, which found that some of the mutual funds divested of tobacco have outperformed the market, and the Domini 400 SRI Index, which never included tobacco securities, has always beaten the S&P500 Index since its inception of May 1990. "It was great stuff and I really learned a lot about responsible investing and investing responsibly," he says.

Like most socially responsible investors who've turned to separate accounts, Rush didn't see social investing as a goal in itself. Rather, he was motivated to use his money to make a positive difference: to protest against the tobacco companies that he felt contributed to his loved ones' deaths.

"Look, I'm no altar boy," concedes Rush. "I like a few beers now and then and I've been know to place a bet on the Super Bowl. But what the tobacco companies are doing to the American public is wrong. I'm glad now that I can take some small action to register my disgust with them."

12

SEPARATE ACCOUNTS AND THE WEB: A MARRIAGE MADE IN CYBERHEAVEN

Once technology is out of the jar, you can't put it back in.

ERVIN L. GLASPY

We like to think that technology can help people achieve total liberation. Take U.S. astronaut Bruce McChandless, who on February 8, 1984, walked in space totally free of any connection to earth. No ropes to the spacecraft, no planet beneath his feet. For the first time ever, a human being was completely on his own, completely set free by the wonder of technology.

Technology is setting investors free, too. One of the reasons that separate accounts are growing so much in popularity is that investors have been given the opportunity to enjoy more direct access to Wall Street's once-mysterious machinations.

Thanks to the Internet, investors can easily download company annual reports, check out analyst commentaries on a particular stock's fortunes, open accounts and track portfolios, and execute trades with the flick of a keystroke. All online. All in real time. All at trading costs and portfolio management fees that are lower than at any time in history.

That's been a boon to the financial services industry in general and to managed accounts in particular in recent years. According to Forrester research, equity assets managed on the Internet will grow to $1.56 trillion by 2003, from only $246 billion in 1999 (*Bloomberg Personal Finance*, "Build Your Own Mutual Fund," October 2000). Forrester adds that the number of managed equity accounts will grow from 5.4 million to 20.4 million over the same period (Figure 12-1). These are numbers that CEOs understand just as easily in Silicon Valley as they do on Wall Street. They know that the Internet can do for separate accounts what it has already done for online trading: make it cheaper, more user-friendly, and less mysterious to investors.

As Cerulli Associates says in its "Market Update: The Managed Account and Wrap Industry," online separate accounts have come of age. "Once the exclusive province of upscale New York wirehouses, [separate accounts] are now available via the Internet. Recognizing the growing popularity and mainstream demand for separate accounts, several online providers have emerged that provide the access to institutional money managers, tax efficiencies, and customization that are characteristic of separate accounts."

According to Cerulli, online separate account providers generally offer an aggregation of money managers to the individual investor with the Internet acting as intermediary. To assist the investor with money manager selection, these firms are supplying limited advice and guidance tools. "So far," Cerulli Associates reports, "these tools provide basic information on participating money managers and some risk profiling tools to match investor objectives with appropriate managers."

FIGURE 12-1

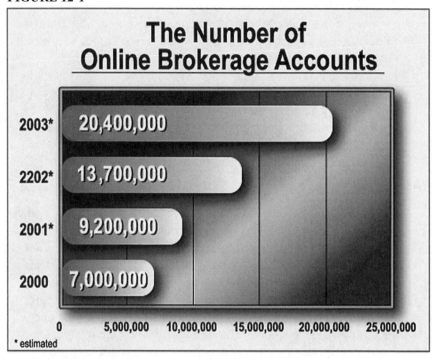

The Number of
Online Brokerage Accounts

2003*	20,400,000
2202*	13,700,000
2001*	9,200,000
2000	7,000,000

0   5,000,000   10,000,000   15,000,000   20,000,000   25,000,000

* estimated

THE INTERNET: A HISTORY

Although we may take what technology and the Internet do for separate account programs—and their customers—for granted, it's easy to forget just how far Wall Street has come as an industry ever since the advent of the Net. According to Denis T. Rice, author of "Cyberspace: New Directions in Capital Markets" (released on April 17, 1999, by the San Francisco chapter of the American Bar Association), the Internet began in the 1960s as a

> **Sidebar I: Succeeding with the SAMBA Technology Platform**
> Not all of the big news being made on the separate account technology front is being made on the Internet. In fact, a good case can be made that customized front- and back-office software applications are driving the real growth of separate accounts both on the Web and off.
> Consider our own SAMBA 3000™ technology platform, which combines state-of-the-art features in the white-hot customer

relationship management technology, unique branding capabilities, and world-class operations into a comprehensive solution. This architecture provides the framework for delivering unique services to both the investor client and business partners.

Simply stated, SAMBA enables financial service firms and professional money managers with the technology and expertise to offer separately managed accounts, dynamically branding their Web site services with the look and feel they want. The technology integrates seamlessly with Investcomm3000™, Separate Account Solutions' state-of-the-art communication center. As a result, financial service firms are able to deliver a unique, dynamically branded, personalized Web interface to manage their client relationships easily, conveniently, and securely.

Using the client Web interface, clients can set up a login ID and password to their account and fill out an account application. The client provides personal information, interaction preferences, and financial profile information through an online dialogue that directs the client through entry and selection screens. The client can save the application at any point in the process, and the next time the client logs into the site, the site will automatically direct them to complete the application beginning where they left off in their last session.

Once clients have established their account, they can use their login ID and password to access their account online. Through this interface, they can review their account balances, holdings, performance, and transaction history. If a client has multiple accounts, he or she can review them all via the single login ID.

With SAMBA, each client receives a quarterly report for each investment account. The quarterly report includes portfolio activity, portfolio holdings, performance, portfolio growth, and a schedule of realized gains and losses. Reports are distributed to the secure client message mailbox in .pdf format. In addition, several reports can be requested for on-demand production through the account team for interim reporting needs. Distribution of the reports is online through the message mailbox. Clients can always view their accounts online through the secure Web site and see current balances, holdings, and transactions. All online account access requires username/password authentication, and all access to the SAMBA Web site is secured by Verisign Secure Server Pro, providing 128-bit encryption of all data transmission.

decentralized, packet-switched network of computers funded by the Department of Defense, intended to facilitate communication in the United States in the event of a nuclear attack. In the late 1970s, universities and other nongovernmental entities started linking with the Department of Defense network. By the late 1980s there were multiple computer networks joined together in an Internet. It allowed e-mail communications to be sent electronically over the Internet to one or more specific addresses or even mass-mailed, (i.e., a message could be sent electronically to large numbers of addresses).

According to Rice:

> The World Wide Web has created a dramatically new environment for companies issuing securities, brokerage firms and other intermediaries, and investors. Web sites, bulletin boards, e-mail and push technology all can and are now used in advertising, offering and selling securities and for disseminating investment advice. They permit communication instantaneously with millions of people worldwide at low cost. They not only allow instant matching of proposed trades and circulation of information in broad-based markets, but permit individuals to access massive amounts of information far more quickly and directly than was believed possible just a few years ago.

Rice ties the recent phenomenon of separate accounts with the rise of online trading systems, which paved the way for the ongoing revolution we're seeing with online trading generally and folio-based trading specifically these days. "Institutional investors have used extranets to support closed trading systems among themselves since the 1970s," Rice says. "The pioneer was Instinet [www.instinet.com], which introduced a closed networked computer system in which a group of institutional members, such as [mutual funds and investment brokers] could trade large blocks of securities electronically among themselves, thereby avoiding brokers in the middle." Operating outside of the established stock exchanges, Rice adds that Instinet has not used the World Wide Web; instead, its members use the more limited electronic linking system of the extranet. Trades are made on an anonymous basis directly between buyer and seller.

In the past few years, other closed electronic services with much broader membership bases have started operating, such as the Island System and the Portfolio System for Institutional Trading (POSIT). While Instinet operates simply by electronically "hitting" offers posted in an electronic order book, POSIT uses a crossing system for batches of orders. Despite the fact that these alternative systems have been limited to institutions, their volume of trading has greatly escalated; the SEC estimated that by 1997, they handled almost 20 percent of the orders in NASDAQ securities and almost 4 percent in New York Stock Exchange–listed securities.

GROWING PAINS

The proliferation of the Internet and the separate account industry has led to some soul searching at financial institutions that have to develop technologies to keep pace with the volume and complexity of Web-based managed account relationships. The good news is that investors are already benefiting from the work that the financial services industry has done on the technology side. "Technology has allowed the brokerage house to bring institutional-quality investment consulting and asset management to the retail level," says Jamie Waller, vice president of CheckFree Investment Services, a service bureau provider of automated investment management, trading, reporting, and performance measurement services.

But the early success of the separate accounts industry has led some to question whether investment firms can find systems that can handle a high volume of individual accounts. "This type of technology requires specialization," says Joe Rosen, managing director and partner, Enterprise Technology Corporation (ETC), a New York City–based technology management consulting firm, in the January 1, 2001, issue of *Wall Street + Technology*. "Having the software to support the separate account business is definitely a concern for both the broker/dealers and money managers. They want sophisticated software that provides speed and flexibility in handling the often many thousands of separately managed accounts," says Rosen, who notes these were the most critical attributes that emerged from a recent vendor search project that ETC conducted for a fast-growing wrap advisor.

> ### Sidebar II: Monkey See, Monkey Do
> Some discount brokerage firms are adopting the "if you can't beat 'em, join 'em" stance and are jumping into the online separate accounts marketplace with both feet.
>
> In August 2000, E*TRADE Group Inc. purchased privately held PrivateAccounts.com, a Minneapolis developer of online separate accounts. Like many online separate account firms, PrivateAccounts.com offers to set up trading accounts for customers with a minimum balance of $100,000. E*TRADE account balances average about $21,000. We expect other online brokers to follow suit.

Fortunately, the industry has ascended at the same time as (many say because of) the simultaneous growth of the Internet. The Net has negated or at least minimized some of the costs of bringing separate accounts to consumers and has increased customer interactivity options, which previously were pretty much limited to walk-in visits or telephone calls.

LOGGING ON AND DIGGING IN

In fact, separate accounts weren't invented with the Internet in mind per se, but it's hard to imagine a better fit for an industry and its consumers. Separate accounts give individuals the power to buy and sell fully diversified portfolios of stocks for a flat fee. All a potential investor has to do is log on, dig through a list of money managers, pick one they like, and complete an online application. Presto, instant customized portfolio management.

Industry observers also see separate accounts as a great alternative not only to mutual funds, but to "traditional" Internet trading tools as well. Separate accounts "represent the beginning of a new phase in the evolution of online investing just when the time is ripe," writes Fred Barbash in the September, 4, 2000, issue of the *Houston Chronicle*. "Growing numbers of mutual fund investors are now complaining—rightly or wrongly—about the fees and tax inefficiency of many mutual funds, which buy and sell stocks feverishly.

"And based on my own anecdotal evidence, plenty of investors are getting fed up or bored or discouraged with the work involved in conventional Internet-based stock trading. Some of the reasons include trades getting messed up or not getting executed, not being able to speak to a human being, and receiving someone else's monthly statement and having someone else get yours."

Plus, Barbash adds, as online investors increase their wealth, their fear of loss may overcome greed. Many will then seek diversification not efficiently achieved at the E*TRADES, the Schwabs, or the Ameritrades on a do-it-yourself basis.

Separate account money managers like Merrill Lynch or Salomon Smith Barney now offer an online blend of educational material, financial planning tools, money manager performance information, and information on particular separate account classes, like growth or balanced portfolios. Online separate account customers can also expect to receive custody and clearance of their securities, quarterly investment statements (although some sites allow customers to check their portfolio performance whenever they want, night or day). Customers can also e-mail their money manager to buy or sell certain stocks or to screen or block the purchase of stocks they may not want in their portfolio for socially responsible or spiritual reasons (e.g., tobacco or alcohol company stocks).

Sidebar III: Chatting Up Online Voice Chat
More breakthroughs online come from the world of telecommunications, where Voice over IP (VoIP) technology is allowing a firm's customers to communicate with it online, from personal computer to personal computer, all in real time. With Online Voice Chat, a firm's clients request a chat session online through a communication center, and a member of the client's account team initiates a voice chat dialogue to the client's PC. The client speaks into the microphone in his or her PC and listens through the PC's speakers, enabling clients to interact verbally and directly with the firm's service professionals without hanging up their online session and calling over the phone. Investors love the fact that they can access their account balances, holdings, and request reports and statements via an Internet connection while talking over the same connection with a customer support team member.

Most online separate account sites also offer call-in centers and online help desks. Your separate account firm's customer service reps can help you with common problems, like tracking your portfolio's performance, or more complex ones, like how to send in more money and have it invested in the same proportion as your existing portfolio or withdraw part of your investment and keep the remainder invested in the same proportion.

LEANING TOWARD ONLINE FOLIOS

One interesting development has been "folios," which are baskets of stocks that investors can buy online with or without the help of an investment advisor and for a price as low as $29.95 per month. It's important to note that folios aren't separate accounts in the truest sense but may serve as the basis for separate accounts with the addition of professional management.

Here's how the average folio works: For a flat annual fee of about $300 (billed monthly), you can assemble up to three investment baskets or folios, each containing up to 50 stocks. You can choose stocks yourself or select from nearly 80 prefab folios—one might hold 30 stocks in the

Dow and another might be a basket of 20 energy companies. You can trade as often or seldom as you like at no extra cost. What's more, you can buy or sell the entire folio or one or more stocks separately, giving you much greater control over your tax bill than a mutual fund can offer. You can invest automatically every month. Special features include portfolio monitoring software that enables you not only to check your asset allocation levels but also track your tax liabilities garnered from your custom-built stock portfolio.

On the downside, some online folio providers place restrictions on when you can trade, often as infrequently as twice a day. This means the costs of trading are automatically included in your account fee, as long as you trade at certain times. Online folio firms do this to seek to match the maximum number of buyers and sellers in-house, which keeps everyone's brokerage costs low. You can, however, pay extra to trade when you want to for a cost of about the average price to execute a discount brokerage trade, or about $15. Separate account companies do allow you to instruct them to cancel a trade automatically if the price of a stock rises or falls by a predetermined amount.

To keep costs down, folio companies use the Internet rather than telephone or postal mail for many of their communications with you. Statements, trade confirmations, and other communications are sent by e-mail. You send in all your instructions through the Internet as well.

PREDICTIONS FOR THE NEAR FUTURE

According to FolioFN and Forrester Research:

- The number of online brokerage accounts is predicted to grow 70 percent to over 20 million accounts by 2003.

- Today e-accounts comprise more than 50 percent of retail stock trades. This trend is expected to continue.

CASE STUDY 11

Benefiting from Online Separate Accounts

Carol Knox had made a nice career out of being a financial advisor. The 33-year-old Ivy League business school grad felt she had the best of both worlds—working with numbers and helping people. "I love the interaction between my clients and myself," she says. "I had a knack for running numbers in my head and had a good memory for clients' preferences. Those are good attributes for a financial advisor to have."

When Knox first heard about separate accounts in the 1990s, she wasn't sure there was a strong market for the product. "Nobody was begging me for access to separate accounts," recalls Knox. "Most of my clients thought that early wrap accounts were out of their league, price-wise. And I couldn't argue with them."

Then the Internet roared onto the landscape, and Knox's business has never been the same. "I built a Web site right away and devoted a portion of it to separate accounts. I knew that the Web was the Great Equalizer and that separate account minimums would go down, as would fees."

In 1999, Knox hooked up with a major national discount broker with a strong online presence to better serve her growing list of separate account customers. Under her managed account service, Knox could choose from about 50 money managers representing over 12 investment styles while working with the brokerage firm under a simplified contractual structure. Minimum account sizes dropped to as low as $10,000. The 1 percent brokerage fee includes services from the money manager, an investment consultant, and the broker, including custody and trading. The total cost to the end investor, after advisors add their fees, was about 1.75 percent, which is "extremely competitive" with the nation's leading wirehouse wrap accounts, says Knox. All of her contact with the broker was done online, including industry updates, capital markets research, and a 2-day in-depth investment consulting course.

"Plus they made it possible for my separate account clients to get online and trade, check portfolios, run sample asset allocation portfolios, and a whole lot more," she adds. "Let's face it. The Internet and separate accounts are a marriage made in heaven."

13

THE FUTURE
OF SEPARATE
ACCOUNTS:
WHAT TO
LOOK FOR

He who does not look ahead remains behind.

SPANISH PROVERB

There's a great line from ice hockey legend Wayne Gretzky about antici-
pating the future in his area of expertise. "What I do is skate to where the
puck is going to be," he says, "not where it's been." Investors would do well
to emulate the Great One's strategy. If better portfolio performance, better

tax structures, better control, and lower management fees are to be found in separate accounts, then why not skate in that direction?

To paraphrase Gretzky, mutual funds are where Wall Street has been and separate accounts are where it is headed. In fact, you can't evaluate the future of the separate account industry without reviewing the long-term prospects for the mutual fund industry. Like the horseless carriage and the combustible engine or the carrier pigeon and e-mail, the future of the separate account and the past history of the mutual fund industry are intertwined, for better or worse.

As we've been saying all along, it's a future that's better for separate account investors and worse for mutual fund investors. For the fund sector, recent years have been the best of times and the worst of times. The best because the industry remained one with a license to print money, thanks primarily to the availability of funds in retirement accounts, a raging bull of a stock market, and the continued commitment to self-directed investing by individual investors. The worst because, for the first time, the industry was losing customers and assets at a rate higher than 10 percent annually.

In a striking article in the May 1, 2000, issue of *Institutional Investor* magazine entitled "Mutual Funds Face the Future," authors Riva Atlas, Rich Blake, and Hal Lux say that mutual funds held close to $7 trillion in assets through May 2000, up from $100 billion in 1980, with 47 percent of all American households owning mutual funds, compared with 5.7 percent in 1980. They write:

> Yet with so much to crow about—first-quarter stock fund inflows soared and profits sizzled, the mood among many mutual fund executives today is more sober than giddy, more studied than ebullient. It's not just the sorry state of stocks since [April 2000], worrisome as that is. Long before the words "bear market" began to stir out of hibernation in the minds of those few remaining fund managers old enough to remember gas lines, industry fundamentals had begun to shift, heralding a new era of unprecedented challenge.

GONE WITH THE WIND

The authors add that the era of unbridled growth is gone. Fierce new competitors are fighting for every investor dollar, and the advent of technological changes like the Internet have caused a profound shift in the distribution of products and control of the customer. "These forces will only accelerate the division of the industry into a handful of very big institutions

Sidebar I: On the Money

According to the Washington, DC–based Money Management Institute, the financial services industry's most successful individual advisors are increasingly interested in offering separate accounts to their clients, with the percentage of interested advisors nearly tripling between 1996 and 1999.

"All indications are that investors will continue to aggressively seek out the benefits of individual managed accounts—and the industry's most successful advisors will be positioning themselves to serve this important and growing need," said Christopher L. Davis, executive director of the Money Management Institute. "This study, coupled with our newly released survey demonstrating strong growth in account assets, suggests that our industry is on track to experience ongoing robust expansion well into the future."

According to the MMI study, interest among the industry's most successful advisors—those earning more than $150,000 annually—in offering managed accounts to affluent clients has grown from 13.2 percent in 1996 to 34.6 percent in 1999. Interest among advisors in the next lower income tier—between $75,000 and $150,000—also grew over the same 4-year period from 7.6 percent in 1996 to 13.2 percent in 1999. Among advisors who earn less than $75,000 annually, interest in the accounts has been relatively stable, increasing from 3.1 percent in 1996 to 3.7 percent in 1999.

"As the financial consulting business becomes even more competitive, advisors will look to their most successful peers for insights into product preferences and trends that translate into success," says Davis. "It is clear that, going forward, the advisor community will be seeking more and more opportunities to deliver individual managed accounts."

Source: The Money Management Institute and *Business Wire*, May 13, 1999.

with scale and diversity and myriad small boutiques with niche expertise or superior performance records."

The evidence for such a profound shift in the fund industry is compelling. Consider the 1-year dip of roughly one-third of total fund inflows, from $18.9 billion in 1998 to $12.1 billion in 1999, according to Financial Research Corporation. Investors fled funds in 1999 and 2000, with 53 percent of all fund companies experiencing net outflows, the highest rate ever. This despite the fact that 58 percent of U.S. mutual fund managers exceeded their industry benchmarks, according to Merrill Lynch.

Those who left their mutual funds went to one of two places: either a larger mutual fund or to brokerage firms, many of whom offered some sort of managed fee or online trading platform. In 1999, 85 percent of net new cash in all long-term funds went to five firms: Alliance Capital Management, Fidelity Investments, Janus Capital Corp., Pacific Investment Management Co., and Vanguard Funds.

While mutual funds enjoyed average profit margins of 41.7 percent in 1998, up from 31.4 percent in 1996, the *Institutional Investor* article questioned how long fund managers could sustain these margins. "Despite price-cutting in many financial sectors, mutual fund expense ratios have stayed remarkably constant in recent years—about 139 basis points on average across all funds—even as costs have risen inexorably," the article states. "Companies must pay up for top talent. And while their technological needs are modest, compared, say, with banks and brokerage houses, marketing and distribution are getting more expensive and more complicated."

Enter increased competition from the large brokerage houses, which market much more than just mutual funds, and one begins to understand how the fund industry might be in trouble. "Now we are seeing the emergence of a new landscape of big product platforms, a world where there's no discrimination between proprietary funds and nonproprietary funds. These structural changes leave fund companies struggling to figure out where they will fit in," says Dean Eberling, a financial services analyst with Keefe, Bruyette & Woods. "Banks lost ownership of assets to funds, and presently we are seeing a sea change in the seat of power. Funds are losing the ownership of assets to the brokerages."

One big reason for this shift in financial services power is that brokerages have taken the lead in marketing fee-based management programs to individual consumers. The link between brokerage firms and separate accounts is a tight one with Merrill Lynch, Morgan Stanley Dean Witter, and Paine Webber, among others, rolling out new asset management programs that offer customers unlimited trading for a flat fee.

With competition of that caliber, and facing higher costs in running its own operations, the fund industry is undoubtedly losing much of the steam it generated in the 1980s and 1990s. Just as undoubtedly, we're witnessing the first days of a new era on Wall Street, a changing of the guard from the mutual fund industry to the managed fee industry, with separate accounts the primary engine fueling that growth (Figure 13-1).

FIGURE 13-1

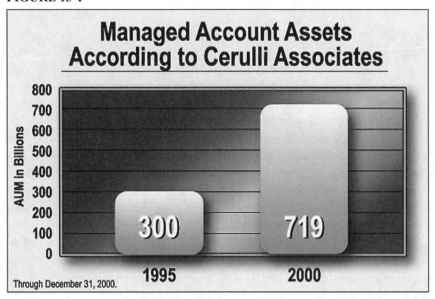

Managed Account Assets According to Cerulli Associates

AUM in Billions — 1995: 300, 2000: 719

Through December 31, 2000.

ERA OF THE INDEPENDENT INVESTOR

As we've said throughout this book, separate accounts appeal to those legions of newly empowered investors who've had a taste of life outside of the mutual fund world, mostly through some combination of online trading, managed-fee-type program investing, or discount brokerage investing. This newfound "independence" will drive the ongoing growth of separate accounts throughout the early portion of the twenty-first century. Let's face it, individual investors like managed accounts because they can be in charge. They have control and power over their affairs if they use managed accounts. They have the power to change managers whenever they think necessary. They can do all of this without losing access to the very top money managers in the investment advisory world.

> *Sidebar II: Johnny-Come-Latelies*
> Increasing competition will bring more pressure in the mutual fund industry. By year's end 1999, the Investment Company Institute counted 7808 mutual funds, including 3964 stock funds, up from 1069 equity and 2900 total funds in 1989. More than half the current mutual fund companies only began operations in the past decade, according to fund consulting firm Strategic Insight.

THE FUTURE OF FINANCIAL SERVICES

Separate accounts will continue to be a big deal to all types of investors because they fit so well into the parameters of the financial services industry down the road. Whatever they do, financial services will need to provide expanded, and more personalized, service to these newly empowered investors. They'll also have to develop more of a relationship with the client, more tax management, and more accountability. As financial firms struggle to win the business of a skeptical new generation of investors, a growing number of them are shaking off old habits. They are earning less from selling stocks and more from managing money. They are making fewer cold calls and spending more time sitting down with clients to discuss long-term financial goals, to set income targets, and then to allocate assets among a range of investments.

The switch could not be more radical in terms of the shift in the "traditional" brokers' financial incentives. It puts the emphasis on performance rather than on the generation of commissions from transactions that may, or may not, be in the client's best interest.

That's where separate accounts come in handy for financial services firms. Many big retail brokerage firms are counting on so-called managed accounts to secure their place in the investing future, which for UBS PaineWebber, Merrill Lynch, and others will largely revolve around managing chunks of the growing mountain of assets that baby boomers are building for retirement.

"What investors are looking for today is a long-term relationship with a well-informed and trusted investment advisor, who is focused on helping them achieve their financial goals," says Peter Russel, vice president and director of Toronto-based Royal Investment Services, in a February 16, 2000, speech at the University of Toronto Capital Markets Institute. "What they don't want is 'good ideas' and someone who can execute or broker a trade for them. Good ideas are a 'dime-a-dozen.' They're available at virtually no cost from a myriad of sources and order execution is $29 per trade through self-serve dealers."

As the population ages and their savings grow, investors will look for people and programs they can trust to help them wade through all that is available to them. Most important, they will want a personalized, comprehensive solution, not a mass-market cookie-cutter approach. They will, in increasing numbers, turn to separate accounts to help them.

"Predicting the future in our industry is extremely tough," says David Annis, chief information officer at The Hartford Financial services. "Financial Services companies that want to come up winners these days

Sidebar III: Price Points to Ponder
A number of new competitors have targeted the managed money market, including some institutionally oriented firms. Although they are competing on service and price and offering separate accounts, commingled accounts, and institutionally priced mutual funds, the pricing differential can be dramatic.

must have an understanding of the Internet economy, invest in a strong technology infrastructure, and learn how to experiment with business models."

Over the course of the last century, he notes, economic power in the United States has evolved from producers like automaker Henry Ford to giant distributors like Home Depot and Wal-Mart. Today, the power base is moving to the customer who "has more information than ever before," Annis says. "We are in the middle of a power shift of enormous proportion. It's a very profound shift and we are not going back. Clearly, the companies meeting customer expectations in our economy are winning."

The Internet is accelerating the shift in power to the customer, Annis adds. Customer expectations are changing, with people demanding 24-hour, 7-day-a-week service, rich information, unbridled communication, and free services. Moreover, the availability of information is driving transparency of price, product features, and competitive alternatives. In this economy, large companies no longer have the deep pockets advantage, with access to capital markets favoring start-ups that are perceived as agile and capable of experimenting.

PREDICTIONS FOR WALL STREET IN THE FIRST YEARS OF THE TWENTY-FIRST CENTURY

Straight from the horse's mouth, here are some predictions from financial services professionals on what Wall Street will look like in the next few years.*

Jim Guillou, CFP, is a producing branch manager with Sutro & Co., in La Jolla, California: "The more complicated investing becomes and the more volatile the markets become, the more people appreciate that it's not

*Source: *On Wall Street*, December 1, 1999, "Peering into Tomorrow: At the Threshold of a New Century, Brokers and Others Discuss Where They Are Going."

as simple as they thought and the more they need a full-service broker. There will be more emphasis on asset allocation and less on short-term trading."

Robert Mills, a broker with Janney Montgomery Scott in Darien, Connecticut, considers himself a market contrarian: "The more our industry is deregulated, the more merger mania and consolidation you'll see. Now that Congress has repealed Glass-Steagall, you're going to see more of those financial supermarket mergers. You could wind up with entities like Chase-Aetna-Merrill. Or Metropolitan Life-Bank of New York-Paine Webber. Insurance companies, banks, and brokerages will crawl all over each other. The longer the market stays above 10,000, the harder it will be for the rest of the mainline firms to resist the E*TRADE trend. But if we get a crash, the people who are buying the most volatile, new-issue, Internet stocks are going to get hurt. And customers are going to flow back to the major brokerage firms."

Matthew Andresen is president of The Island ECN, Inc., one of the largest electronic communications networks: "As the markets become more automated, the importance of the retail broker is growing. The broker's real value lies in being the educated point of contact who can explain everything that's going on and what it all means. I think that someone who can use and explain all the new electronic tools, as well as what's going on in the markets and act as a trusted financial consultant, will be very successful in the new environment."

Don DeWees, Jr., is half of a father-son team at First Union Securities in Greenville, Delaware: "The biggest thing . . . will be to harness the Internet to provide a higher level of service to our clients. We should be able to deliver statements, confirmations, and performance reviews, all electronically in real-time on the Web. Instead of waiting for a quarterly review, we must be able to offer that information in real-time, 365 days a year. There's just too much paper coming to our customers right now."

David Ewing, an Edward Jones broker in Decatur, Georgia: "Every time I meet with an existing or new client, I try to pound home the fact that, on average, the market goes down about one year in every four. I jokingly tell clients a story that's been used at Edward Jones for years. I say, the next time the market goes down and your account is worth less than it was the month before, and you're so angry you want to throw a brick through my window, remember my advice that the best time to buy is when the market occasionally goes down. In fact, when you remember what I told you, I want you to write out a check to buy more stocks, and tie that check to that brick and then throw it through my window. I even have a brick on my desk that says 'One in Four: Ask Me Why.' It's a conversation piece."

Louis Harvey is president of Dalbar, a Boston firm that measures performance of financial professionals: "We're seeing perhaps the most significant transformation ever in the retail business. Historically, the client has been the target. The financial consultant has gone after clients because he wants them to do things, to buy something. But that's now turned around. Now it's the client who wants to find someone to work with him. We first started to see indications of that 4 or 5 years ago. Consumers are actively looking for financial planners, someone to listen to their issues and tell them what to do. I think brokers are up to it, as long as they don't view this opportunity as one to pick their clients' pockets. Because there are certainly individuals out there who are more anxious about the next transaction ticket than they are about helping their clients succeed. We track this stuff every year, and about half the brokers out there are doing both."

Whatever happens in the financial services industry in the coming years, one trend is becoming abundantly clear: There's just no stopping the separate account revolution.

"What was once viewed by many as an experimental concept has since coalesced into a full-fledged industry that's grown to over $600 billion in assets through 2000," says Cerulli Associates. "And everyone wants a piece of the pie, from established firms that have been staples in this arena, to a whole host of new players ranging from fund companies to technology companies to research companies. How large the industry will grow is anybody's guess."

It's Cerulli's guess—and we fully concur with their assessment—that the separate accounts industry will grow to 30 percent of all investable assets within a few years, growing to about $1.4 trillion by 2004. We see assets of over $2.6 trillion by 2010. Where that remarkable growth rate leaves the mutual fund industry is also anyone's guess. No doubt still standing, but out of the spotlight that will soon shine solely upon the separate account.

And that's a sight we can't wait to see.

A P P E N D I X

THE INVESTMENT POLICY STATEMENT

An investment policy statement is an integral part of your separate account investment strategy. It provides you with the same disciplined strategic approach to investing that fiduciaries and investment committees of pension and endowment funds have used for years.

An investment policy statement establishes a blueprint for an investment portfolio and the framework within which all investment decisions can be made. The statement communicates your goals and objectives, risk tolerance, and long-term strategy to your investment advisors and establishes the guidelines for implementing and monitoring the plan.

Here's a sample hypothetical investment policy statement. Read it carefully and you'll understand why professional investors wouldn't dream of parting with one nickel before building an investment portfolio.

Note: Past performance is not a guarantee of future results. All performance numbers are historical, and each security's price, return, and yield will vary. In addition, investors may have a gain or a loss when they sell their securities.

FIGURE A-1

Investment Policy Statement

August 31, 2001

Separate Account Solutions, Inc.

FIGURE A-1 (*Continued*)

Investment Policy Statement

What Is an Investment Policy Statement?

An investment policy outlines a prudent and acceptable investment philosophy and defines your investment management procedures and long-term goals.

Why Have a Written Policy?

The principal reason for developing a long-term investment policy and for putting it in writing is to enable you to protect your portfolio from *ad hoc* revisions of sound long-term policy. The written investment policy will help you maintain a long-term policy when short-term market movements may be distressing and place your policy in doubt.

The development of an investment policy follows the basic approach underlying financial planning: assessing your financial condition, setting goals, developing a strategy to meet the goals, implementing the strategy, regularly reviewing the results and adjusting the strategy or the implementation as circumstances dictate. *Having and making use of an investment policy encourages you to become a more disciplined and more systematic investor, thus improving the probability of satisfying your investment goals.*

The purpose of this Investment Policy Statement (IPS) is to establish a clear understanding between you ("Investor") and Separate Account Solutions, Inc. ("Advisor") as to the investment goals and objectives and management policies applicable to your investment portfolio ("Portfolio"). This Investment Policy Statement will:

➤ Establish reasonable expectations, objectives and guidelines in the investment of the Portfolio's assets

➤ Create the framework for a well-diversified asset mix that can be expected to generate acceptable long-term returns at a level of risk suitable to you, including:

♦ Describing an appropriate risk posture for the investment of the portfolio;

♦ Specifying the target asset allocation policy;

♦ Establishing investment guidelines regarding the selection of investment managers, permissible securities and diversification of assets;

♦ Specifying the criteria for evaluating the performance of the Portfolio's assets;

➤ Define the responsibilities of you and your Advisor

➤ Encourage effective communication between you and the advisor(s)

This IPS is not a contract; it is intended to be a summary of your investment philosophy and the procedures that provide guidance for you and your Advisor. The investment policies described in this IPS should be dynamic. These policies should reflect your current status and philosophy regarding the investment of the Portfolio. These policies will be reviewed and revised periodically to ensure they adequately reflect any changes related to you, the Portfolio, and the capital markets.

It is understood that there can be no guarantee about the attainment of the goals or investment objectives outlined herein.

FIGURE A-1 (*Continued*)

Client Overview

Client Profile

Client	Joseph Sample 1990 Sample Street Anywhere, TX 77097
Current Investable Assets	$375,000
Investment Horizon	20 Years or more
Withdrawal Requirements	None
Investment Constraints	None
Custodian	Yyy Securities
Account Number	0801-2324
Social Security Number	999-99-9999
Advisor	Separate Account Solutions, Inc.
Authorized Decision Maker	Joseph Sample

Current Portfolio	
Large Cap Growth	$225,000.00
Large Cap Value	0.00
Mid Cap Equities	78,000.00
Small Cap Equities	81,000.00
International Equities	0.00
Domestic Bonds	75,000.00
Cash	300,000.00
Total	$759,000.00

Investment Objective

The objectives for your assets under this Investment Policy Statement shall be to achieve relatively stable growth with a low level of income. Based on your risk profile, you should have a moderate tolerance for risk and/or a long-term investment horizon. Your main objective is to achieve steady portfolio growth while limiting fluctuations to less than those of the overall stock markets.

Investment Time Horizon

For the purposes of planning, the time horizon for these investments will be in excess of 10 years. Capital values do fluctuate over shorter periods and you should recognize that the possibility of capital loss does exist. However, historical asset class return data suggest that the risk of principal loss over a holding period of at least three to five years can be minimized with the long-term investment mix described in this Investment Policy Statement.

An annual review will be conducted each year to determine if any changes in your needs and/or investment objectives have occurred. If appropriate, the portfolio and IPS will be updated to reflect these shifts. The first annual review meeting is scheduled for June 14, 2002.

Additionally, an initial meeting to discuss and review your first Quarterly performance report will be scheduled for July 19, 2001.

FIGURE A-1 (*Continued*)

Risk / Volatility

Investment theory and historical capital market return data suggest that, over long periods of time, there is a relationship between the level or risk assumed and the level of return that can be expected in an investment program. In general, higher risk (e.g. volatility of return) is associated with higher return.

Given this relationship between risk and return, a fundamental step in determining the investment policy for the Portfolio is the determination of an appropriate risk tolerance. There are two primary factors that affect your risk tolerance:

> ➤   Financial ability to accept risk within the investment program, and;

> ➤   Willingness to accept return volatility.

Taking these two factors into account, you have rated your own risk tolerance as <u>moderate</u>. You have recognized that higher returns involve some volatility and have indicated a willingness to tolerate declines in the value of this portfolio.

Asset Allocation

Research suggests that the decision to allocate total assets among various asset classes will far outweigh security selection and other decisions that determine portfolio performance. After reviewing the long-term performance and risk characteristics of various asset classes and balancing the risk and rewards of market behavior, the following asset classes and allocation were selected to achieve the objectives of your Portfolio.

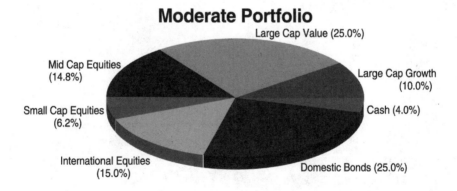

Diagram 1: Your proposed asset allocation.

No guarantees can be given about future performance based on historical returns, and this Investment Policy Statement shall not be construed as offering such a guarantee.

A portfolio of assets combined in a manner consistent with the normalized weightings suggested above and using standardized figures for each represented asset class based on historical norms and adjusted for today's environment allow for the performance results to be reasonably projected as follows on the Approximated Future Returns Chart on the next page.

FIGURE A-1 (*Continued*)

Approximated Future Returns

For Investor's Allocation proposed above

	One Year	Ten Year
Maximum for Period	37.52%	19.22%
Expected Return	12.50%	11.69%
Minimum for Period	-9.44%	4.46%
Worse Case Conditions	-28.44%	-3.03%

All return calculations herein include price appreciation/depreciation, income distributions and capital gains distributions. Above figures based on 90% statistical likelihood, except for those of "Worse Case Conditions," the returns of which are to be exceeded all but 5% of the time. Calculations do not include the impact of management fees, transaction costs or taxes.

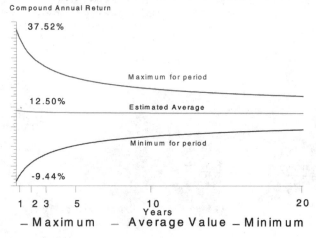

Diagram 2: Approximated future returns over a 20 yr period for your portfolio

On average over long periods of time, this portfolio design can be expected to experience losses one in eight years. In such cases, it should take an average of somewhat less than ten months to recover such losses. Over a five-year period, such a portfolio's performance should exceed inflation 93% of the time.

Updated Allocations

From time to time, it may be desirable to update the stated allocation policy or calculations. When such changes are made, updates will be attached to this Investment Policy Statement, and will be considered part of this Investment Policy Statement.

FIGURE A-1 (*Continued*)

Frequency of Review

You recognize that all investments go through cycles and, therefore, there will be periods of time in which the investment objectives are not met or when specific managers fail to meet their expected performance targets within their investment style. Recognizing that no manager is perfect all the time and that good years help to make up for bad ones, you acknowledge the principle that managers must be given an opportunity to make up for poor periods. Unless there are extenuating circumstances, patience will often prove appropriate when the manager's performance versus their peers in the same style discipline has been disappointing.

On an overall portfolio basis, you established a goal of achieving the stated investment return objectives over a five-year period of time. Reviewing manager performance over short time periods contradicts the principles of long term investing.

Liquidity

You have determined that sufficient dependable income and liquidity are available from other sources such that you do not need to maintain cash balances among these assets, except as may be dictated for investment or operational reasons, such as payment of quarterly fees.

Diversification

Based on the review of your current portfolio, we have determined the following separate account styles and the respective amounts to invest that are necessary to complete the implementation of your asset allocation. The selected money manager(s) for each style are listed in the right hand column below:

Selected Separate Account Categories

Style	Dollars	Money Managers
Large Cap Value	$175,000	Navellier Large Cap Value
International Equities	$100,000	Manager B Global Emerging Markets ADR
Domestic Bonds	$100,000	Manager C Taxable Bond

Permitted Security Type

The Portfolio Manager(s) will determine, in their sole discretion, to invest and reinvest the assets in the Account in equity or debt securities; common or preferred stock; convertible stocks or bonds; options; warrants; rights; corporate, municipal or United States government bonds, notes or bills; any other security or investment instrument of any kind; and in mutual funds (collectively, "Securities") consistent with your investor profile.

FIGURE A-1 (*Continued*)

Selection/Retention Criteria for Investments

Investment Management Selection

Investment managers shall be chosen using the following criteria:

➤ Past performance, considered relative to other investments having the same investment objective. Consideration shall be given to both performance rankings over various time frames and consistency of performance.

➤ Length of time the fund has been in existence and length of time it has been under the direction of the current manager(s) and whether or not there have been material changes in the manager's organization and personnel.

➤ The historical volatility and downside risk of each proposed investment.

➤ How well each proposed investment complements other assets in the portfolio.

➤ The likelihood of future investment success, relative to other opportunities.

Investment Monitoring and Control Procedures

Reports

1. Separate Account Solutions, Inc. shall provide you with a report each quarter that lists all assets held by, values for each asset and all transactions affecting assets within the portfolio, including additions and withdrawals.

2. You shall receive no less frequently than on a quarterly basis and within 30 days of the end of such quarter the following management reports:

   a) Portfolio performance results over the last quarter, year, 3 years and 5 years

   b) Performance results of each individual manager for the same periods

   c) Performance results of comparative benchmarks for the same periods

   d) Performance shall be reported on a basis that is in compliance with Association for Investment Management and Research (AIMR) standards.

   e) Any recommendations for changes of the above

Communication Between Investor and Advisor

As a matter of course, Separate Account Solutions, Inc. shall keep you apprised of any material changes in the Separate Account Solutions, Inc. outlook, recommended investment policy, and tactics. In addition, Separate Account Solutions, Inc. shall contact you no less than annually to review and explain the Portfolio's investment results and any related issues. Separate Account Solutions, Inc. shall also be available for communication via telephone or text chat when needed.

FIGURE A-1 (*Continued*)

Duties and Responsibilities

The Advisor

Separate Account Solutions, Inc. is a Registered Investment Advisor and shall act as the investment advisor and fiduciary to the Investor until the Investor decides otherwise.

Separate Account Solutions, Inc. shall be responsible for:

1) Designing, recommending and implementing an appropriate asset allocation plan consistent with the investment objectives, time horizon, risk profile, guidelines and constraints outlined in this statement.

2) Advising the Investor about the selection of and the allocation of asset categories.

3) Helping identify specific assets and investment managers within each asset category.

4) Monitoring the performance of all selected assets.

5) Recommending changes to any of the above.

6) Periodically reviewing the suitability of the investments for the Investor, being available to discuss with the Investor at least once each year, and being available at such other times at the Investor's request.

7) Preparing and presenting appropriate reports.

The Investor

shall be responsible for:

1) The oversight of the Portfolio.

2) Defining the investment objectives and policies of the Portfolio.

3) Directing Separate Account Solutions, Inc. to make changes in investment policy and to oversee and to approve or disapprove Separate Account Solutions' recommendations with regards to investment manager selection, policy, guidelines, and objectives on a timely basis.

4) Providing Separate Account Solutions, Inc. with all relevant information on the investor's financial conditions and risk tolerances and shall notify Separate Account Solutions, Inc. promptly of any changes to this information.

Adoption

Adopted by the below signed:

Date:

Investor:

Advisor:

Trustee(s):

B

SEPARATE
ACCOUNT
PROPOSAL

Once you've begun shopping for a separate accounts manager, you'll undoubtedly be buried in glossy marketing brochures and shiny "We're the Separate Accounts Firm for You" pamphlets. They're all well and good, but the document you're really looking for from a prospective separate accounts manager is the "investor proposal." In it, you'll find good information on the company, data on its investment performance, a sample hypothetical investment policy statement (see Appendix A, Figure A-1), and some information on its money managers.

You'll also get a good idea about how the company might handle your separate account's asset allocation strategy along with some potential investment sectors the firm specializes in. All in all it's a good and worthwhile read. Figure B-1 on the pages following is a sample investor proposal.

Note: Past performance is not a guarantee of future results. All performance numbers are historical, and each security's price, return, and yield will vary. In addition, investors may have a gain or a loss when they sell their securities.

VIP PRIVATE CAPITAL

Separate Account Proposal

Prepared for

Joseph Sample

August 31, 2001

FIGURE B-1

FIGURE B-1 (*Continued*)

Reaching Your Financial Goals:

There are four steps that we need to take to help you reach your financial goals:

1) Evaluate your Investment Profile

2) Develop an Asset Allocation

3) Determine your Money Manager Allocation

4) Implement the Plan

FIGURE B-1 (*Continued*)

Investor Profile and Policy Statement

Step 1: Evaluate your investment profile

Our first step was to examine your investment objectives, investment time horizon, and tolerance for volatility or risk in your investments. Additionally, we evaluated your current holdings and discussed any limitations that you wanted placed on how the money would be invested. We have incorporated all of this information into the process that we used to complete the following steps. Please review the investment profile below for accuracy, and notify us of any changes that are necessary.

Joseph Sample
1990 Sample Street
Anywhere, TX 77097

Total Investment Portfolio:

Current Portfolio	
Large Cap Growth	$225,000.00
Large Cap Value	0.00
Mid Cap Equities	78,000.00
Small Cap Equities	81,000.00
International Equities	0.00
Domestic Bonds	75,000.00
Cash	300,000.00
Total	**$759,000.00**

Current Investable Assets:
$375,000

Investment Horizon:
20 Years or more

Investment Volatility Tolerance: Moderate

Determining your Risk Type is essential to the development of an appropriate Asset Allocation. Based on the responses to the questionnaire and on previous information you have provided concerning investment time horizon and cash flow needs, your Investment Volatility Tolerance classification would be as a Moderate investor.

Investment Objective:

As a moderate investor, you are seeking relatively stable growth from your investable assets offset by a low level of income. Your objective is to achieve steady portfolio growth while limiting fluctuations to less than those of the overall stock markets.

Withdrawal Requirements:
None

Investment Constraints:
None

FIGURE B-1 (*Continued*)

Asset Allocation

Step 2: Asset Allocation

An asset allocation strategy takes into account the historical performance of stocks, bonds, and cash and exploits their different return characteristics to improve the probability of achieving a desired long-term total return. Stocks, bonds, and cash do not always gain or lose value at the same time, so setbacks in one category can be offset by gains in another. Historically, volatility has been reduced over time by holding multiple asset classes in a portfolio. Below is a comparison of your existing portfolio versus the proposed (model) asset allocation portfolio that we have created for you. For a further explanation of asset allocation, please see appendix A-1.

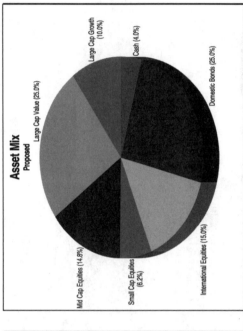

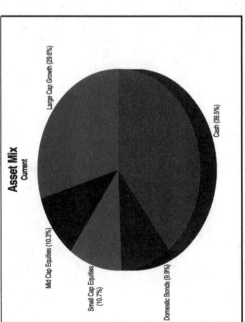

FIGURE B-1 (*Continued*)

Asset Allocation

Your Current and Proposed portfolios are depicted on the Efficient Frontier line below as labeled points. The Efficient Frontier line represents Portfolios with the highest possible return for each level of risk (standard deviation), given the capital market assumptions and constraints being used. As you can see, Asset allocation benefits you by reducing the volatility in your portfolio while also attempting to maximize your portfolio return within the limits of your accepted level of risk.

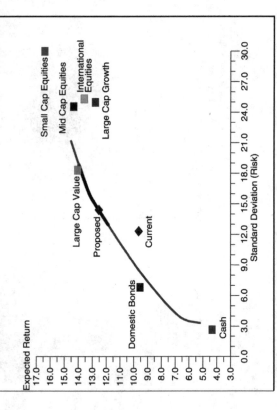

This Efficient Frontier was created by Mean Variance Optimization (MVO) using data believed to be reliable. Past performance is not a guarantee of future results.

FIGURE B-1 (*Continued*)

Asset Allocation

The Return Percentiles Comparison Graph and Table illustrate the hypothetical returns of your Current and Proposed Portfolios. Each shaded area represents a range of the compound annual returns for these portfolios. When you compare the Current and Proposed portfolios, you can see the differences in the range of hypothetical returns. Based on this historical data, there is a 90% probability that the returns for these portfolios will fall within the ranges listed for each timeframe. The best and worst return levels each have a 5% chance of being realized.

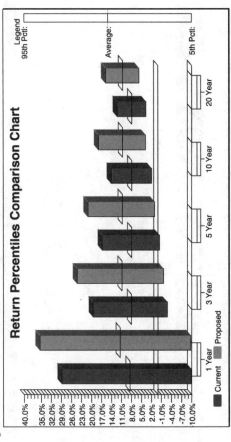

Return Percentiles Comparison Chart

	1 Year		3 Year		5 Year		10 Year		20 Year	
	Current	Proposed	Current	Proposed	Current	Proposed	Current	Proposed	Current	Proposed
95th	28.83	35.35	19.48	24.25	16.74	21.01	14.04	17.85	12.17	15.65
Average	8.42	11.37	8.00	10.81	7.91	10.70	7.85	10.62	7.82	10.58
5th	-9.82	-9.74	-2.76	-1.67	-0.48	0.96	1.88	3.67	3.57	5.64

FIGURE B-1 (*Continued*)

Manager Allocation

Step 3: Manager Allocation

Now that we have developed an appropriate asset allocation, and reviewed the expected returns, we must determine the appropriate manager allocation within the asset allocation. This first table is a comparison between your Current and Proposed Portfolios. It illustrates the amount of each asset class that would need to be bought and sold to get from the Current Portfolio to the Proposed Portfolio.

	Current Portfolio		Proposed Portfolio		Change	
	$	%	$	%	$	%
Large Cap Growth	225,000	29.64	75,900	10.00	-149,100	-19.64
Large Cap Value	0	0.00	189,750	25.00	189,750	25.00
Mid Cap Equities	78,000	10.28	112,469	14.82	34,469	4.54
Small Cap Equities	81,000	10.67	46,851	6.17	-34,149	-4.50
International Equities	0	0.00	113,850	15.00	113,850	15.00
Domestic Bonds	75,000	9.88	189,750	25.00	114,750	15.12
Cash	300,000	39.53	30,430	4.01	-269,570	-35.52

We have selected the money managers that most closely fit your investment profile, and are best suited to help you reach your financial goals. Based on your investable assets, and the money managers' minimum initial investment requirements, the chart below reflects our recommendation to you.

Style	Percentage	Dollars	Money Mangers
Large Cap Value	46%	$175,000	Navellier Large Cap Value
International Equities	27%	$100,000	Manager B Global Emerging Markets ADR
Domestic Bonds	27%	$100,000	Manager C Taxable Bond

FIGURE B-1 (*Continued*)

Implementation

Step 4: Implementation

The final, and most important, step in the process is the implementation of your new investment strategy. We will assist you in reviewing the following information on the portfolios suggested above, and finalizing the manager allocation decision. Additionally, we will provide you with an Investment Policy Statement (IPS) that outlines your investment philosophy and defines the investment management procedures and long-term goals. The IPS will also provide you with a tangible tool to help you maintain a long-term investment perspective during volatile market conditions. If there are any changes in your financial situation or needs, you will want to notify me of those changes as soon as possible. I will update your IPS accordingly. This is especially important since the IPS will be the tool that we will use to monitor the ongoing success of your investment strategy. The worksheet below describes the changes to your portfolio that are necessary to fund your separate account.

Worksheet:

Total Investable Assets: **$375,000**

Current Holding(s) to Liquidate:

Dollars	Holdings
$270,000	Cash
$105,000	Large Cap Growth
$375,000	**Total**

Investment into Separate Accounts:

Dollars	Money Mangers
$175,000	Navellier Large Cap Value
$100,000	Manager B Global Emerging Markets ADR
$100,000	Manager C Taxable Bond
$375,000	**Total**

FIGURE B-1 (*Continued*)

Introduction to Asset Allocation

For any investor, it is important to develop a solid investment strategy to achieve their long-term goals. One way an investor can do this is by comparing their current portfolio to a portfolio with an ideal asset allocation model. This introduction is meant to show you the benefits of using asset allocation in a portfolio.

An asset allocation strategy takes into account the historical performance of stocks, bonds, and cash and leverages their different return characteristics to improve the probability of achieving a desired long-term total return. Stocks, bonds, and cash do not always gain or lose value at the same time, so setbacks in one category can be offset by gains in another. Historically, volatility has been reduced over time by holding all three asset classes in a portfolio.

It is important to note that asset allocation is not the same as diversification, which allows an investor to spread risk within a single asset class. Though diversification is also an important tool in the toolbox of investing, relying on it alone causes an investor to ignore other asset classes that could help them achieve their long-term goals. For example, many people invest with mutual funds and say, "I am diversified, I invested in three different mutual funds." While in reality, if we look closely at the mutual funds that investor holds, we may discover that all three of those funds are Large Growth Funds and those funds own many overlapping securities. This investor is not invested in any other asset classes such as Large Cap Value, Small Cap Equities, International Equities or Fixed Income. They are spreading their risk in just a small section of the overall market.

Asset allocation differs from simple diversification because it involves being diversified in more than one asset class—not only in managed portfolios, such as large cap growth and value, but also, for example, in fixed income, whether it be a federal or a corporate issue. Diversification within an asset class is important, but it is equally important to spread risk among various asset classes. Asset allocation benefits an investor by reducing the volatility in their portfolio while also attempting to maximize their portfolio return within the limits of their accepted level of risk.

Investors must realize that investment returns vary from a short to a long time frame. They must also understand the risk in their investment choices and set realistic expectations for the growth of their assets. By applying the concept of asset allocation to a portfolio, an investor will reduce portfolio volatility by spreading risk over various asset classes. Asset allocation also structures an investor's assets to help them achieve their goals with a minimum level of risk. This should give investors confidence that their money will grow over time at an expected level and be there when they plan on needing it.

Please note that results might be different from a full financial plan that considers information such as financial net worth analysis, insurance requirements, detailed tax situations, and estate planning. Recognizing that past performance does not guarantee future results and that indices differ from actual portfolios, data presented is based on the relationship of various indices representing asset classes. There may be a low correlation between the index and a client's portfolio consisting of securities. The market indices do not contain transaction costs.

FIGURE B-1 (*Continued*)

SAMPLE MONEY MANAGER REPORT: NAVELLIER LARGE CAP VALUE

NAVELLIER & ASSOCIATES, INC.

ABOUT US:

Navellier considers its investment selection process as "dynamic". It is this dynamic process which Navellier believes separates itself from its peer group. Navellier's dynamic process is designed to lock in on what fundamental characteristics are currently attractive on Wall Street. Each quarter, after earnings announcements, Navellier "backtests" various fundamental characteristics in an attempt to identify and select which characteristics are driving stock prices higher. Characteristics such as analyst earnings revisions, earnings surprise, earnings growth relative to P/E, return on equity, etc. are tested each quarter and applied to stock selection. By being "dynamic" and shifting its stock selection basis, Navellier is able to capitalize on "what is working on Wall Street" and enhance returns.

LARGE CAP VALUE:

The Large Cap Value Portfolio is designed for more conservative investors seeking steady returns. This is a lower turnover, more tax-efficient Portfolio that is designed to provide long-term capital gains. The Large Cap Value Portfolio is designed to provide superior long-term performance particularly during weak stock market environments. This portfolio only invests in established large capitalization companies that are familiar to many investors and provides the highest dividend yields of all of Navellier's Equity Management Portfolios. The Large Cap Value Portfolio is designed for more conservative investors that desire the security that is associated with investing in large, well-known companies with a history of steady and rising dividends. Typically, the Large Cap Value Portfolio will invest in approximately the top 20 to 50 stocks that pass Navellier's stringent fundamental value criteria. Navellier's primary performance benchmark is the Russell 1000 Value index.

Firm Characteristics	
Parent Company (if applicable)	N/A
Date Firm Founded	01-01-1987
Previous Name of Firm (if applicable)	N/A
Total Assets Managed	4,348mm
Average Years of Industry Experience	12.5
AIMR Compliance	*Yes
Benchmark	Russell 1000 Value
Number of Investment Professionals	6
Institutional Client List (five)	American Association of OBGYN Foundation

Portfolio Characteristics	
Total Assets in Style	17mm
Benchmark	Russell 1000 Value
Top Five Holdings	Reliant Energy Inc. El Paso Corp Dominion Res. Inc. Firstenergy Corp. Sbc Comm. Inc.
Average Number of Holdings	34
Average Dividend Yield	Higher than the Russell 1000 Value
Median P/E Ratio	Lower than the Russell 1000 Value
Cash Level Over Market Cycle	5-10%
Risk-Standard Deviation	Higher than the Russell 1000 Value
Annual Turnover Rate	%
Capitalization	Large Value

FIGURE B-1 (*Continued*)

Investment Process

Navellier's *Equity Management* program is designed to achieve the highest possible returns, with controlled risk. Navellier is dedicated to finding and exploiting inefficiencies in the market through a comprehensive quantitative and fundamental screening process. We believe that disciplined quantitative analysis can select stocks which will significantly outperform the overall market with a market cycle of three to five years. Navellier has a proven fifteen year track record for it's *Small to Mid Cap Growth composite* in which it has outperformed most broad market indices. Navellier believes it will continue to be successful due to its state-of-the-art research techniques that are continually adapting to changes on Wall Street.

Navellier implements its philosophy through a combination of quantitative and fundamental analysis. Our process begins with a computer driven analysis based on Modern Portfolio Theory. We calculate reward (alpha) and risk (standard deviation) characteristics for a universe of over 9,000 stocks. These quantitative characteristics are calculated and back-tested over the preceding 12 & 36 months for each stock, then combined to produce a reward/risk ratio. The top 5% of these stocks, based on their reward/risk ratios, are then reviewed on fundamental analysis. The fundamentals that are reviewed and measured are based on Navellier's proprietary analysis as to what is currently "in favor" on Wall Street. A variety of fundamental screens are reviewed, weighted and scored versus our entire universe of stocks. The idea is to "stack the odds in our favor" by selecting the top 1% of our universe for the small and mid cap growth and value styles, and the top 5% for the large-cap growth style based on superior fundamental characteristics. Navellier's dynamic approach is very quantitative in nature. Navellier does not deviate from this investment discipline.

Annualized Performance Comparison As of 3/31/01		
	1YR	3YR
Portfolio	-7.19	0.39
Index	0.27	3.85
Difference	6.92	3.46

INVESTMENT ADVISORS

There's no shortage of investment advisors to help separate account investors out. Take Möbius Group's M Search Product. The separate accounts portfolio manager works with hundreds of advisors on client separate account portfolios. Take a look at the list and see why, when it comes to separate accounts, there are plenty of investment advisors looking to help you out.

CURRENT AS OF Q2 2001

1

1838 Investment Advisors

A

A I M Private Asset Management

A.N. Culbertson & Company, Inc.

Abacus Financial Group, Inc.

Aberdeen Fund Managers, Inc.

ABN AMRO Asset Management (USA) Inc.

Abner, Herrman & Brock Asset Management

Acadian Asset Management, Inc.

Acorn Derivatives Management Corporation

Addison Capital Management, LLC

Adell, Harriman & Carpenter, Inc.

Advanced Investment Management, L.P.

Advanced Investment Technology, Inc.

Advantus Capital Management, Inc.

Advent Advisors, Inc.

Advent Capital Management

Advisers Capital Management, Inc.

Advisory Research, Inc.

Aegis Asset Management, Inc.

Aegon Asset Management, UKPLC

AEGON Institutional Markets

AEGON USA Investment Management, Inc.

Aeltus Investment Management, Inc.

AEW Capital Management

Aexpert Advisory Inc.

AFA Financial, Inc.

Affinity Investment Advisors

AFL-CIO Housing Investment Trust

Agincourt Capital Management, LLC

AIB Govett, Inc.

AIG Global Investment Corp.

AIS Capital Management LLC

Al Frank Asset Management, Inc.

Albriond Capital Management, LLC

ALC Investment Advisors, LLC

Alexander & Muckermann

Alexander Capital Management

Alhambra Capital

Alla Investment Management, Inc.

Allegiance Capital, Incorporated

AllianceBernstein Institutional Investment Mgmt

Allied Investment Advisors, Inc.

Allmerica Asset Management, Inc.

ALM Advisors, Inc.

Alpha Capital Management, Inc.

Alta Capital Management, LLC

Amalgamated Bank of New York

AmalgaTrust Company, Inc.

Ambs Investment Counsel, LLC

American Advisors Corporation

American Blue Chip Investment Management

American Century Investment Management, Inc.

American Express Asset Management

American Express Financial Advisors, Inc.

American Express Portfolio Mgmt Group (AEPMG)

American Fund Advisors, Inc.

American General Investment Mgmt, L.P.

American Guaranty & Trust Co.

American Realty Advisors

AmeriCap Advisers, LLC

Amerindo Investment Advisors Inc.

Ameristock Corporation

Amervest Company, Incorporated

Amivest Capital Management

AMR Investment Services, Inc.

AmSouth Bank NA

Analytic Investors, Inc.

Anchor Capital Advisors, Inc.

Anna Corporation

Apex Capital Management, Inc.

Apodaca Investment Group, LLC

Appleton Partners

APS Asset Management

APS Asset Management Pte Ltd.

Arbor Capital Management, LLC

Arcadia Investment Management Corporation

Argent Capital Management LLC

Argus Investors' Counsel, Inc.

Ariel Capital Management, Inc.

Ariston Capital Management

Ark Asset Management Company, Inc.

Arlington Capital Investors Ltd.

Armstrong Shaw Associates Inc.

Arnhold & S. Bleichroeder, Inc.

Arnold Investment Counsel Inc.

Aronson + Partners

Arrowstreet Capital, L.P.

Artemis Investment Management LLC

Artisan Partners, L.P.

ASB Capital Management, Inc.

Ascent/Meredith Asset Management, Inc.

Ashfield & Co., Inc.

Ashland Management Inc.

Ashmore Investment Management Ltd.

Atalanta/Sosnoff Capital Corporation

Atlanta Capital Management Company

Atlantic Asset Advisors, Inc.

Atlantic Asset Management, LLC

Atlantic Capital Management, LLC

Atlantic Capital Management, Ltd.

Atlantis Investment Company, Inc.

Aurora Investment Counsel

Austin Calvert & Flavin, Inc.

Auxier Asset Management, LLC

Avanti Investment Advisors

Avatar Associates

Avatar Associates Capital Management Group

Avenir Corporation

Awad Asset Management, Inc.

AXA Rosenberg Investment Management

Axe-Houghton Associates, Inc.

Axiom International Investors, LLC

B

Babson-Stewart Ivory International

Badgley, Phelps and Bell, Inc.

Bahl & Gaynor

Bailard, Biehl & Kaiser, Inc.

Baillie Gifford Overseas Limited

Baird Advisors

Baird Investment Management

Banc of America Capital Management, LLC

Banc One Currency Advisors, Inc.

Banc One Investment Advisors Corporation

Banca IMI Securities

Bank of Ireland Asset Management (U.S.) Ltd

Barclays Global Investors

Barep Gestion

Baring Asset Management

Barnett & Company, Inc.

Baron Capital Management

Barrett Associates, Inc.

Barrow, Hanley, Mewhinney & Strauss, Inc.

Bartlett & Company

Batterymarch Financial
Management, Inc.

Bay Harbour Management, L.C.

Beach Investment Counsel, Inc.

Beacon Asset Management, LLC

Beacon Fiduciary Advisors, Inc.

Beacon Investment Company

Beacon Street Research

Bear Stearns Asset Management Inc.

Becker Capital Management, Inc.

Benefit Concepts Group, Inc.

Bennett Lawrence
Management, LLC

Benson Associates, LLC

Berents & Hess Capital
Management, Inc.

Berger LLC

Berger/Bay Isle LLC

Berkeley Capital Management

Bermuda Asset Management Ltd.

Berno, Gambal & Barbee, Inc.

Bessemer Trust Company, N.A.

Birmingham Capital
Management Co. Inc.

Bishop Street Capital Management

BlackRock

Blairlogie Capital Management

Blue Rock Advisors, Inc.

BNP Paribas AssetManagement, Inc.

BNY Asset Management

Bob Gordon & Co.

Bogle Investment Management

Boston Advisors, Inc.

Boston Company Asset
Management, LLC

Boston Financial Management, Inc.

Boston Partners Asset
Management, L.P.

Boston Private Bank & Trust
Company

Boston Private Value Investors

Boulder Asset Management

Bowling Portfolio Management, Inc.

Boyd Watterson Asset
Management, LLC

Boys, Arnold & Company

BPI Global Asset Management LLP

Brad Peery Capital

Bradford & Marzec, Inc.

Brandes Investment Partners, L.P.

Brandywine Asset Management

Breckinridge Capital
Advisors, Inc.

Bridgewater Associates, Inc.

Brinson Advisors, Inc.

Brinson Partners, Inc.

Brown Brothers Harriman &
Company

Brown Capital Management, Inc.

Brown Investment Advisory &
Trust Company

BT Funds Management BTFM(I)L

BTR Capital Management

Buckhead Capital Management

Buford, Dickson, Harper &
Sparrow, Inc.

Bull Group Advisors Ltd.

Burney Company (The)

Burnham, Sullivan & Andelbradt

Burridge Group LLC (The)

Bush/O'Donnell

C

C.S. McKee & Company, Inc.

C.W. Henderson & Associates, Inc.

Cabot Money Management

Cadence Capital Management

Cadinha & Co., LLC

Calamos Asset Management, Inc.

Caldwell & Orkin, Inc.

Calvert Asset Management Company, Inc.

Calvert Group

Calvert Investment Counsel

Cambiar Investors, Inc.

Cambridge Asset Management, Inc.

Cambridge Equity Advisors

Cambridge Financial Group, Inc.

Camden Asset Management, L.P.

Campbell Cowperthwait

Campbell Newman Asset Management, Inc.

Cannon Tingey Investment Advisors, Inc.

Capital Advisors, Inc.

Capital Advisors, Inc. (FL)

Capital Counsel LLC

Capital Guardian Trust Co.— Personal Inv Mgmt

Capital Guardian Trust Company

Capital International, Inc.

Capital Inv. Services of America, Inc.

Capital Management Associates Inc.

Capital Management Corporation

Capital Marketing Associates Inc.

Capital Research & Management Company

Capital West Asset Management, LLC

CapitalWorks Investment Partners

Capitol Investment Advisors

CAPROC LLC

Capstone Asset Management Company

Cardinal Capital Management, Inc.

Cardinal Capital Management, LLC

Carr & Associates, Inc.

Carret and Company

Cascade Investment Counsel, LLC

CASE Management, Inc.

Cashen Investment Advisors, Inc.

Cashman and Associates Capital Management L.P.

Castle Ark Management, LLC

Caterpillar Investment Management Ltd.

Cavanaugh Capital Management

Caywood-Scholl Capital Management

CDC Investment Management Corp.

Cedar Capital Management

Cedar Hill Associates, Inc.

Central Plains Advisors, Inc.

Century Management

Certus Asset Advisors

CFSC Wayland Advisers, Inc.

Chandler Asset Management, Inc.

Chapman Capital Management, Inc.

Charlotte Capital LLC

Charter Financial Group, Inc.

Chartwell Investment Partners

Chas. P. Smith & Associates, PA, CPAs

Chase Asset Management
Chase Fleming Asset Management
Chase Investment Counsel Corp.
Check Capital Management, Inc.
Chelsea Management Company
Cheswick Investment Company, Inc.
Chicago Asset Management
    Company
Chicago Capital Management, Inc.
Chicago Equity Partners, LLC
Chinook Capital Management LLC
Church Capital Management
Churchill Management Group
CIC Asset Management
CIC/HCM Asset Management, Inc.
Cincinnati Asset Management
Citigroup Asset Management
Citizens Advisers
City Capital Counseling, Inc.
City of London Investment
    Management Co., Ltd.
Claremont Investment Partners
Clarion CRA Real Estate Securities
Clay Finlay Inc.
Clemente Capital Inc.
Clifton Group (The)
Clinton Group (The)
Clover Capital Management, Inc.
Cobblestone Capital Advisors
Coen & Densmore, Incorporated
Cohen & Steers Capital
    Management
Cohen, Klingenstein & Marks
    Incorporated
Coho Partners, Ltd.

Colchester Global Investors Limited
Coldstream Capital Management
Colonial Advisory Services, Inc.
Colony Capital Management
Columbia Management Co.
Columbia Partners, LLC Invest-
    ment Management
Columbus Circle Investors
Comerica Bank
Commerce Bank
Commonfund
Companion Capital
    Management, Inc.
Compass Bank Asset
    Management Group
Compass Capital Management, Inc.
Concord Investment Company
Concorde Investment Management
Congress Asset Management
    Company
Connecticut Investment
    Management
Conning Asset Management
    Company
Connors Investor Services Inc.
Conseco Capital Management, Inc.
Consistent Asset Management Co.
Constitution Capital Corp
Constitution Research &
    Management, Inc.
Cook Mayer Taylor
Cooke & Bieler, L.P.
Corbin & Company
Corcoran Jennison Institutional
    Services
Cordillera Asset Management

Cornell Capital Management
Cornercap Investment Counsel
Cornerstone Capital
    Management Inc.
Cortland Associates
COZAD Asset Management
Crabbe Huson Group, Inc.
Cramer Rosenthal McGlynn, LLC
Crawford Investment Counsel
Credit Suisse Asset Management
Credit Suisse First Boston
Crestwood Asset Management
Cullen, Fortier Asset Management
Cumberland Advisors
Cummer/Moyers Capital
    Advisors, Inc.
Cutler & Company, LLC
CWH Associates, Inc.
Cypress Asset Management
Cypress Asset Management (TX)
CypressTree Investment
    Management Company

D

D.B. Fitzpatrick & Co.
Daedalus Capital, LLC
Daiwa SB Investments Ltd.
Dalton, Greiner, Hartman,
    Maher & Co.
Dana Investment Advisors, Inc.
Darrell & King Co.
Daruma Asset Management, Inc.
David J. Greene & Company, LLC
David L. Babson & Co.
Davidson & Garrard Inc.
Davidson Capital Management

Davidson Investment Advisors
Davis Selected Advisers, L.P.
Davis, Hamilton, Jackson &
    Associates, L.P.
Dawson-Giammalva Capital
    Management
Dean Investment Associates
Dearborn Partners LLC
Delafield Asset Management
DeLaroche & Company, Inc.
Delaware Capital Management, Inc.
Delaware International Advisers Ltd.
Delaware Investment Advisers
Delta Asset Management, Inc.
Delta Capital Management
Delta Financial Management
DENALI Advisors, LLC
Denis Wong & Associates
Denver Investment Advisors LLC
DePrince, Race and Zollo Inc.
Deutsche Asset Management
Diaz-Verson Capital
    Investment, LLC
Dimensional Fund Advisors, Inc.
Disciplined Growth Investors, Inc.
Disciplined Investment Advisors
Diversified Investment Advisors
Divi-Vest Advisors, Inc.
Dodge and Cox
Dollins Symons Management
Dominick & Dominick
    Advisors LLC
Donald Smith & Co., Inc.
Douglas Capital Management
Dover Partners, Inc.

Dreman Value Management, LLC
Dresdner RCM Global Investors
Dreyfus Investment Advisors, Inc.
Driehaus Capital Management, Inc.
DSI International
Duff & Phelps Investment
    Management Co.
Duncan-Hurst Capital
    Management Inc.
DuPont Capital Management Corp.
Dwight Asset Management
    Company, Inc.
Dyer, Robertson & Lamme, Inc.

E

Eads & Heald Investment Counsel
Eagle Asset Management Inc.
Eagle Capital Management
Eagle Global Advisors, LLC
Eagle Growth Investors
Earl M. Foster Associates
EARNEST Partners LLC
East Side Capital Corp.
Eastover Capital Management
Eaton Vance Management, Inc.
Eclipse Funds
Edgar Lomax Company (The)
Edgewood Management Company
Edinburgh Fund Managers plc
EDMP, Inc.
EGM Capital
EGS Partners, LLC
Elias Asset Management Inc.
Elijah Asset Management
Ell Realty Securities, Inc.
Emerald Advisers, Inc.

Emerald Capital Management
Emerging Mkts Inv Corp-Emerging
    Mkts Mgmt, LLC
Emerson Investment
    Management, Inc.
EQSF Advisers, Inc.
Equinox Capital
    Management, LLC
Equity Assets Management
Equity Investment Corporation
Equity Research
    Management, Inc.
Ernst Research &
    Management, LLC
ESSEX Investment Management
    Company, LLC
Estabrook Capital
    Management, LLC
Eubel Brady & Suttman Asset
    Management, Inc.
Evaluation Associates
Evergreen Capital Management
Evergreen Investment Manage-
    ment Company (VA)
Evergreen Investments
Excalibur Management Corporation

F

Fairview Capital Investment
    Management
Farr, Miller & Washington, LLC
Farrell-SL Investment
    Management, Inc.
Fayez Sarofim & Co.
FCA Corp
Federated Investors
Fenimore Asset Management, Inc.

Ferguson Investment
  Consultants, Inc.
Ferguson Wellman Capital
  Management, Inc.
Fidelity Inst'l Retirement Svcs Co.
  (FIRSCO)
Fidelity Management Trust Com-
  pany
Fiduciary Asset Management
Fiduciary Asset Management, Inc.
Fiduciary Capital Management, Inc.
Fiduciary Management Associates
Fiduciary Management, Inc. of
  Milwaukee
Fiduciary Trust International
Fifth Third Bank
Fifth Third/Maxus Investment
  Advisors
Financial Counselors, Inc.
Financial Management
  Advisors, Inc.
FinArc, LLC
First Albany Asset Management
First American Capital Management
First Austin Capital Management
First Fiduciary Investment Counsel
First Financial Investment Mgmt
First Financial Trust, N.A.
First Honolulu Asset Management
First Investment Group
First Madison Advisors
First Midwest Trust Company
First Pacific Advisors, Inc.
First Quadrant Corp.
First Trust Advisors LP
Firsthand Capital Management, Inc.

Fischer Financial Services, Inc.
Fischer Francis Trees & Watts, Inc.
Fisher Investments, Inc.
Flagship Capital Management
Fleet Investment Advisors
Flippin, Bruce & Porter, Inc.
Foothills Asset Management, Ltd.
Foreign and Colonial Emerging
  Markets Limited
Forest Investment Management
Forstmann-Leff Associates, LLC
Fort Washington Investment
  Advisors, Inc.
Fortaleza Asset Management, Inc.
Founders Asset Management LLC
Fountain Capital Management
Fox Asset Management
Frank Russell Trust Company
Franklin Advisers, Inc.
Franklin Portfolio Associates
Franklin Private Client Group
  (FPCG)
Fred Alger Management, Inc.
Freedom Capital Management
  Corporation
Freeman Associates Investment
  Mgmt LLC
Friedman, Billings, Ramsey
  Investment Mgmt. Inc.
Friends Ivory & Sime, Inc.
Friess Associates Inc.
Froley, Revy Investment Company
Frontier Capital Management
  Company, LLC
Frontier Investment Management
Frost National Bank

Fuller & Thaler Asset
Management, Inc.
Fulton, Breakefield,
Broenniman, Inc.
Furman Selz Capital
Management LLC

G

G E Asset Management
Gabelli Asset Management
Company
Gabelli Fixed Income LLC
Gabelli Funds, Inc.
Galliard Capital Management, Inc.
Gannett Welsh & Kotler, Inc.
Gardner Lewis Asset Management
Garner Asset Management
Company, L.P.
Garrison, Bradford &
Associates, Inc.
Gartmore Global Partners
Gateway Investment Advisers, L.P.
Geewax Terker & Company
GEM Capital Management, Inc.
Gemini Investments
General Motors Asset Management
Genesis Asset Managers Limited
Geneva Capital Management Ltd.
GeoCapital LLC
George D. Bjurman & Associates
Gilkison Patterson Investment
Advisors
Glenmede Trust Company (The)
Glickenhaus and Co.
Global Asset Management

Globalt, Inc.
Globalvest Management
Company, L.P.
GlobeFlex Capital, L.P.
Godsey & Gibb Associates
Gofen & Glossberg, LLC
Golden Capital Management
Goldman Sachs Asset Management
Grace Capital Management, LLC
Granahan Investment
Management, Inc.
Granite Investment Advisors, LLC
Grantham Mayo Van Otterloo &
Company, LLC
Gratry and Company
Great Lakes Advisors
Great Northern Capital
Green Investment Management, Inc.
Greenville Capital Management
Greenwood Capital Associates, Inc.
Greystone Capital
Management, Inc.
Gries Financial LLC
Griffon Capital Management
Groesbeck Investment
Management
Groh Asset Management, Inc.
Groupama Asset Management N.A.
GS Investments, Inc.
GSB Investment Management
Guardian Asset Management Corp.
Guardian Capital, Inc.
Gulf Investment Management Inc
Gulfstream Global Investors, Ltd.
GW Capital

H

H. M. Payson & Co.

Haberer Registered Investment Advisor, Inc.

Hahn Capital Management

Hake Capital Management, Inc.

Haker/Zellmer Investment Management, Inc.

Hallmark Capital Management, Inc.

Hampton Investors Incorporated

Hansberger Global Investors, Inc.

Harbor Capital Management Company, Inc.

Harding, Loevner Management, L.P.

Harleysville Group & Harleysville Asset Mgmt L.P.

Harman Investment Advisors, Incorporated

Harris Associates L.P.

Harris Bretall Sullivan & Smith LLC

Harris Investment Management, Inc.

Hart Advisers

Hart Capital Management

Hartford Investment Management Company

Hartline Investment Corp.

Harvest Capital Management

Havell Capital Management

Haven Capital Management Inc.

Head and Associates

Heartland Advisors, Inc.

Heartland Capital Management, Inc.

Hebert Advisory Services, Inc.

Heitman/PRA Securities Advisors LLC

Henderson Global Investors

Henssler Asset Management, LLC

Heritage Asset Management

HGK Asset Management, Inc.

Hibernia National Bank

Hickory Group, Ltd.

Highland Capital Management Corp.

Highmark Capital Management, Inc.

Hilspen Capital Management, LLC

HLM Management Company, Inc.

HM Capital Management, Inc.

Hoisington Investment Management Company

Holderness Investments Company

Holland Capital Management

Hollingsworth & Company

Holt-Smith & Yates Advisors

Hoover Investment Management Co., LLC

Horizon Investments, LLC

Hough Capital Advisors

Hourglass Capital Management, Inc.

Hovey, Youngman Associates, Inc.

Howard and McInnes, Inc.

Howard Capital Management

Howland & Associates, Inc.

HSBC Asset Management

Hughes Capital Management, Inc.

Husic Capital Management

Hutchens Investment Management

Hyperion Capital Management, Inc.

I

ICC Capital Management, Inc.

ICM Asset Management

IMS Capital Management

Income Research & Management Inc.

Independence Capital Management, Inc.

Independence Investment LLC and Subsidiary

Independence One Capital Management Corp.

ING Pilgrim Advisors, Inc.

ING Pilgrim Quantitative Management Corp.

Innovest Capital Management, Inc.

Insight Capital Research & Management, Inc.

Insinger Asset Management (Asia) Limited

Insinger de Beuafort Asset Management, Inc.

Institutional Capital Corporation

INTECH

Interinvest Corporation

International Investment Group LLC

Intrepid Capital Management, Inc.

Inverness Counsel, Inc.

INVESCO Global Asset Management (N.A.), Inc.

INVESCO, Inc.

INVESCO-National Asset Management

Investment Advisory Corp.

Investment Counsel Co.

Investment Counselors Incorporated

Investment Counselors of Maryland

Investment Management Associates, Inc.

Investor Resources Group

Investors Management Group

Invista Capital Management, LLC

Iridian Asset Management LLC

Ironwood Capital Management, LLC

ITS Asset Management

J

J.M. Hartwell L.P.

J.P. Morgan Investment Management Inc.

J.W. Burns & Company

Jacobs Asset Management

Jacobs Levy Equity Management, Inc.

James C. Edwards & Company, Inc.

James Investment Research Inc.

Jamison, Eaton & Wood Inc.

Janus Capital Corporation

Jarislowsky Fraser Limited

Jennison Associates LLC

JL Advisors, LLC

JL Kaplan Associates, LLC

John A. Levin & Company

John Hancock Advisers, Inc.

John Hsu Capital Group, Inc.

John McStay Investment Counsel

John Morrell Advisory Services Ltd.

Johnson Asset Management

Johnston Asset Management Corp.

Julian's Mutual Funds Tactics

Julius Baer Investment
    Management Inc.
Jumper Group (The)
Jundt Associates Inc.
Jurika & Voyles L.P.

K

Kahn Brothers & Company
Kalmar Investments Inc.
Kanawha Capital Management
Karpus Investment Management
    Company
Kayne Anderson Rudnick Invest-
    ment Management LLC
KBC Asset Management (Int'l)
    Limited
KBW Asset Management, Inc.
KCM Investment Advisors
Keeley Asset Management Corp.
Kellner, DiLeo & Co.
Kempner Capital Management, Inc.
Kenmar group of companies
Kennedy Capital Management
Kensington Investment
    Group, Inc.
Kensington Management Group
Kenwood Group
Kern Capital Management LLC
Kestrel Investment
    Management Corp.
King Investment Advisors, Inc.
Kirr, Marbach & Company, LLC
Kit Cole Investment Advisory
    Services
KLCM Inc.
Knappenberger Bayer

Knelman Asset Management
    Group LLC
Knightsbridge Asset
    Management, LLC
Kopp Investment Advisors
KPH/Invest, LLC
KPM Investment Management
KR Capital Advisors, Inc.
KRA Capital Management
Kramer Capital Management, Inc.

L

L&B Realty Advisors, Inc.
Laidlaw Group, LLC
Laird Norton Trust
Lake Forest Capital Management
Lakefront Capital Investors, Inc.
Landis Associates, Inc.
Lang Asset Management, Inc.
Lanphier Capital Management, Inc.
Lara Group
LaSalle Investment Management
LaSalle Investment Management
    (Securities)
Lateef Management Associates
Laurel Capital Advisors, LLP
Lazard Asset Management
Lebenthal Asset Management
Lee Munder Capital Group
Lee, Danner and Bass, Inc.
Legg Mason Capital Management
Lend Lease Real Estate Investments
Lend Lease Rosen Real Estate
    Securities LLC
Leonard Management Group (The)
Leonetti & Associates, Inc.

Leuthold Weeden Capital Management

Leylegian Investment Management, Inc.

Liberty Capital Management, Inc.

Light Green Advisors, Inc.

Lighthouse Capital Management, Inc.

Lincoln Capital Management Company

Lincoln National Life Insurance Company

Lindbergh Capital Management

Lipper & Company, L.P.

Lloyd George Management

LM Capital Management

Locke Capital Management, Inc.

Lodestar Investment Counsel, Inc.

Logan Capital Management, Inc.

Lombard Odier Int'l Portfolio Management

London Company (The)

Long Wharf Investors

Longfellow Investment Management Co.

Longwood Investment Advisors

Loomis, Sayles & Company, L.P.

Lord, Abbett & Co.

Lotsoff Capital Management

Lowe Enterprises Investment Mgmt, Inc.

Lowe, Brockenbrough & Company, Inc.

LSV Asset Management

Lunn Partners, LLC

Lyon Street Asset Management Company

M

M & I Investment Management Corp.

M & T Capital Advisors Group

M.A. Weatherbie & Co., Inc.

M.D. Sass Group of Companies

M.J. Whitman Advisers, Inc.

MacKay Shields LLC

Madison Investment Advisors Inc.

Magten Asset Management Corp.

Malley Associates Capital Management

Manley Asset Management, L.P.

Manning & Napier Advisers, Inc.

Manulife Financial Group

Marco Investment Management, LLC

Mark Asset Management

Markston International, LLC

Marque Millennium Capital Management Ltd.

Marshall & Sullivan, Inc.

Marsico Capital Management, LLC

Martin Currie, Inc.

Martingale Asset Management, L.P.

Marvin & Palmer Associates, Inc.

Maryland Capital Management Inc.

Mason Hill Asset Management

Mass Mutual Pension Management

Mastholm Asset Management, LLC

Mastrapasqua & Associates

Matrix Asset Advisors, Inc.

Mazama Capital Management, Inc.

MBIA Capital Management Corp.

McDonald Capital Investors, Inc.

McGahan, Greene, McHugh Capital Mgmt, LLC
McGlinn Capital Management, Inc.
McHugh Associates, Inc.
McKee Investment Management Co. Inc.
McKinley Capital Management, Inc.
McLaughlin Investment Group, LLC
McMillion Capital Management
McMorgan and Company
MDL Capital Management Incorporated
MDT Advisers, Inc.
Mellon Bond Associates
Mellon Capital Management Corporation
Mellon Equity Associates, LLP
Mellon Private Asset Management
Mench Financial, Inc.
Mercantile-Safe Deposit & Trust Co.
Mercator Asset Management, L.P.
Merganser Capital Management L.P.
Meridian Management Company (AR)
Merrill Lynch Investment Managers
Mesirow Asset Management
Messner & Smith Investment Management, Ltd.
Metropolitan Life
Metropolitan West Asset Management
Metropolitan West Capital Management, LLC
MFM Capital Management

MFS Institutional Advisors, Inc.
MidCap Investors LLC
Mid-Continent Capital, LLC
Middleton and Company
Miller/Howard Investments, Inc.
Minton Investment Management
Missouri Valley Partners
Mitchell & Henry, Inc.
Mitchell Capital Management
Mitchell Group, Inc.
Monetta Financial Services, Inc.
Montag & Caldwell, Inc.
Montag Management Corporation
Montgomery Asset Management, LLC
Montgomery Investment Management Inc.
Moody, Aldrich & Sullivan, LLC
Moody, Lynn & Co.
Morgan Dempsey Capital Management, LLC
Morgan Stanley Investment Advisors, Inc.
Morgan Stanley Investment Management
Morley Capital Management, Inc.
Morris Capital Advisors
Morse, Williams & Company, Inc.
Mount Vernon Associates, Inc.
Muhlenkamp & Co.
Munder Capital Management
Murphy Investment Management Company
Murray Johnstone International Inc.
Mutual of America Capital Mgmt Corp.

N

National City Investment
   Management Company
National Investment Services, Inc.
National Life Investment
   Management Company
Navellier & Associates, Inc.
NCM Capital Management
   Group, Inc.
Nelson Capital Management, Inc.
Nelson, Benson & Zellmer, Inc.
Netfolio, Inc.
Neuberger Berman, LLC
Neumeier Investment Counsel
NeuWorld Financial
New Africa Advisors, Inc.
New Amsterdam Partners, LLC
New Century Investment
   Management, Inc.
New Providence Advisors, Inc.
NewBridge Partners, LLC
Newell Associates
Newgate LLP
Newport Pacific Management
NewSouth Capital
   Management, Inc.
Next Century Growth Investors
NFJ Investment Group
Nicholas-Applegate Capital
   Management
Nikko Global Asset Management
   (U.S.A.), Inc.
NISA Investment Advisors, LLC
NMF Asset Management
Nomura Asset Management
   USA Inc.

Nomura Corp. Research & Asset
   Management Inc.
Normandie Capital
   Management LLC
Noroian Capital Management
North Central Trust Co.
Northern Capital Management
   (North Dakota)
Northern Capital Management, LLC
Northern Trust Global
   Advisors, Inc.
Northern Trust Global Investment
   Services
Northern Trust Value Investors
Northpointe Capital
NorthStar Asset Management
Northwest Investment
   Counselors LLC
Nottinghill Investment
   Advisers, Ltd.
Numeric Investors, L.P.
Nuveen Asset Management
NWQ Investment Management
   Company
Nye Parnell & Emerson Capital
   Management, Inc.

O

Oak Associates, LTD
Oak Ridge Investments
Oak Value Capital
   Management, Inc.
OakBrook Investments, LLC
Oaktree Capital Management, LLC
Oberweis Asset Management, Inc.
Oechsle International Advisors

OFFITBANK
OFI Private Investments, Inc.
O'Herron & Company
Oppenheimer Capital
Oppenheimer Investment Advisers
OppenheimerFunds, Inc.
Opportunity Asset Management
Optimum Investment Advisors
Orbitex Management, Inc.
Orleans Capital Management
Osprey Partners Investment
    Management
Oxford Capital Management

P

Pacific Financial Research (PFR)
Pacific Income Advisers
Pacific Investment
    Management Company
Paladin Investment
    Associates, LLC
Palisade Capital Management, LLC
Palladian Capital Management
Palladium Capital Management
Palley-Needelman Asset
    Management
Palo Alto Investors
PanAgora Asset Management, Inc.
Paradigm Asset Management
    Company, LLC
Paradigm Capital Management, Inc.
Parametric Portfolio Associates
Paramount Capital Asset
    Management
Parcon Advisory Group LLC
Pareto Partners

Parker/Hunter Asset Management
Parnassus Investments
Pattern Recognition Fund
Patterson Capital Corporation
Patton Investment Management
Payden & Rygel
Peachtree Asset Management
Pell, Rudman Trust Company, N.A.
Peninsula Asset Management
Penn Capital Management
Pennsylvania Trust Company (The)
Pentecost Capital Management, Inc.
Peregrine Capital Management
Performance Enhancement
    Technologies, Ltd.
Perritt Capital Management, Inc.
Peter Cundill & Associates, Inc.
Peter Uys Partnership, Ltd.
Philadelphia Investment
    Management Group
Philadelphia Trust Company
Philippe Investment Management
Phillips & Drew
Phoenix Investment Counsel
Pictet International Management
Piedmont Investment Advisors, LLC
Piedra Capital, Ltd.
Pilgrim Baxter & Associates, Ltd.
Pillar Capital Advisors, LLC
Pillar Point Capital
    Management, Inc.
Pillar Point Equity
    Management, LLC
PIMCO Equity Advisors
Pinnacle Associates Ltd.

Pinnacle Investment Advisors (OK)

Pioneer Investment
Management, Inc.

Pitcairn Trust Company

PMG Advisors

Polaris Capital Management,
Inc. (MA)

Polaris Capital Management,
Inc. (NY)

Polen Capital Management

Polynous Capital Management, Inc.

Portfolio Advisory Services, LLC

Portfolio Capital Management

Potomac Fund Management, Inc.

PPM America, Inc.

Presque Isle Capital
Management, Inc.

PRIMCO Capital Management

Prime Advisors, Inc.

PRIMECAP Management
Company

Principal Capital Income
Investors, LLC

Principal Life Insurance Company

Principal Real Estate Investors

Pritchard Investment
Management, Inc.

Private Capital Management

Private Management Group, Inc.

Providence Capital Management

Provident Investment Counsel, Inc.

Prudential Investment
Management, Inc.

Prudential Private Placement
Investors

Prudential Real Estate Investors

Prudential Timber Investments, Inc.

P. Schoenfeld Asset
Management, LLC

PSI Minneapolis Portfolio
Management Group

Pugh Capital Management, Inc.

Putnam Investments, Inc.

PVG Asset Management
Corporation

Pyrford International PLC

Pzena Investment
Management, LLC

Q

Q.E.D. Investments LLC

QCI Asset Management, Inc.

Quaker Capital Management
Corporation

Quant Funds

Quantitative Strategies

Quest Investment Management, Inc.

Quintus Asset Management, Inc.

R

R. Meeder & Associates, Inc.

Radnor Capital Management

Rainier Investment Management

Rampart Investment Management
Company, Inc.

RDM Capital Associates, Inc.

Reams Asset Management
Company, LLC

Redstone Advisors, Inc.

Reed, Conner & Birdwell, Inc.

Regent Inv Svcs—A Divtston of
Alliance Cap Mgmt L.P.

Reich & Tang Capital Management

Reinhart, Mahoney & Bryden Capital Mgmt, Inc.

Renaissance Investment Management

Retirement System Investors Inc.

Rexiter Capital Mangement Limited

Reynders, Gray, Prince & Gottlieb

RhumbLine Advisers

Rice Money Managers, Inc.

Rice, Hall, James & Associates

Richard J. Fruth & Associates, Inc.

Richmond Capital Management, Inc.

Richmont Investment Management, LLC

Rigel Capital Management, Inc.

RIMCO (Riggs Investment Mgmt Corporation)

Rittenhouse Advisors Incorporated

Rittenhouse Financial Services, Inc.

Riverbridge Partners, LLC

Riverplace Capital Management, Inc.

RM Investment Management Inc.

RNC Capital Management LLC

Roanoke Asset Management

Robert Bender & Associates

Robert E. Torray & Co., Inc.

Robert Harrell Inc.

Robinson Wilkes, LLC

Robshaw & Julian Associates

Rochdale Investment Management Inc.

Rock Capital Management

Rockefeller & Co., Inc.

Rockhaven Asset Management

Rockwood Capital Advisors

Roger Engemann & Associates, Inc.

Roger H. Jenswold & Company, Inc.

Rogge Global Partners

Roll & Ross Asset Management

Ronald Sadoff's Major Trends

Rorer Asset Management, LLC

Rothschild Asset Management Inc.

Rothschild International Asset Mgmt, Ltd.

Roulston & Company, Inc.

Roxbury Capital Management

Royce & Associates, Inc.

RREEF

RRZ Investment Management, Inc.

RS Investment Management

RTE Asset Management

Rutherford Investment Management, LLC

Rutland, Dickson Asset Management

Ryan Labs, Inc.

S

S.R. Schill & Associates

SAFECO Asset Management Company

Sage Advisory Services LLC (TX)

SAGE/America

SAI Capital Management, LLC

Salus Capital Management

Sander Capital Advisors

Sanderson Asset Management

Sanderson Capital Management, Inc.

Sands Capital Management, Inc.

Santa Barbara Asset Management

Sapourn Financial Services, LLC

Sasco Capital Inc.

Sawgrass Asset Management LLC

SC Fundamental, LLC

Schafer Cullen Capital Management

Scharf Investments

Schneider Capital Management

Schroder Investment Management
North America

Schuylkill Capital
Management, Ltd.

Schwendiman Partners

Schwendiman Technology
Management Co., LLC

Schwendiman Technology
Partners, LLC

SCI Capital Management, Inc.

Scottish Widows Investment
Partnership Ltd.

SeaCap Investment Advisors

SEB Asset Management
America Inc.

Sector Capital Management, LLC

Security Atlantic Capital
Mgmt LLC

Security Capital Global Capital
Management Group

Segall Bryant & Hamill
Investment Counsel

Seix Investment Advisors

Select Equity Group, Inc.

Seligman & Co., Inc.

Sena Weller Rohs Williams, Inc.

Seneca Capital Management LLC

SF Sentry Securities

SG Cowen Asset Management, Inc.

SG Pacific Asset Management, Inc.

Shaker Investments

Shamrock Asset Management, LLC

Shapiro Capital Management
Company, Inc.

Shay Assets Management, Inc.

Sheard & Davey Advisors, LLC

Sheer Asset Management

Shenkman Capital
Management, Inc.

Sierra Investment Partners, Inc.

Silchester International Investors

Simms Capital Management, Inc.

Siphron Capital Management

Sirach Capital Management, Inc.

Sit Investment Associates, Inc.

Skandia Asset Management, Inc.

SKBA Capital Management

Skyline Asset Management, L.P.

Smith Affiliated Capital Corp.

Smith Asset Management
Group, L.P.

Smith Breeden Associates, Inc.

Smith, Graham & Co.

Smithbridge Asset
Management, Inc.

Snyder Capital Management, L.P.

Social Responsibility Investment
Group, Inc.

Societe Generale Asset
Management

Sosnowy Investment Management
Company, Inc.

Sound Shore Management, Inc.

South Street Advisors, LLC

Southeastern Asset Management, Inc.

Sovereign Advisers

Sovereign Asset Management Corporation

Sparrow Capital Management Incorporated

Special Assets Limited

Spectrum Asset Management, Inc.

Spectrum Asset Management, Inc. (CT)

Speece Thorson Capital Group, Inc.

Sprucegrove Investment Management LTD.

SSB Citi/Smith Barney Asset Management PPG

SSCM LLC

SSI Investment Management Inc.

St. John's Investment Management

St. Denis J. Villere & Company

Stacey Braun Associates Inc.

Stafford Capital Management, LLC

Stamper Capital & Investments Inc.

Standard Asset Group

Standish, Ayer & Wood, Inc.

Starbuck Tisdale & Associates

Stark Capital Management

State Street Global Advisors

State Street Research & Management Company

Stein Roe & Farnham Incorporated

Stein Roe Investment Counsel LLC

Steinberg Asset Management Co.

Steinberg Global Asset Management

Stephens Capital Management

Sterling Capital Management (NC)

Sterling Johnston Capital Management, Inc.

Steven Charles Capital, Ltd.

Steward Capital Management

StoneRidge Investment Partners

Strategic Fixed Income, LLC

Stratton Management Company

Street Asset Management, LLC

Strong Capital Management, Inc.

Sturdivant & Co.

STW Fixed Income Management, Ltd.

Suffolk Capital Management, Inc.

Summit International Investment, Inc.

Summit Investment Management, Ltd.

Sun Capital Advisers

Sun Valley Advisors, Inc.

Swarthmore Group, The

Sweetwater Investments, Inc.

Symmetric Advisors, Inc.

Systematic Financial Management, L.P.

T

T. Rowe Price Associates, Inc.

T. Rowe Price International, Inc.

T.H. Fitzgerald & Company

T.O. Richardson Company, Inc.

TAMRO CAPITAL Partners LLC

Tanaka Capital Management

Tandem Financial Services, Inc.

Taplin, Canida & Habacht

Target Investors, Inc.

Tattersall Advisory Group, Inc.

TCW Group

Tealwood Asset Management

Telegraph Hill Investment Counsel

Tempest Investment Counselors

Templeton Private Client Group (TPCG)

Templeton/Franklin Templeton Institutional

Thomas White International, Ltd.

Thompson, Plumb & Associates

Thompson, Siegel & Walmsley, Inc.

Thompson/Rubinstein Investment Mgmt, Inc.

Thomson Horstmann & Bryant, Inc.

Thornburg Management Company

TimberVest

TimesSquare Capital Management, Inc.

Timucuan Asset Management

TIP (Bermuda) Limited

TIS Group, Inc.

Tocqueville Asset Management L.P.

Todd Investment Advisors

Tom Johnson Investment Management, Inc.

Towle & Co.

Towneley Capital Management Inc.

Trainer, Wortham & Company

Transamerica Investment Management, LLC

TranSierra Capital, LLC

Trend Dynamics

Trent Capital Management

Trevor Stewart Burton & Jacobsen

Triad Investment Advisors Corp.

Trias Capital Management, Inc.

Trillium Asset Management Corporation

Trilogy Capital Management, LLC

Trinity Investment Management Corp.

Trusco Capital Management, Inc.

Trust & Investment Advisors

Trust Fund Advisors

TT International Investment Management

Tucker Hargrove Management, Inc.

Tukman Capital Management

Turner Investment Partners, Inc.

Tweedy, Browne Company L.P.

Twin Capital Management, Inc.

U

UAS Asset Management

Ulland Investment Advisors

Ultra Finanz, LLC

Unibank Investment Management

Union Heritage Capital Management

Union Labor Life Insurance Company

Uniplan, Inc.

United States Trust Company of Boston

Unity Management Inc.

Urdang Investment Management, Inc.

U.S.Bancorp Piper Jaffray Asset Management, Inc.

U.S. Trust Company, N.A.

U.S. Trust Company of New York

Utendahl Capital Management, L.P.

V

Valenzuela Capital Partners, LLC

Valley Forge Asset Management

ValueQuest/TA, LLC

ValueWorks

Valu-Trac Investment Management Ltd.

Van Deventer & Hoch

Van Kampen Management Inc.

Van Kasper Advisers

Vanderbilt Capital Advisors, LLC

Vanguard Group, Inc. (The)

Vaughan, Nelson, Scarborough & McCullough

Vector Money Management

Veredus Asset Management LLC

Victory Capital Management Inc.

Victory Gradison Capital Management

Victory SBSF Capital Management

Viewpoint Investment Partners

VMF Capital, LLC

Vontobel USA, Inc.

Voyageur Asset Management

W

W. G. Trading Co., L.P.

W. H. Reaves & Co., Inc.

W. P. Carey and Company, Inc.

Wachovia Asset Management

Waddell & Reed Asset Management Group

Wafra Investment Advisory Group, Inc.

Wagner Investment Management, Inc.

Waite and Associates

Wall Street Associates

Walnut Asset Management, LLC

Walter Scott and Partners LTD

Wanger Asset Management, L.P.

Ward & Company, Ltd.

Ward & Wissner Capital Management, Inc.

Warren D. Nadel & Company

Warwick Capital Management, Inc.

Wasatch Advisors Incorporated

Wayne Hummer Management Company

WCM Investment Management

Weatherfield

Weatherly Asset Management

Weaver C. Barksdale & Associates

WEDGE Capital Management LLP

Weiss, Peck & Greer, LLC

Wellington Management Company, LLP

Wells Capital Management

Wentworth, Hauser & Violich

West Chester Capital Advisors, Inc.

West Ellis Investment Management, Inc.

WestAM

Westcap Investors

Westcliff Capital Management, LLC

Western Asset Management

Westfield Capital Management
Westpeak Investment Advisors, L.P.
Westridge Capital Management, Inc.
Westwood Management
    Corporation
WHB / Wolverine Asset
    Management, Inc.
Whitehall Asset Management
Widmann, Siff & Company, Inc.
Wilbanks, Smith & Thomas Asset
    Mgmt, LLC
Wilkinson O'Grady & Co., Inc.
William Blair & Co.
William D. Witter, Inc.
Wilmerding & Associates, Inc.
Wilmington Trust Company
Wilshire Asset Management
Wilson/Bennett Capital
    Management, Inc.
Windham Capital Management
Windsor Financial Group LLC
Winslow Asset Management, Inc.
Winslow Capital Management, Inc.
Winslow Management Company
Wood Asset Management, Inc.

Woodford Capital
    Management, LLC
Woodley Farra Manion Portfolio
    Management, Inc.
World Asset Management
WorldInvest Limited
Wright Investors' Service

Y
Yacktman Asset Management Co.
Yeager, Wood & Marshall Inc.

Z
Zacks Investment Management, Inc.
Zak Capital, Inc.
Zazove Associates, LLC
Zeliff Wallace Jackson Investment
    Counsel, Inc.
Zephyr Management, L.P.
Zevenbergen Capital Inc.
Ziegler Asset Management, Inc.
Zimmerman Investment
    Management Company
ZPR Investment Management
Zurich Scudder Investments, Inc.
Zweig-DiMenna Associates

M-Search v.1.10 Copyright Möbius 1995, 2000. M Search is a registered trade-mark of Möbius Group Incorporated.

D

PERFORMANCE REPORTING

When managing your own separate accounts portfolio, you want your performance statements to be as accurate and as detailed as possible. Consider this sample separate account quarterly report from a hypothetical company. In it, you'll find everything you need to know about your separate account's activity, including performance numbers, growth rate, account holdings, asset allocation distribution, and a summary of your account activity. The company even includes estimated realized portfolio gains and losses.

Note: Past performance is not a guarantee of future results. All performance numbers are historical, and each security's price, return, and yield will vary. In addition, investors may have a gain or a loss when they sell their securities.

FIGURE D-1

VIP PRIVATE CAPITAL

Quarterly Report
December 31, 2000
Pam Q Public
25000639

Performance Review
Executive Summary
Portfolio Holdings
Portfolio Growth
Activity Summary
Schedule Of Realized Gains & Losses

FIGURE D-1 (Continued)

Pam Q Public
25000639

Performance Review

December 31, 2000

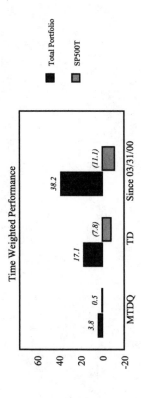

Time Weighted Performance

- Total Portfolio
- SP500T

	60	40	20	0	-20

MTDQ: 3.8, 0.5
TD: 17.1, (7.8)
Since 03/31/00: 38.2, (11.1)

Sector	Month to Date	Quarter to Date	Year to Date	Inception to Date
Total Portfolio	3.82	17.10	(N/A)	38.21
Cash Equivalents0	.00	483.21	(N/A)	483.21
Equities	6.32	(14.21)	(N/A)	48.46
Fixed Income	(2.87)	(N/A)(	N/A)	(2.87)
S & P 500 Total0	.49(	7.82)	(9.11)	(11.14)

FIGURE D-1 (*Continued*)

Pam Q Public
25000639

Executive Summary

December 31, 2000

Sector	Market Value	%MV% Last Quarter	MV Current Quarter	Annual Income	Yield
Cash Equivalents	34,330	1.2	4.9	2,746	8.0
Equities	513,888	98.8	73.3	11,336	2.2
Fixed Income	153,000	0.0	21.8	10,875	7.1
Grand Total	**701,217**	**100.0**	**100.0**	**24,957**	**3.6**

Accrual   1,737

Grand Total Plus Accrual   **702,954**

Current Quarter
As of 12/31/00

Cash Equivalents 5%

Fixed Income 22%

Equities 73%

Last Quarter
As of 09/30/00

Cash Equivalents 1%

Equities 99%

FIGURE D-1 (Continued)

Pam Q Public
25000639

Portfolio Holdings

December 31, 2000

Units	Security Description	Cost	Market Value	% Market Value	Purchase Date
	CASH EQUIVALENTS				
	Cash	34,330	34,330	4.9	
	EQUITIES				
	BANKS				
1,500	Bank One Corp	44,820	54,938	7.8	07/17/00
1,000	Citigroup Inc Com	43,690	51,063	7.3	05/26/00
2,000	Royal Bk Cda Montreal Que Co	43,760	67,750	9.6	03/21/00
	TOTAL	132,270	173,750	24.7	
	ENERGY				
700	Chevron Corp	54,117	59,106	8.4	07/25/00
700	Exxon Mobil Corp Com	52,325	60,856	8.7	03/22/00
5,000	Frontier Oil Corp Com	30,000	34,375	4.9	05/03/00
1,000	Phillips Petroleum Company	41,440	56,875	8.1	03/17/00
	TOTAL	177,882	211,213	30.0	
	FOOD AND BEVERAGE				
600	Quaker Oats Co	40,350	58,425	8.3	07/31/00

FIGURE D-1 (*Continued*)

Pam Q Public
25000639

Portfolio Holdings

December 31, 2000

Units	Security Description	Cost	Market Value	% Market Value	Purchase Date
	HOTEL AND RESTAURANT				
2,000	Starwood Hotels & Resorts Wo	48,380	70,500	10.0	03/30/00
	TOTAL EQUITIES	**398,882**	**513,888**	**73.1**	
	FIXED INCOME				
	MUNICIPAL BONDS				
150,000	Alameda County Ca 7.250% 12/01/05	153,339	153,000	21.8	11/06/00
	Accrual		1,737	0.2	
	Grand Total	**586,551**	**702,954**	**100.0**	

FIGURE D-1 (Continued)

Pam Q Public
25000639

Portfolio Growth

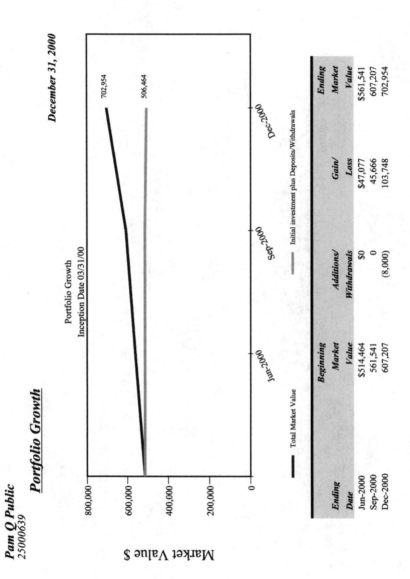

December 31, 2000

Portfolio Growth
Inception Date 03/31/00

Market Value $

— Total Market Value   — Initial investment plus Deposits/Withdrawals

Ending Date	Beginning Market Value	Additions/ Withdrawals	Gain/ Loss	Ending Market Value
Jun-2000	$514,464	$0	$47,077	$561,541
Sep-2000	561,541	0	45,666	607,207
Dec-2000	607,207	(8,000)	103,748	702,954

FIGURE D-1 (*Continued*)

Pam Q Public
25000639

Activity Summary

December 31, 2000

Units	Security Description	Cost	Proceeds	Gain/ Loss	Trade Date
Purchases					
150,000.000	Alameda County Ca 7.250% 12/01/05	153,338.96			11/06/00
	Total Purchases	**$153,338.96**			
Sales					
1,000.000	Intel Corp Com	43,310.00	46,558.44	3,248	11/06/00
1,000.000	Cisco Sys Inc Com	50,550.00	55,128.16	4,578	11/06/00
2,000.000	Qwest Communications Intl In	82,260.00	91,496.95	9,237	11/06/00
	Total Sales	**$176,120.00**	**193,183.55**	**17,064**	
Contributions/Withdrawals					
2,000.000	Qwest Communications Intl In	82,260.00			05/24/00
	Total Contributions/Withdrawals	**$82,260.00**			
Cash Contributions/Withdrawals					
	Client W/D	(8,000.00)			12/22/00
	Total Cash Contributions/Withdrawals	**($8,000.00)**			

FIGURE D-1 (*Continued*)

Pam Q Public
25000639

Schedule Of Realized Gains & Losses

December 31, 2000

Security				%			Short	Long
Units	Description	Cost	Proceeds	Gain/ Loss	Purchase Date	Sale Date	Term	Term
1,000	Cisco Sys Inc Com	50,550	55,128	9.06	05/23/00	11/06/00	4,578	
1,000	Intel Corp Com	43,310	46,558	7.50	09/26/00	11/06/00	3,248	
2,000	Qwest Communications Intl In	82,260	91,497	11.23	05/24/00	11/06/00	9,237	
	Total Gain						17,064	0
	Total Loss						00	
	Grand Total	176,120	193,184				17,064	
	Net Gain/Loss						$17,064	

GLOSSARY

annual report — an often glossy publication, put out by management, that summarizes the performance of a company or mutual fund over 1 year (calendar or fiscal) and discusses future prospects; also a public relations device to attract new investors.

appreciation — an increase in the basic value of an investment.

bear market — a market characterized by generally falling prices over a period of several months or years.

blue chip — the common stock of a company known nationally for the quality of its products and its profitability.

boiler rooms — fraudulent schemes operated by high-pressure salespersons working out of rooms equipped with many telephones, offering phony investment opportunities.

bond — a certificate representing a loan of money to a corporation or government for a specific period in exchange for a promise to repay the bondholder the amount borrowed plus interest.

broker — a representative who handles transactions related to investors' orders to buy and sell securities. Brokers charge a fee, known as a commission, for this service. Brokerage firms currently dominate the separate accounts marketplace.

bull market — a market characterized by generally rising prices over a period of several months or years.

business failure risk — the risk that the business will fail and the investment will be worthless or that a business will be less profitable than expected.

capital — the wealth of a business or an individual in terms of money or property.

capital gain — the gain realized when a security is sold for more than its purchase price.

capital loss — the loss realized when a security is sold for less than its purchase price.

capitalism — the economic system practiced in the United States which allows individual ownership of land, buildings, and equipment.

caveat emptor — a Latin phrase meaning "Let the buyer beware."

CFA — chartered financial analyst. The Chartered Financial Analyst Program is a global standard for measuring the competence and integrity of financial analysts. Three levels of examination measure a candidate's ability to apply the fundamental knowledge of investment principles at a professional level. The CFA exam is administered annually in over 70 nations worldwide.

CFP — certified financial planner; an individual who has completed the educational requirements of the International Board of Certified Financial Planners (IBCFP) which covers all facets of financial planning, from taxes to investments.

CFTC — Commodity Futures Trading Commission; the federal regulatory agency that monitors the futures and options market.

ChFC — chartered financial consultant; a designation earned by individuals who successfully complete the financial training program offered by the American College in Pennsylvania.

commission — a broker's fee for buying or selling securities for an investor or earned by a real estate agent for selling property.

commodity — an article of commerce or a product that can be used in commerce, such as agricultural products, metals, petroleum, foreign currencies, financial instruments and indices.

common stock — the most basic form of corporation ownership. Owners of common stock have a claim on the assets of a company after those of preferred stockholders and bondholders.

compound interest — the interest earned on interest, which is added to the principal.

consultant wrap accounts — the name for separate accounts given by investment monitoring firm Cerulli Associates.

convertible bond — a bond that an owner can exchange for stock before maturity.

coupon rate — the fixed annual interest rate quoted when a bond is issued.

deep discount bonds — *see* zero coupon bonds.

discount — the sale of a bond at a price less than face value.

diversification — spreading investment funds among different types of investments and industries.

dividend — the payment received by stockholders from the earnings of a corporation.

dollar cost averaging — investing the same fixed dollar amount in the same investment at regular intervals over a long period of time.

Dow Jones Industrial Average — the price weighted average of 30 actively traded stocks.

ethical views — widely held opinions about what is right and wrong, good and bad.

exchanges — marketplaces for transactions such as the New York Stock Exchange, the American Stock Exchange, and the Chicago Board of Trade.

face value — the amount a bond is worth when it matures.

FDIC — Federal Deposit Insurance Corporation; an agency of the federal government created to guarantee bank deposits.

financial planner — a person who advises others about financial issues.

folios – baskets of securities (stocks, bond funds, etc.) that can be bought in one step and are directly owned by individual investors; folios also serve as a basis for separate account programs and other brokerage offerings.

fraud — the act of deceiving or misrepresenting the truth.

fraud risk — the risk that an investment deceives or misrepresents facts.

full-service brokers — people who buy and sell securities or commodities to investors and offer information and advice.

futures contract — a legal commitment to buy or sell a commodity at a specific future date and price.

goal — a specific statement about a preferred future condition.

growth stock — shares, usually in small companies with potentially bright futures and fast growth.

hedging — the process of protecting an investment against price increases.

index — a way to measure market performance as a whole based on a set of stocks, such as the Dow Jones Industrial Average or the Standard & Poor's 500.

index fund — a mutual fund that strictly invests in shares of a particular stock index, such as the S&P 500 or Russell 2000. These funds generally have low costs and fees.

individual retirement account (IRA) — a special savings account that allows individuals to contribute money for retirement without paying taxes on either the money that is added or the interest that is generated. In general, money from IRAs cannot be removed until age 59.5 without paying a 10 percent penalty.

inflation — a general rise in the prices of goods and services that reduces the purchasing power of money.

inflation risk — the risk that the financial return on an investment will lose purchasing power due to a general rise in the prices of goods and services.

infomercial — a radio or television program with both an information and advertising component.

insider trading — the illegal use of investment information not generally known to the public.

interest — the payment received from a financial institution for lending money to it.

interest rate risk — the risk that the value of a long-term fixed return investment will decrease due to a rise in interest rates.

investment advisor — an individual who helps you develop your investment objectives, determines the appropriate asset allocation to achieve your objectives, selects the investment managers and investment vehicles to implement your plan, and then monitors and reports back to you on the progress of your portfolio. An investment manager is responsible for a specific segment of your portfolio, such as large capitalization growth stock.

investment objective — the broad goals of a separate account or other investment. In general, portfolios seek income (blue chip), capital appreciation (growth stock), safety (bonds), or some combination of these three.

investment policy statement (IPS) — a written document that defines your investment goals, what strategies to use to achieve those goals, and how to adjust for changes. Written policy statements are de rigueur for separate account investors.

IRA — *see* individual retirement account (IRA).

junk bonds — high-risk bonds issued by corporations of little financial strength. Interest rate is high, but default rate is also high.

life cycle — the pattern that identifies common tasks at various stages of life, such as the 18 to 24 age group.

limited partnership — an investment vehicle formed of a general partner and limited partners.

liquidity — the ease with which an investment can be converted into cash.

load fund — a mutual fund purchased directly by the public that charges a sales commission when bought.

market price — the price the seller will accept and the buyer will pay.

market risk — the risk that the price of stocks, real estate, or other investments will go down due to business cycles or other causes.

MMI — Money Management Institute. MMI, located in Washington, DC (www.moneyinstitute.com), is the national organization representing the managed account industry and includes as members major sponsor organizations like Merrill Lynch, Morgan Stanley, and Salomon Smith Barney as well as major money manager firms like Alliance, Brandes, or Rittenhouse/Nuveen. MMI serves as the Industry's advocate with financial/investment reporters, regulators and public policy makers.

mutual fund — a company that invests the pooled money of its shareholders in various types of investments. Generally, a mutual fund allows for investors to buy or sell their interest at any time. Thus, investors may be subject to the tax consequences of buying and selling in the portfolio even though the investors have not sold their interest in the fund.

NASAA — North American Securities Administrators Association; an organization of securities administrators charged with enforcing securities laws and protecting investors from fraudulent investments.

NASD — National Association of Securities Dealers; the securities industry's largest self-regulatory agency. Parent corporation of NASD Regulation and the NASDAQ stock market.

NASD Regulation — the NASD subsidiary that carries out regulatory functions, including on-site examinations of NASD member firms, continuous automated surveillance of markets operated by the NASDAQ subsidiary, and disciplinary actions against broker/dealers and their professionals.

NASDAQ — the world's largest screen-based stock market built totally out of telecommunications networks and computers.

NASDAQ Composite Index — a market-value-weighted index measuring more than 5000 NASDAQ-listed common stocks.

NCUA — National Credit Union Administration; a federal government agency created to guarantee credit union deposits.

NFA — National Futures Association; a congressionally authorized self-regulatory organization for the futures industry.

NICE — National Institute for Consumer Education; an educational program with an emphasis on consumer, economic, and personal finance education.

no-load fund — a mutual fund purchased directly by the public that does not have a charge for buying.

odd lot — a unit of less than 100 shares of stock.

offering circulars — disclosure documents provided to investors by the company seeking capital.

P/E ratio — price/earnings ratio; the price of a stock divided by per share earnings. A figure used to evaluate the value of a stock. Also referred to as the "multiple," that is, the number of times by which the company's latest 12-month earnings must be multiplied to obtain the current stock price. Obtained by dividing the current earnings into current market value.

penny stocks — high-risk stocks that generally sell for less than $3 and are not listed and traded on any exchange or stock market. (Con artists often deal in penny stock frauds.)

political risk —the risk that government actions such as trade restrictions will negatively affect the price of an investment.

Ponzi scheme — an illegal investment scam named for its inventor, Charles Ponzi.

portfolio — the total investments held by an individual.

preferred stock — ownership in a corporation which has a claim on assets and earnings of a company before those of common stock-holders but after bondholders.

premium — the sale of a bond at a price greater than face value.

prospectus — a legal document describing an investment offered for sale.

pyramid scheme — a fraudulent scheme where an investor buys the right to be a sales representative for a "product." Those in the scheme early may profit; those in late always lose.

rate of return — a combination of yield (dividends or interest) and appreciation (increase in basic value of the investment).

redemption fee — a charge levied by a mutual fund when shares are sold.

return — the total income from an investment; it includes income plus capital gains or minus capital losses.

risk — in an investment, the uncertainty that you will get an expected return. In insurance, the uncertainty whether a loss will occur.

risk tolerance — a person's capacity to endure market price swings in an investment.

round lot — 100 shares of one stock.

Rule of 72 — a mathematical tool used to determine the length of time needed to double an investment at a given interest rate.

savings — money set aside to meet future needs with very little risk to principal or interest.

SEC — Securities and Exchange Commission; a federal agency established to license brokerage firms and regulate the securities industry. The SEC helps curb investment fraud, but the individual investor, not the SEC, must judge the worth of the security offered for sale.

securities — a broad range of investment instruments, including stocks, bonds, and mutual funds.

separate account — a portfolio of individual stocks, bonds, and/or derivatives managed by an investment manager for a client. There is no pooling of the investments with other clients. Separate accounts are generally considered more tax efficient than mutual funds

SIPC — Security Investors Protection Corporation; a nonprofit corporation created by Congress. It insures investors in SIPC-insured firms from financial loss due to financial failure of the brokerage firm up to $500,000 per customer.

socially responsible investing – the incorporation of an investor's social, ethical, or religious criteria in the investment-making process.

SRO — self-regulatory organization; securities industry regulatory bodies are under the jurisdiction of the SEC. Futures industry regulatory bodies are under the jurisdiction of the CFTC.

stock — an investment that represents ownership in a company; also known as a share.

street name — securities held in the name of the broker rather than the investor.

tax-exempt investments — investments that are not subject to tax on income earned.

time value of money — an increase in an amount of money over time as a result of investment earnings.

values — beliefs or ideas that are considered desirable and important.

wrap accounts — investment accounts "wrapped' under one fee. Traditional wrap accounts offer a full range of securities, along with the expertise of outside money managers with different investment styles. These traditional wrap accounts are customized according to your investment horizon, goals, and risk tolerance. Mutual fund wrap investments are made up of only mutual funds. These wrap accounts are generally based on an asset allocation selected from several noncustomized allocations generated by a computer program.

yield interest or dividend generated by the investment — an amount of money generally calculated as a percentage of the amount invested; see also *rate of return*.

yield to maturity — the total annual rate of return on a bond when it is held to maturity, considering the purchase price, time to maturity, value at maturity, and the annual dollar amount of interest earned.

zero coupon bonds — bonds issued for less than face value; they pay no interest income. Return to the investor occurs when the bond is sold or redeemed; also known as *deep discount bonds*.

Index

About the Authors

Erik Davidson, CFA, and **Kevin Freeman, CFA**, cofounded *Separate Account Solutions* (www.SeparateAccounts.com) to help large-scale financial institutions offer this innovative financial service to their customers. They are recognized authorities on separate accounts, featured in numerous articles and conferences. Their strong advocacy has earned them the reputation as the "Evangelists of the Separate Account movement."

Davidson previously worked in the private client division of Franklin Templeton (Templeton Portfolio Advisory) as managing director of portfolio operations. There, he codesigned, implemented, and was responsible for oversight of the division's more than 2,500 separate account portfolios representing nearly $2.5 billion in assets under management. Prior to joining Franklin Templeton, he served as an executive with First Boston on Wall Street as well as in Tokyo. Davidson earned his MBA from the Anderson School of Management at UCLA and currently resides with his wife and four children in Carmel, California.

Freeman is the former managing director for Templeton Portfolio Advisory, the separate accounts division of Franklin Templeton. He was personally selected by John Templeton to write and implement the business plan that enabled Templeton to be the first major mutual fund complex to offer separate accounts. Supported by his strategic leadership and investment knowledge, in less than a decade, the firm attracted and managed nearly $2.5 billion of separate account assets. Freeman's other business ventures include Carmel Creamery, Capitalist Publishing Co., and The Adam Smith Foundation. Freeman resides with his wife and daughter in Keller, Texas.

Brian O'Connell is a freelance business writer who has written numerous books on financial topics including *CNBC Creating Wealth: An Investor's Guide to Decoding the Market* and *The 401(k) Millionaire*. O'Connell resides in Doylestown, Pennsylvania.